Praise For *My Father*

D0790598

"For one generation it's a return to an earlier home, for another it's a discovery of a new one. *My Father's Daughter* is a meditative travel memoir that speaks to all Baby Boomers in clear voice with new understandings about the past. Syverson takes you on a trip to Italy that renews her sense of self and family—one that creates a longing for more. There are no easy lessons here and through it all she finds a new self through watching her parents. In the process, she revives a passion for life by making the old country new, and finding a place for herself in it all."

~ **Fred Gardaphé, Distinguished Professor of Italian American Studies, Queens College/CUNY.**

"At age 50, Gilda Morina Syverson knows it is time to transform her relationship with her father by casting off her role as argumentative child and by healing the rifts that divide them. *My Father's Daughter* tells the story of that inner transformation that slowly unfolds with discoveries about ancestry, family, culture, and connection to Italy… A Novello Literary Award Book finalist, *My Father's Daughter* is a mosaic of travel memoir, identity writing and family stories. Syverson's stories will resonate with millions of Italian American Baby Boomers who grew up influenced by Italy in their most intimate family relationships."

~ **Review by Kirsten Keppel, *Ambassador Magazine*, NIAF (National Italian American Federation)**

"Gilda Morina Syverson makes me wish I were Italian.
Oh, those ancient Sicilian villages.
Oh, those fragrant family feasts.
Oh, the way Italians greet their long-lost relatives from the U.S.
Syverson tells a good story – the joy of watching her parents as they visit the old villages – … It's no accident that after a long search for a title, she landed on *My Father's Daughter* …
Not only are the hills in the villages steep, so is Syverson's learning curve: 'Perhaps by accepting all of who my father is, I can forgive

him for not being what I thought he should have been …' I applaud Syverson for opening her heart wide to the reader and saying, *Entrate! Entrate!"*

~ **Dannye Romine Powell,** *Charlotte Observer,*
The News & Observer, **Raleigh, NC**

"My Father's Daughter is a memorable and insightful journey that bridges the past, the present and the future. Going back to the old country *with one's parents* - now that's something many of us dream about or dread . . . or both. Beyond the descriptions of tourist spots, and reconnecting with relatives in hometowns, Gilda Morina Syverson passionately illustrates the beauty and challenges of family."

~ **Licia Canton, editor-in-chief of** *Accenti Magazine,*
Montreal, Canada

"Gilda Morina Syverson reaches for bottom and is richly rewarded with renewed love for her family and Sicily, the island of her ancestry. Her multi-layered memoir, part family history and part travelogue is a compelling read. Syverson's writes from her heart and her honesty and integrity touched mine."

~ **Venera Fazio, past president, Association of Italian**
Canadian Writers and co-editor of *Sweet Lemons 2:*
International Writings with a Sicilian Accent

"Long after I finished reading this delicious memoir, I could still taste the flavors brought to mind by a story ripe with lush details, bracing wit, and bold pleasures. Embarking on Syverson's journey is like traveling the world with a treasured friend. This is an experience to be savored."

~ **Amy Rogers, author of** *Hungry for Home: Stories*
of Food from Across the Carolinas; **publisher,**
Novello Festival Press

"Syverson took her elderly parents back home to visit the 'old country' after decades of living in America : their journey offers a rich

set of first-person insights and experiences cemented by warm family relationships and a sense of place. If it's a travelogue alone that is desired, move on; but if it's a wide-ranging discussion of the heart of both Italian and family connections, then the richness of *My Father's Daughter* is a pleasure not to be missed, recommended for readers who want both personal observations and experiences and fun cultural interactions under one cover."
~ **Diane Donovan,** *California Bookwatch*

"My Father's Daughter, From Rome to Sicily is rumination on how worlds Syverson has inhabited *relate* her, not just *to* her… To read this book is to know that the places we've lived, the places we've known, the places and people we come from stick with us in ways we don't always understand. Her work is the stuff of houses and homes and the fixtures they contain, a mapping of experience and how we share it, a way of, as the Syverson herself has put it in her poetry, "seeking our own kind" from wherever we happen to be."
~ **Bryce Emley,** *Raleigh Review*

"Gilda Morina Syverson's beautiful memoir, *My Father's Daughter, From Rome to Sicily*, is so rife with Italianate passion and sentiment that I was often spirited away – not just to Rome and Sicily, but to my parents' kitchen, and the precincts of my past I most cherish… *Bravissimo*!"
~ **Joseph Bathanti, North Carolina Poet Laureate, 2012-2014**

"Travel south from Rome with Gilda Morina Syverson. Let her show you her ancestral land through the eyes of her closest ancestors, her parents, who travel with her and her husband. It's a trip well worth taking… The only thing better would be a trip to Italy."
~ **William Martin,** *New York Times* **Bestselling Author of** *Cape Cod* **and T***he Lincoln Letter*

My Father's Daughter
From Rome to Sicily

Gilda Morina Syverson

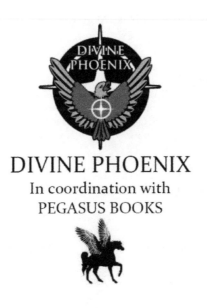

DIVINE PHOENIX
In coordination with
PEGASUS BOOKS

Copyright © 2014, 2016 by Gilda Morina Syverson

All Rights Reserved. No part of this book may be produced or transmitted in any form or by any means, electronic or mechanical, including photocopying, recording or by an information storage and retrieval system—except by a reviewer who may quote brief passages in a review to be printed in a magazine or newspaper—without permission in writing from the publisher.

Divine Phoenix Books
2985 Benson Road
Skaneateles, NY, 13152
www.divinephoenixbooks.com

First Edition: December 2014

Published in North America by Divine Phoenix and Pegasus Books. For information, please contact Divine Phoenix c/o Laura Ponticello, 2985 Benson Road, Skaneateles, NY, 13152.

This book is a work of creative nonfiction. The events are portrayed to the best of Gilda Morina Syverson's memory. While all the stories in this book are true and the author tried to portray the events as accurately as possible, Gilda Morina Syverson at times has condensed conversations or summarized scenes. Given each person may remember incidences and occurrences differently, this is the Author's story.

Library of Congress Cataloguing-In-Publication Data
Gilda Morina Syverson

My Father's Daughter *From Rome to Sicily*/Gilda Morina Syverson— 1st ed

p. cm.
Library of Congress Control Number: 2014956758
ISBN – 978-1-941859-10-0
1. BIOGRAPHY & AUTOBIOGRAPHY / Personal Memoirs. 2. TRAVEL / Europe / Italy. 3. BODY, MIND & SPIRIT / Inspiration & Personal Growth. 4. BIOGRAPHY & AUTOBIOGRAPHY / Cultural Heritage. 5. FAMILY & RELATIONSHIPS / Life Stages / Mid-Life. 6. LANGUAGE ARTS & DISCIPLINES / Composition & Creative Writing.

10 9 8 7 6 5 4 3 2 1

Comments about My Father's Daughter *From Rome to Sicily* and requests for additional copies, book club rates and author speaking appearances may be addressed to Gilda Morina Syverson directly at www.gildasyverson.com.

Also available as an eBook from Internet retailers and from Divine Phoenix Books

Printed in the United States of America

Dedicated to:

Mom & Dad
Mary & Nicholas Morina

and

Nonna Nicolina & Nonno Antonio Morina
&
Nonna Egidia & Nonno Francesco Stagnitta

and

To my very American husband,
Stu

In this nonfiction memoir, **My Father's Daughter** *From Rome to Sicily*, by Gilda Morina Syverson, we are captivated by a trilogy travel adventure, with ancient sites of Rome, contrasting the landscape of a picturesque countryside, the seaside villages of Sicily, and olive trees in the valley of Mount Etna.

This *Novello Literary Award* Book Finalist exudes passion, eloquence, heartfelt language and ancestral roots. Reader discussion questions are included for book clubs, reading groups and libraries.

ACKNOWLEDGEMENTS

I gratefully acknowledge the editors of Novello Festival Press for having selected this manuscript as a Novello Literary Award Finalist, when entitled *Finding Bottom, an Italian-American woman's journey to the old country.* I am grateful to the editors of the following publications in which portions of this book originally appeared, some in different forms—*Wellspring, Iodine Poetry Journal, Main Street Rag, and Novello Festival Press,* and to the Charlotte Writers Club for a non-fiction award for a chapter's excerpt.

Now where it all began, with gratitude to relatives, here and on the other side—of the veil and Atlantic—for their inspiration that drove me to travel back to Italy and Sicily.

A special gratitude to you, Mom and Dad, and my siblings—Nicki, Anthony, Fran, Teresa, Gerard, JoAnne, Bridget and Ann Marie, plus the sister who told me through a psychic reading to never forget her—Mary, who died the day she was born. You, your spouses, children, and grandchildren are always in my heart. You have forced my soul to grow through joys, sorrows and love.

Thank you also, to both my grandmothers and grandfathers, *Nonne and Nonni,* aunts and uncles, including the greats, *cugini* (many of them), *paesani,* who sat around tables talking about villages, people left behind, mountain springs, volcanoes, umbrellas, donkeys, gardens and the deep, teal blue sea.

Your inspiration came from "blood" and "land." Aunt Mary and Uncle Peter Colosi, I am forever grateful for having lived with you in Gualtieri Sicaminò, as well as for my sister, Teresa Morina DeWitt, and cousin, Marisa Villani Marron, for that summer we landed in Palermo and ended in Lake Como, and to my sister, Nicki Morina Richards, for allowing me to publish her poem, *Nonna's Hands.*

To Laura Ponticello, Divine Phoenix Books—I imagine you as a relative from a distant time. I prayed for an editor and publisher who believed in my journey as an Italian-American, female, writer, and lo and behold the angels pulled you and I together in a small upstate New York spa, in the town where I once-upon-a-time attended summer camp.

I would also like to thank the team at Pegasus Books for their amazing support to help edit and produce my book, including an outstanding cover design and incredible editorial support. Thank you Chris Moebs, Caprice De Luca and Marcus McGee.

It is with sincere humility and gratitude that I thank all those who have been supportive and provided endorsements for this book. And to the many publishers, both in the United States and in Canada, I am grateful that you saw the passion I have for my heritage.

To those who provided great feedback—Betty Pendle White, Ann Campanella, Brenda Graham, Suzanne Baldwin Leitner, (Ione) Tootsie O'Hara, Irene Honeycutt, Naomi Myles, Mary Wilmer, Maureen Ryan Griffin, Christine Pearson, Susan Shevlin, Pam Dykstra, Francine Morina Levato, and the members of my Lake Norman Poetry group. An extra-special thank you to Ann Campanella and Maureen Ryan Griffin for the additional care they took in sitting across the table with me over and over again.

Thank you to the writers and artists in the Carolinas who have been such an encouragement, including supporters of the arts—friend and translator, Giovanni Labardi and his wife Jill, my first Italian teacher. They believed in this story, as did many friends, including Rosemary Broton Boyle and Jackye Zimmermann, and all of my life timers.

To my memoir students—you have kept me humbled and honest as we sat in circles and around tables at Queens University, at The Warehouse Performing Arts Center, Myers Park Baptist Church and Davidson Parks and Rec. You have made me a better writer.

Now, to the person who has been there on one long, amazing journey—he's my laughter and delight, despite my Italian/Sicilian angst. If it weren't for my husband, my parents and I would never have taken the trip that became this memoir. You're the humor and joy in this story and in my life. An editor once said, "Stu is my favorite character."

Mine, too!

Thank you, Stu, for your unconditional love, for your constancy, for traveling this road with me. I could never have done this creative life if it wasn't for your endless support.

Ti amo, I love you.

"... And the end of our exploring
will be to arrive where we started
and know the place for the first time ..."

"Four Quartets"[1]
T.S. Eliot

---

[1] Eliot, T.S., "Little Gidding," *Four Quartets*, New York, Harcourt, 1943

1) Wake-Up Call

Sunday, October 15

Bright lights on the digital alarm blink 5:00 a.m. Five o'clock? What in the world am I doing awake? And what is this inner voice nagging me about room reservations in Rome? Something doesn't feel right. Today? Sunday. Tomorrow is Monday. We're leaving—Mom, Dad, Stu and me—for our trip to Italy and Sicily.

Why this message now and not when the itinerary arrived two months ago? Wait. I did wonder why the address for the hotel was different from what Carol, our travel agent, gave me on the phone. Why didn't I pay attention to those feelings when the reservations first arrived?

I've been to Italy half a dozen times. Anything's possible there. The building could be on a side alley, the address on the main road. Carol referred to the place as Hotel Columbus, and in her next breath called it *Hotel Cristoforo Colombo*.

It didn't seem unusual to hear her use English and then Italian. After all, we both have Italian backgrounds. That's why I used Carol to make the flight arrangements. I even chuckled when she rolled those rich flowing vowels off her tongue. Maybe I shouldn't be so friendly and focus strictly on business.

One night on the Internet, I looked up the Hotel Columbus. Just like Carol had said, the address was *Via della Conciliazione, Numero 34*. The ad even touted that they were only blocks from the Vatican. I assumed the street address on the itinerary was simply an error. How many Christopher Columbus Hotels could there be, anyway? It wasn't a chain—that much I knew.

At different times in my life, I've learned to let go and let others do things for me. But it didn't come easy. Being the second oldest of eight children, I've often felt overly responsible.

I can't be in charge of absolutely everything. At least that's what I've tried to tell myself after having moved away from my large Italian-American family. Besides, our agent is not just any fly-by-night. She's been in the business for over thirty years specializing in trips to Italy.

Now, here I am the morning before we're supposed to leave, and I can't stop churning. If I don't get back to sleep, I'll wake my husband. There's no sense in both Stu and me being sleep deprived. I slip out of bed, climb the stairs to my art studio and quietly close the door. I hate following up after Carol, but I'm calling that hotel in Rome.

"*Buon giorno,*" I say in my best Italian. "*Parla Inglese?*"

I've learned that if anyone there admits to speaking English, his or her verbal skills are much more fluent than my broken Italian. Luigi, the person on the other end of the phone, takes my last name and my parents' name, then asks for our reservation numbers.

"*No problema,*" Luigi says in his rich accent; we are booked.

To be absolutely sure, I say, "Now this is the Hotel Columbus two blocks from the Vatican, correct?"

"No, not correct," Luigi replies. "We are about fifteen kilometers from the Vatican."

Fifteen kilometers doesn't register. I envision fifteen yards, fifteen feet, fifteen anything but kilometers.

"*Si,*" I repeat, "fifteen kilometers is right down the street from the Vatican, correct?"

"No, not correct," he says again. "Kilometers, kilometers," he repeats, pronouncing each syllable—*key lom e tours.*

And then it hits me.

"KILOMETERS?" I bellow, "But my travel agent said that you were in walking distance of the Vatican."

"We are not," he says. "You will have to take a bus or a *tassi.*"

Frantic, I hang up furious with myself for not having listened to my intuition after the itinerary arrived months ago. I ignored that internal voice trying to tell me something was awry and assumed my imagination had gotten the best of me, as I've been told most of my life it did.

I click on the Internet and find the phone number for the other Hotel Columbus and call. A woman named Stefania also replies *yes* to my question about speaking English.

"I'm sorry, Madam," she says, "We do not have your name."

She doesn't have the reservation number that I read off either. Obviously, the confirmation system at one hotel is different from another. But I am grasping here. It's pretty apparent that our reservations are with the first place I called.

I'm going to Rome with my mother and father, seventy-three and seventy-six, respectively. Although they're not old, they're not young and used to traveling either. And we're not even staying close to the Vatican.

My father attends Mass every day, sometimes twice. Mom is not compulsive about daily Mass, but she is excited about being within walking distance from what we've always been taught is the seat of Catholicism.

Thanks to Stu, my Episcopalian husband, we're scheduled to see Pope John Paul II in St. Peter's *piazza* the morning after we arrive in Italy. Stu's nephew's wife's father, a colonel in the U.S. Army, had once been stationed at the American Embassy in Rome, and he was able to arrange a papal audience for us. Well, the four of us and about 8,000 other people.

The plan is to walk to the *piazza* from our hotel. Since the year 2000 is the Catholic Church's Jubilee Celebration, we do not want to fight the traffic with the thousands of pilgrims who will be flooding Vatican City from all areas of the capital. Even though the main impetus for the trip is to visit my parents' ancestral towns in Sicily, how can we go to Italy with my folks and not visit Rome?

Now on the other end of the phone, Stefania, the woman from the hotel near the Vatican, is trying to calm my rattled nerves.

"Madam, stay in the hotel that you have a reservation for and then try to find another place after you arrive. Rooms are scarce here," she continues. "You are lucky to have one at all."

Lucky is not how I'm feeling. I explain to Stefania how my parents are older, that it's my mother's first trip abroad, and we are willing take any available rooms. After several apologies and her sympathy, Stefania says they are totally booked. Exasperated, I go back to bed and crawl beneath the covers. So much for trying not to rouse my husband.

"Stu," I whisper, "Those hotel reservations in Rome... they're not at all near the Vatican."

His eyes pop open.

Now we're both awake for the day. I wait until almost 8:30 before I call our travel agent at home. Carol and I spend most of Sunday on and off the phone. Even though she looks on numerous Internet sites for another place near the Vatican, none of her attempts meet with success.

****

For almost twenty years, I've begged my father to travel with me to the town in Sicily where he was born. Going with Dad, who knows the ins and outs of the customs there, would provide more information than I would ever be able to find on my own.

But my father has always made excuses for not going. Early on, he said that he hated puckering up for all those kisses his cousins would expect. Eventually he switched to, "I could never travel with you. We'd kill each other."

There's probably more truth to us killing each other. Dad has always been patriarchal and more conservative. After having left home over thirty years ago, I've discovered a more feminist outlook. It's made for a rather fiery relationship between my father and me. We've argued over women's issues, the hierarchy of the church, and my profession as an artist.

I've even reached the point where I refuse to answer my father when he asks how much I make on a piece of art. He's been known to scoff at the amount, throw his hands in the air and say something irritating about how much more money he makes cutting hair.

"And I didn't even have all those years of college and graduate school."

Dad also squirms when I encourage my mother to stand her ground against him. One day, when I was visiting, my father stood up from the dinner table, like he's always done and headed for his recliner.

"Mary, bring me my coffee," he called out to my mother.

Using every expression my eyes and brow would allow, I mouthed the words dramatically, for only my mother to see.

"Tell him to get it himself."

With me there as support, Mom held her head high and proudly called back.

"Get it yourself, Nick."

My father turned around quickly, his face a red flame. He stared at her with his mouth open, then calmed down, looked over at me and pointed.

"You, you, I know you were behind this!"

I shrugged my shoulders and smiled. My mother laughed all the way to the coffee pot. She poured a cup and laid it on the TV table next to him. I just shook my head.

Despite my father's opinion that my career choices as an artist, writer and teacher would never bring in large amounts of money, I've managed to get myself to Italy and other countries in Europe numerous times. Of course he attributes this to Stu's income, even though that's not always been the case.

Twice, I have traveled with my husband to Italy. Stu likes to brag about how I could get us through the country with what he thinks is good Italian. But even Stu always said that he would only travel to Sicily if my father agreed to go, since the language barrier is more challenging in the smaller *paesi,* or villages, on the island.

So during Easter weekend of 2000, while driving from our home outside of Charlotte, North Carolina to see my parents in Syracuse, New York, Stu and I conjured up a plan to trick my father into going to Sicily. Knowing how vital money is to the Italian mindset, we were about to make my father an offer he'd hate to refuse.

"Dad, want to go to Sicily with us?" I asked soon after we arrived.

He responded with one of his usual smart remarks.

"Only if you pay."

"You're on, Dad."

Speechless, which was rare for Dad, he stood smiling. Even though he can be a curmudgeon at times, I also knew my father's generous spirit would never allow us to pay for everything. My response intrigued him.

"You're going to pay my way?" he asked.

"We'll pay if you go."

"Your mother, too?"

"Of course," I said, and looked over toward Mom standing at the stove, stirring a pot of boiling pasta.

She scrunched her face in uncertainty, wrinkles in her forehead appeared. Her mouth turned into a half smile.

"You game, Mom?" I asked.

"Whatever your father says."

Poor Mom. I knew she had little desire to go to Italy or anywhere abroad. She has never been crazy about flying, period. As part of the World War II generation of Italian-American women, she believes in doing whatever her husband says. She may complain about my father to one of my sisters or to me—sometimes even in hearing range of Dad's chair—hoping to elicit an ally. But whatever conversation transpires doesn't matter. My mother still goes along with my father's decisions.

It took time for Mom to warm up to the idea of traveling overseas. One day in midsummer, about three months before our trip, I noticed while talking to her on the phone that her demeanor had changed.

She actually seemed excited about seeing where her parents, older brother, aunts and uncles were born. Her family's *paese*, Linguaglossa, sits at the foot of Mount Etna, only a two-hour car ride from my father's hometown of Gualtieri Sicaminò, outside of Messina, Sicily.

Mom informed me that she began preparing for the trip by walking Sunnycrest Park with a friend at least four times a week. If it rained, they strolled Shoppingtown Mall. She started with twenty minutes and built up to forty. Mom bought new walking shoes and a lightweight purse to strap over her shoulder.

She asked my sister, Teresa's husband, Jimmy, a leather craftsman, to make passport holders and a rectangular wallet to carry her *lire*. Jimmy also made leather key chains and small change purses that Mom could give away as gifts to relatives that she would meet for the first time.

****

Sunday night, before our departure, my parents sound eager on the phone as they review what they packed in their luggage and what they'll carry on the plane. There's no reason to tell them about the hotel not being close to the Vatican until I see them face-to-face tomorrow in Philadelphia, where we'll meet for our overseas flight.

After I hang up, my sister, Teresa, calls. She's number five out of eight children and the only one still in Syracuse, two blocks from Mom and Dad's house.

"Aren't you excited about leaving tomorrow?" she asks.

"I think I'm more nervous," I say.

I spare her the news of the hotel mishap. Although delighted about their trip, Teresa is also apprehensive that my parents will be so far away. There's no need to add to her angst.

Teresa and I traveled to Italy and Sicily in 1983 with one of our cousins, Marisa. It was Teresa's first time abroad, and although she still talks enthusiastically about that trip, like my parents, she's not crazy about being too far from home. They prefer to host Stu and me, our slew of siblings, in-laws, nieces, nephews and any other relatives who visit Syracuse.

Teresa remembers every detail and every next of kin from that year we traveled together—including many relatives we never knew existed. She swears she will return after getting her four children through college.

My sister sounds more enthusiastic about our trip than I do. I mention to her how responsible I'm feeling about traveling with Mom and Dad. Being the second oldest in a large family, I used to pride myself as being my mother's helper, taking on tasks of feeding and bathing my younger siblings, cleaning the house, ironing and helping with dinner and kitchen duties.

But not having lived in Syracuse for three decades, not having children of my own to care for, and not being around to help my folks in unexpected situations makes this responsibility for my parents seem overwhelming. I'm not about to say much to Teresa, knowing all that she does for our mother and father.

****

During months of planning the trip, each time I made some arrangement, I also prefaced it with, "Now I'll be traveling with my elderly parents, so I'll need…" and I filled in the blank with whatever obsessive concern emerged at the time—twin beds, airline seats together, a comfortable car.

Of course, I was a bit over the top, since my parents are hardly elderly. They were older, but not in need of much assistance. Having felt accountable for every detail, I even returned to my therapist for perspective.

She suggested that I delegate some duties. Stu, who already knew he'd be driving the rental car in Sicily, agreed to plan the routes from town to town. Like his astrological sign, Taurus, Stu is calm, steady, and down to earth.

My mother was delighted to have a job—getting the gifts that Italians bring when visiting. She drove to Oneida in upstate New York and picked up pieces of silverware, ladles and serving utensils, to be given along with the leatherwork that Teresa's husband, Jimmy, made. Mom found socks, too, with the label "Made in U.S.A."

"Just a little something extra," she said. "You know, for my two male cousins that I'll be meeting for the first time."

About a month before leaving, I called my father on the phone.

"Dad," I said, "I'm giving everyone something to be in charge of."

"Oh, really. Your mother, too?"

"Yes, Dad. Mom, too," I answered, knowing that if he had a task, she better be assigned one as well.

"What am I in charge of?" he asked.

"You're in charge of the language," I said, unsure what his response would be.

Dad's mood could change in a second, and we have been known to come head-to-head over the simplest comments. The Italian language is so natural to my father, though, that it seemed like a reasonable undertaking and a fair request.

Dad burst out laughing

"You're kidding?"

"No, Dad. I haven't had time to practice. So can you take on the language?"

Still snickering, he said, "I thought that was why you were bringing me to begin with."

What a relief!

****

With this hotel thing hanging over my head, my stress level is at its peak. Maybe my therapist was right when she suggested I go on the drug, Zoloft. I opted for the herb, Suma, instead, which isn't strong enough to get me through the agent's recent call to announce, that after scouring the Internet, there still is no other available hotel in Rome.

Carol is going to her office early tomorrow morning and will call us before we leave at 11 a.m. for the airport. She's hoping to have better luck finding something with the resources available at her agency.

As I climb into bed, suitcases packed and ready to go, I realize more than ever that I need to write five things to be grateful for today. It's a ritual I started a few years ago. Having carried the worry gene for so long, I am determined to see the good in life.

1) I am so glad I followed the hunch, the voice, the whatever that woke me, and called the hotel in Rome. It's a lot better to find out at this end where we're staying, before taking a cab to the wrong place in a foreign country after having flown all night.

2) I am grateful for my conversation this afternoon with Bridget. Although my sister, Bridget, is nineteen years younger, she has the wisdom of the Goddess Sophia. Her astrological sign is the same as Stu's—Taurus. She's as down to earth as he is and was the one who pointed out that at least we had a place to stay when arriving.

3) Thank God for the long, hard walk around the park. There, I beat the pavement and let out the frustrations of my day.

4) I'm grateful for the herb, Suma to curb my anxiety.

5) Last but not least, I wrote, Stu, Stu, Stu. He hung in there, rubbed my head and shoulders. He listened to me fret as we walked the park together.

I also like to write one awareness that I had each day and one request. Today, I learned, again, to pay attention to my own intuition. It did try to get my attention about the hotel in Rome months ago.

The one request that I am now asking, this Sunday night, from God, Spirit or whatever Divine force exists, is for help in resolving our room situation in Rome before we leave in the morning. After tossing and turning for what seems like hours, I finally fall asleep.

2) Departure

Monday, October 16

Lights on the digital alarm glimmer 4:15 a.m. That same nagging voice again says, "Call Rome." What? I need rest, not some crazy inner prattle, tempting me out of bed. I'll only pace the floor and continue worrying. It's bad enough that I'm awake. I don't want to wake Stu up again.

However, no matter how much I try to get comfortable, I can't get back to asleep. So I gently pull back the covers, step out of bed, put on my robe and climb the stairs to the studio. It's almost five o'clock our time and close to eleven a.m. in Rome. I close the door and dial the number of the hotel near the Vatican.

"Buon giorno, parla Inglese?" I begin, with my usual four words of Italian.

"Yes, Madam," the person on the other end says.

I recognize the same woman's voice from twenty-four hours earlier.

"Stefania?" I ask. "Is this you?"

Lucky for me, it is. I tell her I'm taking a chance that somebody may have canceled their reservations. She remembers me.

"Wait one minute, Madam," she says, and puts me on hold.

A little embarrassed about my persistence, I'm relieved that I'm not there face-to-face with her. My behavior must appear obsessive. I ignore my self-consciousness in the hope that rooms will appear. I haven't been a dreamer all of my life for nothing.

"Madam," Stefania says, returning to the phone, "Would you be willing to take a small apartment with two bedrooms and share a bath?"

Bells chime in my head. There are often twelve to twenty-four people sharing two and a half baths at my parents' house in Syracuse, during the holidays. Four people for one facility will feel like luxury accommodations.

I jump at the offer without even asking the cost. I'm taking those rooms no matter what. Yet just before I hang up, my Italian upbringing rears its head. I can't help myself. I ask the price. The apartment is more expensive than the two rooms at the other hotel by the airport, which makes it 80,000 *lire* more per night, forty American dollars, and worth every penny.

When I crawl back into bed, Stu puts his arms around me. For a nanosecond, we lay together like spoons, before I flip my face back towards his.

"We got the rooms in Rome."

"What?" Stu stammers, half sleeping.

"We have rooms in the hotel near the Vatican. I just spoke to the woman there."

He sighs a breath of relief and one eye opens wide.

"How did you do it?"

"I'll tell you when we get up," I say, and feel his whole body relax.

We sleep soundly until the alarm rings at seven. Soon after, I call our travel agent to tell her the good news. To be sure that the other reservations are definitely canceled, she suggests I call the first hotel, so that we don't get stuck paying two hotel bills. After speaking to Luigi at the *Hotel Cristoforo Colombo*, I settle down, confident that nothing could go wrong now.

It won't even matter if I get my menstrual period on the plane. It's been one of many things I've fretted about over the past weeks. My worry stems back to the flight I took to Italy in '83, with my sister and cousin. The toilets were stopped up, and we held our breaths when entering any of the aircraft's bathrooms. Although none of us had our periods, we discovered that not all of the women on the plane were that fortunate—it's one of those bloody images I've never quite shaken.

I'm slowly realizing that periodic bouts of PMS have added to my anxiety about details I can't do a thing about: hailing down the right taxi from the da Vinci airport to the hotel after we arrive, getting another cab to the train station the morning we leave for Sicily, and of utmost concern, my parents' safety in the large city of Rome.

The sense of responsibility I've been feeling about my parents has been unrelenting. Now with the synchronicity of the hotel in Rome falling in place, maybe my fears will melt away. On route to the airport in Charlotte, I announce to Stu,

"We are about to embark on a blessed trip."

Stu smirks and says, "I hope so."

He knows me too well. My mood, like Dad's, can shift in a second.

****

There are a handful of cities where I feel I belong. Rome is one of them. I went to a psychic once, who told me that in a previous life, I was the widow of an aristocrat in ancient Rome. As a patron of the ceramic arts, the Roman community held me in high esteem. According to the psychic—after my spouse died, I became a lonely woman who took to walking the streets, past the Coliseum, The Roman Forum, the Pantheon and other ancient ruins. This makes more sense to me than any other reason I can come up with.

I love traveling to Rome. I can't always stay there for long periods of time, though, because of the current, frenzied pace. Cars and Vespas are driven insanely over curbs and onto sidewalks. Whenever I'm there, I revisit at least one of the Roman ruins, an Early Christian, Renaissance or Baroque church, and always the Fountain of Trevi.

I throw in my coins like they did in the 1954 movie, *Three Coins in the Fountain*. It's my assurance that I will return to Rome again someday. I've never mentioned to my parents the psychic's interpretation of my love for Rome. Actually, I've never even told them that I go to psychics.

****

The arrival time of Mom and Dad's flight from Syracuse to Philadelphia has been changing every ten to fifteen minutes. Syracuse is holed up in rain and fog. I just told the airline representatives they need to make arrangements for the four of us to travel tomorrow because I cannot leave for Rome without my folks. One attendant gets a bit indignant. Another says, "You're way ahead of yourself."

I'm trying to keep in mind what I said to Stu this morning about our trip being blessed. Remaining calm is not my forte, but I'm giving it my all as I wait for Mom and Dad's flight from Syracuse. Funny— Stu, who rarely worries, is sitting across from me, fiddling with his hands, crossing his legs again. That's a switch in character, for the both of us.

In thirty minutes, our overseas flight is scheduled to depart, just as Mom and Dad come walking down the jetway. They half-turn around and say goodbye to a couple they must know from Syracuse, and then they stretch up to see us.

Mom never looks away while putting on her sweater and waving all at the same time. Dad smiles. An airport employee appears with a passenger cart to pick up my parents and another older couple. We quickly hug each other, and then we help them onto the cart.

The driver honks the alarm and off she goes moving as fast as pedestrian traffic will allow, as she heads toward the international concourse for the flight to Rome. Stu and I trot behind.

Once at the International gate, we discover that the seats assigned when booking the flight are not the seats we're in. Throughout months of planning, I envisioned Mom and me sitting in the center four seats in the middle of the plane, Dad and Stu on either end.

On board, all I can see of my parents are the back of their heads, eight rows in front of us. I muster up the courage and ask the woman sitting on my right if she and her husband would consider changing seats with my folks.

Not only are they willing, but eager. It turns out they did not get their request for a left aisle seat, which the man needs to protect his injured arm. A left-aisle seat is exactly where my father is sitting.

After my parents settle in the row with us, we compare notes about our connections into Philadelphia. Thunderstorms in upstate New York delayed all air travel. After my folks' plane took off, the captain announced that their flight was the only one that was getting out of Syracuse today. Finally, I fill them in about the room mishap and how I was awakened two mornings in a row to call Rome. Mom listens with interest. Dad, with his own prophetic dream world, smiles as his eyebrows lift. He's intrigued.

****

Once, during my teenage years, when most things my parents said were of little interest to me, Dad woke up and told us he'd dreamt the lyrics and music to a song. He taught the song to my younger sisters and cousins.

Over the years, the singing of *Walking on the Stars toward Heaven* became part of family gatherings. Often Dad woke up, having had a significant dream. Sometimes, he'd tell us about it. More times than not, he kept the dream a secret, leaving everyone on the edge of curiosity, while he waited to see if it came true.

My father owned a hardcover black book that included the meaning of dreams, which I frequently looked through. There were other topics, from Astrology to Yoga that also piqued my interest. I'm not sure Dad read about all of them: Numerology, Chakras, Handwriting Analysis, Telepathy and others.

I was enamored with all the various subjects, including the visual images in the Palmistry chapter, portraying drawings of different types of hands and information on how to figure out my life, head and heart lines. The full shape of a person's hand could represent such types as Philosophical, Inspirational, Pointed and Elementary.

Dad and I both fell between the Conical Hand (inspirational), which tapers gently from base to fingertips and the Pointed Hand (idealistic). The second type has been known as the Psychic Hand. Fingers are pointed and the hand is long, narrow and thin.

When I would sit and listen to Dad's numerous dreams, my mother would tell my father to stop filling my head with his crazy ideas, since she could tell that I was one to sit and take in any mystical information Dad would offer. One day, Dad said that I was not allowed to look in his book anymore.

By then I was hooked—not only on Dad's dream life and the new material I was reading, but also on my own dream world. Even though I was a rather obedient child, when Dad was at work at the barbershop, I would sneak many a peak in his "infamous" book.

The day I left for college, my father actually handed me his black hardcover book, *The Complete Illustrated Book of the Psychic Sciences*, by Walter & Litzka Gibson, published in 1966.

****

On the plane, Mom and I talk like we always do. Dad does his typical sleep act, although it's not an act. He can fall asleep anywhere, at any time. Stu appears relaxed and seemingly unaffected by the tension of the last two days. After dinner, Stu, Mom and I watch Julia Roberts in *Erin Brockovich* on the miniature screens in the back of the seats. Once the cabin lights are totally dim, we all take a nap.

Dozing in and out of awareness, I think of the message that awakened me earlier in the day saying, "Call Rome." I can't help feeling that we are embarking on some kind of soul journey.

In Nomine Patris

Another sermon
on the pope's visit,
his processions
through major cities
enclaved by bishops
and cardinals, moving
past nuns pressed
behind wooden barriers.

"Awake From Your Slumber"
the priest first bellowed
marching down the aisle,
dressed in gold-brocade,
lead by cross bearer,
altar boys, the female lector
hoisting above her head
a large red book,
readings from Matthew,
Mark, Luke and John.

The homily, and there's no
Catherine of Siena communing
with forest creatures
on the road to Avignon
to advise church leaders.
No Hildegard of Bingen,
drawings of heavenly images,
symphony of seraphs singing.
No Teresa of Avila pierced
with angel's arrows
entering a trance, writing
inspired words.

3) In Rome

Tuesday, October 17

Minutes after walking into the da Vinci airport, early morning—Rome time, my father tries to track down a cousin he was told worked there. When a man in baggage claim says there are hundreds of people who work at the airport, Dad gives up.

We stop at the money exchange and trade some American traveler's checks for *lire*. Before long, I'm bartering for a *tassi* into the city with the first driver who meets us at the swinging doors. His quote, 175,000 *lire*, or $82.50, will take us to any hotel near the *Vaticano*. I walk away.

The guy puts his hands on his hips and pushes his chin out. Then he starts calling after me in English with a heavy Italian accent.

I flip around and lash back in my fractured *dialetto*, or dialect.

"We paid half that amount the last time we visited Rome."

It was only Stu and me, not four of us, but even then, I thought we were ripped off. Since I've done my share of negotiating in Italy before, there is no way I'm giving this taxi driver the upper hand. My father could arrange the deal in Italian, but he's not the barterer that I am.

Growing up, I learned how to bargain from my mother's mother, my grandmother, *Nonna* Egidia. And it comes back when needed—at flea markets, antique stores and especially when traveling in Italy.

The driver walks over and tries to appeal to my father and the sense of patriarchy rooted in Dad's DNA. It's the way the Italian male-mind thinks. Fathers, brothers, husbands, priests—bottom line—men are the only ones who could or should make decisions.

"When was the last time *you* were in Rome?" the cab driver calls after me when I turn away, as if I owe him, a complete stranger, an explanation.

The guy quickly engages my father in conversation, raises his hand to his head and turns his finger around his temple indicating to my own parent that I must be *pazza*, or crazy. Instead of defending me, my father walks over, trying to reconcile in favor of the driver.

I'm offended, but I don't have time to deal with it right now. By the time Dad reaches me, I've already arranged for another ride into the city for the four of us. The price—80,000 *lire*—less than half of what the first driver quoted.

"Now who exactly is the one that's nuts here, Dad?" I say, glaring at the guy who is escaping into the terminal.

My father's face takes on a look of delightful surprise when he hears the amount I bargained for. I must admit, I did catch a smirk on Dad's tired mouth when I was haggling with the first driver. Perhaps I misjudge my father, because eventually he tells me he's impressed that I have the guts to speak up. Now speaking up, I learned from him.

As we drive into the city and through rounded arches in the walls that surround Rome, Franco, our driver, beeps his horn. He drives over street dividers, passes Romans on bicycles and scooters, and calls out the window in colorful Italian expletives to "move over!"

The closer we get to Vatican City, the more my father's olive complexion changes to grayish white. It was me who got carsick growing up—never any of my siblings, and definitely not my parents. Dad, who was always in charge, decided the route, drove and, most of the time, chose our destination.

Soon after, I notice my father's pallid appearance against the white dome of St. Peter's Basilica in the distance. Oddly, Tuesday morning's traffic is more congested the closer we get to Vatican City.

Franco rolls down his window again and asks a guy on the street why the delay. To Franco's and our chagrin, Queen Elizabeth II of England is visiting Pope John Paul II this very morning. As my father's face gets more washed out, security gets tighter and cars begin to back up, bumper-to-bumper.

In my head, I picture us moving along quickly as we pass landmarks that I recognize—the bridge I traveled over in the past and the tunnel that will lead us around and away from the Basilica itself. Despite my visualizations, traffic is jam-packed. Franco zooms down a narrow alley, looking for a shortcut, only to come up behind other cars in the same predicament.

By now, Dad is totally silent. Mom grows quiet, too, picking up, as she does, all of my father's behaviors. Suddenly, our driver cuts through a couple of narrow alleyways that could be driveways, for all I know.

He takes a sharp left, pulls the van up onto the sidewalk, follows a running brick wall, and stops. Puzzled, I look up at the moment Franco points to a sign above an arched opening. *Hotel Columbus.*

Dad quickly maneuvers himself out of the van, fumbles through his pocket for *lire* and hands it to Mom, insisting she pay the fare. We encourage Dad to go on ahead into the lobby for the *toilette*, while Stu and the driver pull out the luggage.

The bellhop runs over and stretches out his hand, motioning for us to enter through the archway. A few blocks down looms St. Peter's Basilica.

Franco apologizes for the first driver back at the airport, then holds out his business card.

"Call, call," he repeats, "call when you fly back to the United States."

And I agree that we will, not really knowing if we can or not.

Stu, Mom and I follow an old chipped and broken walkway, through a barrel-arch. Behind the busy *Via della Conciliazione* lays an enclosed garden of various plants, trees, bushes and a large flowing fountain. It's a respite from the hubbub of the street a few steps behind.

To the left is the door of a once-upon-a-time monastery turned hotel. Stefania, the woman I talked to on the phone, is on duty, along with two well-dressed men. She smiles and reaches over the counter. We shake hands firmly.

While the four of us sit on the couches in the lobby, waiting for the apartment to be ready, I use a hotel phone to call the American Embassy, and I talk to a woman named Stephanie. She and I had communicated by email and phone.

I met Stephanie in 1996 at Stu's nephew's wedding in Rome. Paul's father-in-law had been stationed at the American Embassy back then, and Stephanie, his former assistant, had arranged for our Papal Audience tickets.

Now, Stephanie gives me directions to a convent on *Via dell'Umiltà*, where we can pick up the tickets after four this afternoon. The two of us chat a few minutes about the flight, about how we've been since we met four years ago and about our predicament with the rooms in Rome. I tell her about the voice that woke me from sleep two mornings in a row, saying to call Rome. She seems as intrigued as I've been.

"You have no idea how lucky you are," Stephanie says. "We've struggled here at the embassy to find a decent room, any room sometimes, even for dignitaries. There's been a shortage of places to stay in Rome all year."

We talk as if we've known each other a good deal of our lives and end with the hope that someday we'll meet again.

On the third floor, halfway down the long corridor, we open and enter through a thick mahogany door. Two steps up, and we're standing in a three-by-three-foot hall. The door on our immediate right opens to the narrow, rectangular bathroom we will all share.

Mom and Dad take the room straight ahead. Stu and I settle in the one on the left. Our apartment, or what in America would be called a suite, fits us perfectly—very European and very Italian—decorated in plush, heavy, purple-floral drapes that hang from ceiling to floor. Pushed to the side, they expose expansive vertical windows, overlooking the monastery gardens.

In the distance, I see part of the facade of an early-Baroque church standing on the other side of the hotel wall. Each of our rooms has twin beds, cloak closets and television sets, although, neither Stu nor I are interested in any programs or news. Even with the noise of traffic beyond the wall, we decide a nap is in order, at least until lunch—Rome time.

Years earlier, I was warned not to nap when first arriving from the states and to get on local time as soon as possible. Yet snoozing is a pastime for Dad, who is still trying to get over the aftermath of the nausea he had in the van.

My siblings and I have taken hundreds of pictures of my father, sleeping everywhere—at the beach, on couches, in chairs, at airports. If Stu, Mom and I are tired, I'm sure Dad is too, no matter how long he slept on the plane.

With a little prodding, he opens his mouth and lets me drop in some homeopathic liquid that I brought along for upset stomachs. Dad falls asleep before I leave the room. Mom says she's going to lie there and try to rest, something she wants to make clear she never does at home in the middle of the day.

Being the first to wake, I call out Stu's name, step out of bed, pull back the thick heavy drapes and open the window to the end of a light rain shower. I go next door to rouse Mom and Dad.

"If we're going to eat lunch, we better do it somewhere before three in the afternoon, when the *ristoranti* and *trattorie* close," I say, suggesting we could even do something more casual than a restaurant.

Owners of Italian eating establishments will head home to eat their own meals before reopening for dinner, sometime after seven. I learned the Italian eating style the hard way while traveling with my sister and cousin in 1983.

We tried to eat our meals on American time, but we found out quickly that there are no early five o'clock meals at a place like Denny's or Shoney's. It was a good lesson on the phrase, "When in Rome…"

We could sleep through the day and stay on U.S. time, but it's my mission to get us on Italian time. Since I'm the self-appointed tour guide, I know that if I stay on schedule, the rest of them will too. Besides, we have Papal Audience tickets to pick up at four in an old convent near the Trevi Fountain.

Across the wide *Via della Conciliazione* and down two streets, we find a bustling *trattoria*, that small less formal restaurant. The establishment sits on a corner, flanked by lots of little shops and tourist joints. It appears that the *trattoria* has mostly Italian clients inside. I always look to find where the locals eat, since it's usually the best food. As it turns out, we are the last party they agree to sit. Italians are independent souls, even in business.

Our waitress looks to be around nineteen or twenty, attractive, about 5'7" including tall heels, slick jet-black hair, heavy eyeliner to match, and a tight mini skirt. She rolls her eyes as the owner sits us at her table. I bet she was hoping her shift was over.

Dad immediately speaks Italian to her, explaining how he hasn't been in Italy for a while and apologizes for any mistakes he makes with the language. The waitress warms right up to him.

It's easy to do when Dad puts on the charm, even though I know how fast his disposition can change. But for now, he's gracious, helping the waitress and the rest of us with any language barrier.

My father and I order soup—chicken broth with small *pastina,* or little pasta, and chopped vegetables. It hits the spot for sensitive stomachs. I never take a chance on spicy foods before or after a long flight.

The *vitello arrosto,* or veal roast, which Dad and I share, has the protein we need to carry us through the rest of the day. Mom and Stu have tortellini, stuffed with cheese and covered with a light, zesty, pink marinara sauce.

Both my mother and husband have ironclad stomachs. It isn't the first similarity I've seen over the years. Parallels between my father and me, too, have often been pointed out, something I've tried hard to dispute.

Although we cashed traveler's checks earlier at the airport, we begin wondering if we'll need more *lire* before leaving for Sicily the day after next. So after lunch, we head for another bank down the street, but we miss getting inside within minutes of it closing at three.

No matter how many times I've been to Italy, I'm still never sure when banks open and close. It seems to vary from city to city, town to town. I have my suspicions that they have their own secret system that I'll never be privy to.

We stroll on down the road and try to figure out the best way of getting to the Trevi Fountain, where the convent on *Via dell'Umiltà* is located and where we'll pick up the papal audience tickets. I recognize the bus stop that Stu and I used back in 1996, at the time of his nephew's wedding.

Before we even get across the street, it begins to rain. From awning to awning, we follow Dad, who heads directly to a shop with a stack of umbrellas stuffed in a large ceramic pot sitting in a doorway.

"How about a Jubilee umbrella?" the shopkeeper asks my father in Italian, pointing to a white umbrella, plastered with the papal insignia.

Although my conversational Italian is weak, I can understand most of what he says. Mom, who grew up speaking her parents' dialect, can also talk if she chooses to. Stu, the only one in the dark, doesn't seem at all concerned since he's been in the country with me before and is now overly confident with, what he thinks, are three interpreters.

In the past, I've tried to tell him that my Italian is not that proficient. But he's easily impressed with the little I know. He didn't believe me then and doesn't now. Plus, he is even more secure, with a father-in-law who understands and speaks the language effortlessly.

The shopkeeper seems delighted talking to us about how the city of Rome has been preparing for the Jubilee celebration. Monuments and buildings had been washed and cleaned, and all tourists' attractions geared up for the onslaught of pilgrims heading to the Catholic Mecca.

According to the shopkeeper, the Vatican receives a cut on any items sold that portray their motif or the papal insignia.

The man tells us lots of tales about the pilgrims who've been flocking here since January, about how he lived in the U.S. for a short time and about the orders he's received for souvenirs that he sent over to, of all places, Atlantic City.

He switches to English and glances at Stu to be sure he's being understood, when he demonstrates how gamblers place medals of their favorite saint in their pocket for good luck.

Just like Dad's command of Italian, the shopkeeper has a fine grasp of English. Both speak with an Italian accent, Dad's not nearly as heavy. My father never really lost his accent, even after emigrating from Sicily more than sixty years ago.

I enjoy watching Dad interact with the shopkeeper, the cab driver who drives us over toward the Trevi fountain and the woman working in the *cambio,* or change center, near the corner *piazza.* After retrieving our Papal Audience tickets at the convent, Dad shows no hesitation as he walks up to a number of money exchange sites. Each one is a narrow opening, with a window tucked in between shops and businesses.

Dad easily asks for change from paper money to coins. Of course, the rest of the immediate world flocking to the infamous fountain has the same request, a constant bombardment of tourists from all over the world. My father is a take-charge person—not one who easily accepts "no" for an answer. Even if he only gets a few coins, he achieves something and moves onto another window until there is enough change for all four of us to throw into the water.

I watch Mom and Dad, like a mother duck protecting her young. Despite my love of Rome, it is still a city, like any other major metropolis, where I've learned to be cautious. Besides, I have seven siblings back home to answer to, each just as protective. Stu, having been married to me for twenty-three years, is used to our family dynamic.

He finds our emotional responses entertaining and chuckles most times or cracks a joke. He humors me when I motion with my hand for him to watch my parents carefully, as they walk down the steps toward the Trevi Fountain.

I hope to prevent anyone from knocking Mom off-base and grabbing her purse. Dad assures me that he came prepared and shows me the zipper that Jimmy, Teresa's husband, sewed on the back pocket of his jeans. From a distance, I take a picture of them throwing their coins in the water.

With all the tourists and hawkers in one location, I feel like a stuffed anchovy in a flat metal container. I maneuver my way between the crowd and down the steps to participate in the time-honored practice.

The sounds and sights of the strong gushing water, pouring out and around the twisted sculptural forms of the fountain, reflect the energy of this city. Thrilled to be back in Rome, I throw in three Italian coins and three American pennies, assuring another return to the grand capital. Is it from my past visits, the genetic inheritance of the country from where my family originated, or have I really walked these streets some other lifetime ago?

****

Later, back at the hotel after everyone else is asleep, I lay in bed and journal about the long day, from the morning call to Stephanie here at the Hotel Christopher Columbus, to the flights from Charlotte to Philly onto the daVinci airport. I write about our ride through the Roman thoroughfares and walking the streets of the grand capital.

In reviewing the long day, I'm reminded how determined I am to avoid confrontation with my father. I've struggled for so long with having grown up under his authoritarianism, his strict rules, and his ways of taking control like the men of his culture.

Dad is a typical Italian father who would say, "If you have a problem making a decision, come to me and I'll give you the right answer," rather than encouraging independent thinking. Having rejected that stance years earlier, I've spent a good deal of my adulthood arguing with Dad about the different ways he and I see the world.

To hold him responsible for the entire patriarchy permeating everything and everywhere is unfair. Now here in, of all places, Rome, Italy, right down the street from the most patriarchal site of my upbringing—the Vatican—I am determined to break that pattern of conflict and stop blaming my father for the woes of mankind.

Maybe it was my soul that wanted to be in the right Hotel Columbus—close to St. Peter's—to help in shattering the old dynamic with Dad once and for all. Heaven knows that at fifty years old, it is time for me to shift from being his child—arguing with his every word—to being an adult who accepts my father for who he is, despite our differences.

As I lie in bed still awake at 1:30 a.m., I think of Dad asking for change near the Trevi Fountain. Finally, I see value in his ongoing resolve to get things accomplished—even a simple task of exchanging money in a place that may or may not be accommodating.

That doesn't matter to my father. He's not run his life by how other people perceive him. Instead, Dad can ask for what he needs. He didn't necessarily get all the *lire* he wanted exchanged, but he got enough, and it was more than what he had to begin with.

In the past, I might have gotten angry with Dad too, after he fell asleep in the chapel at the convent on *Via dell'Umiltà*, when we picked up the Papal Audience tickets. Dad snoozed as a young priest explained how the building became a school for other American priests traveling to Rome to study canon law. My father would have gone off the deep end if I, or any of my siblings, fell asleep in a chapel or in the presence of a priest talking.

Instead of getting mad this afternoon, I took another photo of Dad to show those back home—his head hanging in front of a side altar in the middle of the elaborate frescoes adorning the space. Even as adults, he still insists that we kneel erect and pray. We laughed, Mom and me, watching him sound asleep. Stu smiled, always having understood Dad in a way that I've found puzzling. Maybe it's the way men understand life.

At one time, I would have accused Dad of being self-centered. And I can't be sure that I won't think that again. For now, I appreciate his ability to be clear about his wants, needs and beliefs. Maybe by accepting my father for who he is, I'll learn to focus on my own desires, and I'll grow less concerned with others' approval.

I've also been thinking about the tickets we were given at the convent. Instead of receiving the yellow ones like everyone else, a Monsignor called us aside and handed us green tickets, saying that the pope wanted us nearby. I knew that had been arranged by Stephanie from the Embassy.

The pope doesn't really know who we are, but being able to sit close to him delights my folks, and that makes it exciting for Stu and me, too. The Monsignor also encouraged us to arrive early tomorrow morning so that we will not be far from the front, since there will be a few hundred other people sitting in an area near the Pontiff.

I am thrilled for my parents, knowing how much Catholicism has been a central part of their lives and my upbringing. I can't say that all my siblings and I have followed or stayed with the church as closely as my father might have wished.

I'm not going to think about that right now. We have green tickets in hand and plan to be in St. Peter's piazza when the gates open, first thing in the morning.

4) Papal Audience

Wednesday a.m. October 18

I don't do mornings well. Night is my time, when most people are asleep, their energies subdued. I can ruminate. Dressing up for the pope and arriving by eight o'clock to get front row seats in the green section is enough for me to handle. Before leaving our apartment, Dad keeps flipping back and forth about whether or not he wants to wear a sweater under his suit jacket.

When I suggest he carry the sweater, he throws his right hand up in the air and says, *"uffa!"*—his Italian expression for any number of things. I know this time he means, "leave me alone and let me do what I feel like doing!" So, what's new?

The hotel's breakfast is not the typical *prima colazione* of *biscotti* and *caffè*. The lavish buffet, more like an American brunch, includes hard-boiled eggs, salami, mortadella and other cold cuts, along with croissants and a huge variety of breads and pastries, fruits and juices, coffees and teas. Since there is no way of knowing how long the Papal Audience with all its festivities will take, we eat heartily.

My stomach takes longer than a day or two to settle into another time zone. There's no way I'm going to pour myself a cup of the heavy-thick coffee that Italians prepare, whether it's *espresso* or not. And the strong liquid reminds me of the way my maternal grandfather, *Nonno* Stagnitta, made coffee until, as the family tale goes, he brewed it so long his teaspoon stood straight up by itself.

Mom and Dad pour themselves a cup. After they each have a sip, they add boiling water and lots of milk. I choose *camomilla* tea, and Stu stays with his old faithful, *succo d'arancia,* or orange juice.

Once outside and halfway down the first block, Dad decides he wants his sweater after all. I want to scream. It wasn't like I hadn't told him. Stu offers to run back to the room, and I do all in my power not to lash out. I must have temporary amnesia, forgetting those insights about my father just six hours earlier. Typical Dad. He expects to be catered to by Mom and anyone else around.

I hold back from saying that we are not *his* papal entourage, there to serve his every need. Biting my lip, I suppose what I really need is more sleep or a slurp of that thick-black coffee, since all of my positive revelations about Dad are floating down the *Via della Conciliazione.*

Hurrying to be one of the first people through the security gate has become pointless. I specifically arranged our trip around Rome, so that Dad, the staunch, devout Catholic, could see the pope during the Jubilee year. Now here we are running late because of his sweater. The judgmental part of me rears its ugly head. Once Stu catches up, he quietly reprimands me.

"He only wanted his sweater."

Feeling irritated and guilty all at the same time, I attempt to listen, while hurrying toward the Vatican.

"It wasn't such a big deal for me to run back up to the room," Stu murmurs.

"Yeah, if I hadn't told Dad to bring the sweater with him," I lash back, now feeling agitated with my husband, too.

By the time we arrive at the colossal columns of St. Peter's *piazza*, people are already moving through the security gates, posted between the pillars. Even though the pope is not scheduled to arrive until eleven, I wanted to be here at the stroke of eight, like the Monsignor from the convent on *Via dell'Umiltà* suggested. Obsessive about following directions, I blame that trait on my religious upbringing. But I'm not off-base. The *piazza* is filling up early, as we were told it would, and we aren't even close to our seats.

I snap at Stu when he insists that the entrance the Monsignor told us to use is further down and closer to the Basilica. I know I'm taking my frustrations out on my husband. He is one of my safe people—even tempered, always in the same place, as I move up and down the emotional scale.

At the same time, after looking at the map we were given yesterday afternoon, I know we're wasting time and there is no entry further down. Stu disagrees and is just as resolute. I've been married to him long enough to know when he's on a mission to do something his way, whether I agree or not. So Mom, Dad and I follow, passing rows of folks entering a number of security sites along the way.

When we come to a dead end and I turn out to be right, Stu and I growl at each other, turn back and queue up in one of the security entrances we'd already passed. Once we finally get through, I dash ahead, gritting my teeth.

I'm pissed at my father and now my husband. *They can catch up with me* is what I think, hammering out my frustrations, pounding the pavement and moving as quickly as possible. What a way to start a pilgrimage!

With green tickets in hand, we march to the front. The guards direct us from the left side of the *piazza*, completely across to the other side of St. Peter's square. We pass the stand, where the pope will sit, and keep walking until we go around and behind the erected stage.

What a surprise to find ourselves up on the stand. My foul disposition shifts to relief as we nab four seats to the immediate left of the pope's throne-like chair. We are only three rows back from a low-wooden barrier that separates us from the dignitary section.

"Just think," Dad, says, "It takes my Episcopalian son-in-law to get us seats close to the pope."

Then he points to the places immediately adjacent to the pope's chair.

"I guess I'd have to be an atheist to get on the other side of that barrier."

****

Throughout the morning, the *piazza* fills with thousands of pilgrims arriving into Vatican City. From our vantage point, we can see an entire panorama of people, walking up the *Via della Conciliazione*, through the massive columns and into the square, lined with hundreds of chairs. I use the camcorder's zoom lens to locate our hotel and pan the entire view to show my siblings back home.

I know some of them wish they could have made this trip with Mom and Dad. Who wouldn't want to be with my parents in Italy, the Vatican and the towns of their ancestry? For the first time, Mom will soon be in the town that her family came from over seventy-five years earlier. Dad, who was fifteen years old when he immigrated to America, hasn't been back to his Sicilian village in thirty-two years. He took that trip right after my youngest sibling, Bridget, was born.

It was impossible for me to include everyone on the trip—not that most of them could have made the journey. They have families still at home. Maybe this is one of God's compensations for not giving me children of my own.

Before having left, I accepted that it would be Stu and me, here with Mom and Dad, and I would videotape my parents as they go from place to place. Microphone on, I talk to my sisters and brothers as if they're here, and in my mind's eye, I envision each of them, their spouses, my eighteen nieces and nephews and even some cousins.

Maybe someday we can get a bus—okay two, *due autobus*—and create a family tour, but for now, the four of us are as much as I can handle.

****

Stu agrees to take charge of still photos at the *piazza*, while I work the camcorder, praying right here—in the seat of Rome—that the thing operates properly. The camcorder belongs to my sister, Fran, and it's the first time I've ever used one. During our two and a half hour wait, there's lots of time to practice.

I snap a shot of the Bishop of Switzerland, who stops in front of us to greet some members of his congregation. I also zoom in on the gold keys St. Peter is holding in the relief sculpture above the basilica's main entrance, after Mom points it out. As quiet as she is most times—with a spouse who takes center stage—I'm careful to be attentive whenever my mother mentions anything that appeals to her.

Sitting opposite us are brides and grooms, clustered in one area, dressed in white gowns and black tuxes. It makes me uneasy. Photos and clips of the Moonie weddings from the church of the Rev. Sun Myung Moon flash in my mind. In their services, young women and men, who hadn't even met each other before their wedding day, are married *en masse* in various stadiums throughout the world.

I feel a sense of relief when people sitting nearby tell us that the couples here at the Vatican are already married, and they are in their wedding garb so the pope can bless their marriages.

Only footsteps away from the Holy See of St. Peter's, and I am questioning how religion can be such an imposing and controlling structure on humankind. While pointing and zooming with the video camera, I give my own personal commentary to my siblings, who've heard me expound before about my stance on the church as an institution. Besides mentioning my initial concern—that the brides and grooms were meeting each other, like in the Moonie weddings—I point out the masses of people flocking to the *piazza*.

"They look a little like cattle, don't they, following mindlessly along? And there's the Obelisk. You're aware of what *that* symbolizes," I say, knowing full well they'll pick up on the phallic imagery.

"And look, the Swiss Guard, all men, scores of them, actually, milling around running the show!"

At least with a video, my siblings will be able to turn me off. We are among all nationalities and races of people, like the French boy sitting in the seat directly in front of us, laughing and talking with his friends. He reminds us of my sister, Fran's oldest child. The French boy's antics, like Joey's, keep us entertained.

An artist approaches the barrier, holding up a portrait of John Paul II. He's elated when one of the security guards takes the piece from him and lays it on a table behind the Pontiff's chair with other gifts that people have brought.

Just before eleven, pockets in the crowd start to stir, as the infamous white Pope-Mobile scoots through the *piazza*. The vehicle rumbles up the stairs and unto the stage, behind the Pontiff's throne-like chair. John Paul II struggles to work his way out of the vehicle, cane in hand. Slumped over with a dowager's hump, the pope approaches his chair slowly, methodically, brushing away any help or assistance.

John Paul II was elected in 1978. Stu and I had been married less than a year. The pope's conservative ways have never appealed to my feminist sensibilities. And as the twenty-plus years of John Paul II's tenure evolved, I questioned more and more where women have been positioned in the church, and worse yet, where they've been left out.

Earlier in the year, I read a book on the legend of a Pope Joan. According to the accounts, any sign or information about her has been eradicated from all church history. There is a place near the Coliseum where she supposedly gave birth en route from the Vatican to The Basilica of St. John Lateran.

I haven't yet talked to Stu about my interest in finding that spot, and I definitely have not mentioned it to my parents. It's a place I have on *my* list to see. For now, here in the *piazza*, only steps outside of the Vatican, I stand with the two people who raised me under a cloak of strong religious beliefs, and I share this extraordinary experience with Mom and Dad.

Sitting on the platform listening to the pope, cardinals and bishops announcing the different groups of pilgrims present, I am acutely aware of the diversity of people. The various languages spoken remind me of the biblical story of the Tower of Babel. I suspect that the different tongues we speak are symbolic of the lack of understanding we still have for each other, our various cultures, customs and mores.

Bells ring. The pope addresses the audience in Spanish, welcoming all those of Spanish-speaking origin. The sun peeks through the cupola-like tent and light shines onto this frail man's slumped form. Various clergymen assist him by taking turns announcing the particular groups of pilgrims present. Cheers of recognition bellow from one end of the *piazza* to the other.

Sitting up close and watching priests and bishops carefully attend to the pope, I realize that his energy is being saved for the greetings he will give in the various languages that he speaks fluently.

"*St. Egidio della Comunità*," the Italian Bishop announces.

Egidia is my maternal grandmother's name. I'm named after her. At birth, my mother called me Gilda, having thought it was the closest derivative. When Stu hears the name over the loudspeakers, he gives me a gentle nudge. Mom smiles. Dad looks at me, and with the tilt of his head, acknowledges the mentioning of my Italian name.

Later, Pope John Paul repeats the group's name again, and I think of how *Nonna* would be pleased that the society from her hometown of Linguaglossa in Sicily happens to be here on the same day that we're present. Next week, we'll be in Linguaglossa, with *Nonna's* people. Is it a coincidence that my maternal grandmother's name rings over the loudspeakers, not once, but twice? Maybe her spirit is here, too.

The smell of roses drifts by. I've heard it said that when one smells roses—that Mary, Christ's mother, is near. I haven't smelled them during the three-plus hours we've been sitting here. I ask Mom and Dad, but neither of them smells anything. Stu admits he had a whiff, but thought it was perfume.

How is it that the patriarchy, with all its pageantry, can be overshadowed for me by the gentle presence of my mother's lineage—first my ancestral grandmother that I'm named after, then the mother of the religion in which I was raised? Even my father's nod is an acknowledgement of my maternal heritage.

When I was a child, I loved the pomp and circumstance of processions—*St. Egidio di Abate's* feast, celebrated every year in early September, where my family marched with other *paesani* from Our Lady of Pompeii church on the Italian Northside. We followed my namesake's sculpture, held high in the air by the men who'd immigrated from Linguaglossa.

When I was six years old, my First Communion class led the entire school procession at Blessed Sacrament—my family's home church. The girls wore white lace dresses and veils, the boys wore white suits and ties.

Oh, how I wanted to be chosen to crown the tall concrete statue of Mary that still sits behind the church back in Syracuse! That summer in July—before all my younger siblings were born—Mom, Dad, my older sister Nicki, younger brother, Anthony, *Nonna* and I drove to Canada to visit numerous cathedrals and marched in various processions.

The most momentous experience for me was the Basilica of Sainte-Anne-de-Beaupré. I climbed up and down the stairs, grasping *Nonna's* hand, while holding a lit candle enclosed in a paper lantern. Memories of past processions continue to creep in as the events continue—white gowns and red collars and beanies for my Confirmation ceremony, The Marian Award for Catholic Girl Scouts and years of May Processions, where each year Mary was crowned by a chosen girl in the school.

When did I lose the passion I once had for my religion? How did I begin to see through and into the patriarchy of the hierarchy's dictates? I push aside my questions and discontent with the church and let myself enjoy the celebration, knowing there'll be times ahead to dwell on the disparities that haunt me.

5) After the Vatican

Wednesday p.m. October 18

The thousands pouring out of the *piazza* are a telltale sign that the ceremonies are over. We stay for a short time and watch the colorful Florentine flag throwers perform for the masses. Brides, grooms and the chosen select who are sitting in front of the wooden barrier march up to kiss the pope's ring.

While people leave St. Peter's Square, the line to John Paul II continues slowly, allowing the official Vatican photographer to take a picture of each person with the Pontiff in his own private outdoor space.

I heard that people could purchase their photographs. Not a bad moneymaking proposition, since I also learned that only an official Vatican photographer is allowed to take pictures of anyone with the pope. Things always seem clearer when privy to behind-the-scenes information. I'm sure my skepticism of the church adds to my periodic cynicism.

Despite the photography rules, I still wish that my parents could shake the pope's hand and buy a glossy photo. It would mean so much to them, especially my father.

Just as we covet the seats beyond the wall in front of us, I know there are probably those in the *piazza* that envy our places. It's the way hierarchies make me feel—a yearning to be one step higher than I am. Is that the result of growing up Italian or growing up Catholic? Or is it human nature?

While working our way through the crowded *piazza*, swarms of tourists fill tables at the eating establishments that we pass along the way. Lines of even more people wait to sit down. We are worn out from the morning's excitement and there's relief knowing the garden restaurant at our hotel lies ahead.

On the way there, we stop at *la Banca* across from our hotel. Because of the sheer numbers of people, each exchange cannot exceed the equivalent of $200 American dollars. The woman teller who doles out most of the currency works faster than any of us can think in foreign-legal tender. Even though rates are posted lower than the exchange at the airport, I eavesdrop on Americans exiting the building who mention additional fees.

Mom and Dad have their own separate traveler's checks and carry out their transactions first. Mom confidentially confessed to me, before we left, that she was bringing extra cash of her own—cash that my father didn't know about. I can tell she's trying to keep it that way, too, while fishing through her half-opened, half-closed purse, so that Dad can't see inside. He's oblivious to what she's doing.

Before the final trade takes place, a $100 American dollar bill appears in Mom's hand. Together with her traveler's checks, she is over the $200 limit. I question her, but she doesn't hear me. She must be concentrating on keeping her secret from Dad, and at the same time, she's trying to figure out how much *lire* she wants. Eventually, I lose track of the amount she's cashing, and I wonder if Dad has, too.

My father is now in his take-charge mode as he completes Mom's transaction. Mom appears to be attempting to uphold an autonomy she's never really established with Dad. I stay out of the middle, a place where I've spent most of my life.

After stopping at our rooms to unload cameras, sweaters and purses, we take the elevator down to the garden *ristorante*. Everyone's quiet, tired, and we order only the *primo piatto*, or first course. Dad wasn't sure that he even wanted to join us, preferring a snooze to food. With adult-onset diabetes, he doesn't really have the luxury of missing a meal anymore. He's compulsive about following directions given by the doctor, about taking his pills exactly a half an hour before he eats.

****

A few weeks before leaving on our trip, I talked to Dad, explaining about how we'd be eating out and how he might not be able to dial in the precise, thirty-minute marker that he strongly adheres to. Back home, my father's pill taking had become a family event for whoever was around.

"Let me know, Mary, thirty minutes before we're going to eat," Dad would announce to my mother. "I have to take my pills."

As if she repeated the same practice every day, whether someone was watching or not, Mom mouthed with her lips, "I know you have to take your pills."

It has been a bone of contention for both of them. Dad insisting that he must take his pills precisely ten minutes before he eats, and

Mom questioning Dad about the difference between thirty minutes or forty.

My mother's plan to serve dinner at 6:30 could change if someone called or a neighbor showed up at the door, or if she decided at the last minute to quickly sauté mushrooms that she remembered having stored in the basement refrigerator.

During holidays in Syracuse, Mom could be serving anywhere from 16 to 40 people, depending upon who made it home. She loves catering to everyone and tries hard to please. Mom might have told Uncle Joe, her oldest brother, that dinner would be around three.

If one of my sisters tried to bow out gracefully, attempting to get her family back home at a decent hour to Massachusetts, Pennsylvania, Connecticut or Maine, Mom would insist that she would have the pasta on the table by two-thirty. All along, she'd told my brother, Gerard, who was driving in from New Jersey on the actual day of the festivities, that she would hold up dinner for him until four, which made it all very difficult to tell Dad exactly when he needed to take those pills.

He's been known to announce loudly, "I should have waited ten minutes before I took my pills."

The last time my brother, Anthony, visited from California for a week, he heard my father proclaim so many times that he should have waited ten minutes, that one night when Mom said, "Nick, take your pills," Anthony chimed in, "No, Dad, wait ten minutes, and the timing will be perfect."

****

Dad does come with us, taking his pills before we leave the hotel room, only to discover that he has to wait at the restaurant before we even order our meals. Although service is not what Italians consider slow, it's also not what my father expects. Italians anticipate their patrons will linger over a drink or two, which we opt not to do. It doesn't matter.

Italian waiters and waitresses have an allotted time that they give, and I learned from my previous travels that they see it as an insult to rush anyone before, during and after their meal. Pills or no pills, Dad will never be able to hurry a staff of Italian servers. Fortunately, there is thick-crusted bread to munch on.

When our meals finally arrive, I'm relieved not only to be rid of the anxiety around Dad's pills, but also to get my first pasta dish of the trip, *penne alla vodka*. I chew the light-pink doughy meal slowly, savoring every mouthful.

When we get back to our suite, Mom calls me out into the small hallway.

"I didn't get the right amount of *lire* at the bank!" she says her eyes wide, her mouth stretched in fear.

I clench my teeth and try to remain calm. As simple as the 2,000 to 1 exchange of *lire* to the dollar is at the time, I can't figure out her receipt. Having observed the scene at the counter when Mom pulled out that $100 bill, I'm not surprised at the discrepancy.

I draw Stu into the conversation to figure out the numbers. Inevitably, Dad overhears us. Although I know Mom wishes she could keep this from him, only my father will be able to speak the language well enough to explain the problem back at the bank.

Stu waits outside the bank, eyeing up the Italian ice cream, *gelato*, that he plans on getting from the street vendor as soon as the dilemma is solved. I go inside with my parents, not knowing if I'm here to referee or lend moral support.

After Dad begins explaining the situation, the guy at the window sticks his head into an office and calls the teller who handled the transaction. She remembers my parents and, without questioning, begins the task of thumbing back through hundreds of traveler's checks.

I suspect my parents' ages have come to their aid, since traditionally elders are highly respected in Italy. At one point, Dad turns to Mom and, under his breath, mutters in English.

"Mary, if you've messed up, and make a fool of me here..."

My father never finishes his statement. His lips tighten and his eyes get wide and fiery. As much as they pick at each other, he rarely gets that furious with her.

I know that he's been frustrated with Mom about money before, and perhaps it conjures up old stuff that spouses can have with each other. The two of them have never quite agreed on how to handle funds—he seemingly more frugal, or at least more organized, while she is more frivolous, yet frugal at times, too. It's a dichotomy I've never figured out. So why try now in Rome?

On vacations or trips, Dad has always been generous, spending whatever it takes. And Mom, she stashes money away for special occasions, so that she has extra to spend, not on herself, but on her children and grandchildren. I can see that look of frustration building up in Dad as he stands in front of the teller, waiting. He clenches his teeth and his cheeks harden.

Mom's fear mounts too, as she stammers when talking. In spite of her dread, she still protects her pocketbook—not so much from any possible thieves that prey on tourists in large cities, but I suspect from revealing any stash that she still has tucked away.

"It's okay Nick, let's go," I hear my mother say.

Let's go? I think, but I keep my mouth shut. I'm surprised Dad doesn't question her. I'm more amazed that she's giving up rather quickly. When it comes to money, my mother can hang on like a fox to a rabbit. Yet, Dad doesn't persist. He must half-suspect that she's found evidence of something in her purse.

"*Scusi*," he says, excusing himself graciously to the teller behind the window, and then he apologizes in flowery Italian for taking up her time.

No words are spoken between my parents as we turn around and walk away. Just before we reach the threshold of the door, Mom whispers to me, "I found that cash in my purse."

I stop breathing. I'm afraid of what will transpire once we get outside. Just before we reach the edge of the doorway, the teller comes running out from behind the divider, calling after my parents.

It appears there was a mistake after all, in spite of the fact that Mom secretly found her $100 bill. The receipt shows that the teller had not given Mom enough *lire* from the checks she did cash. It all sounds rather confusing. Since the teller found an error, Mom gets money back and Dad, who saves face, lets out a sigh of relief.

Once outside, Stu quietly suggests that picking out my favorite flavor of *gelato* is much more important than any amount of money lost or, in this case, not lost. And I am smart enough to listen to my husband and not pursue the exact figures any further. I count this as one of those "blessed" moments in our trip. *Thank God!*

Dad heads back across the street to the hotel. He needs a nap and refuses to take a cab to the Pantheon with us. Although the streets now are not as busy, people still mill around the *Via della Conciliazione*.

Stu, Mom and I walk the two blocks back to the edge of St. Peter's *piazza*, where the cabstand is located.

Queuing up is tenuous at best in Italy, since Italians don't seem to believe in a formal line, per se. We don't realize that the small conclaves of people standing around are in a so-called "line." So when we go to flag down the *tassi*, a woman yells out to us that they are next. Another group makes sure to point out that their little enclave is also part of that line.

Within minutes, four more people walk up—one a priest, who convinces the older woman at the front of the alleged line to let him ahead of her. No one argues. He calls to his three companions. Then he looks around to see if anyone is watching.

He doesn't notice me staring from behind my sunglasses. That's when I see him pointing to his collar and grinning at his companions while slightly lifting one brow. *Why* did I have to see that gesture with my already-existing skepticism in the brotherhood of priests?

Dusk is settling in. Although it isn't as crowded as Vatican City has been all day, *Piazza Rotonda,* where the Pantheon is located, is another place where lots of tourists gather. People are sitting at tables, sipping *caffè* and eating *biscotti* or *gelato*. I'm delighted that the monument is still open, knowing that most of them close by late afternoon.

After admiring all the architectural details inside the building, we talk briefly to a middle-aged Italian-American *professore*, who's been giving his younger brother a history lesson on Garibaldi, an Italian patriot and solider.

Then we park ourselves inside on one of the wooden benches, while the bustle of modern man takes place on the other side of the imposing bronze portal. The three of us sit up against the concrete wall and rest under the cool, quiet dome of 1st century Rome. I feel at home.

Later, on a corner and to the right of the Roman temple, I notice a green sign that says "*Piazza di Spagna*" and an arrow pointing down the street.

"Hey," I say, "there's a sign to the Spanish Steps."

Mom shifts from her quiet demeanor. Her mouth opens into a big "O" as she extends her arms in a welcoming manner. I'm excited about her enthusiasm.

"Oh good," I say, "You know about the Spanish Steps?"

"Yes," she says, "I just saw them on *Everyone Loves Raymond!*"

Speechless, I try to make the connection—*Spanish Steps? Everyone Loves Raymond?*

"You'd love it, Gil," she says with gusto before telling the story about the main character, Raymond, on one of her sitcoms back home.

"Raymond was at the Spanish Steps in the premiere show of the fall season."

I lean against the old stonewall at the corner, and then I mumble something about where in the world has my interest in art come from. Mom gets quiet, and I feel her spirit withdraw.

I try to cover up my condescending remark by laughing and teasing. The more I say, the deeper the hole I am digging. *Darn, I made my mother feel small, and now I feel guilty for putting her down.*

Mom has always had a more tender way about her than Dad. I probably learned the critical commentary I just spewed from him. Dad's the one who sat around the family table, debating any issue—intellectual or otherwise—from his own unique perspective. He never cares what anyone else thinks and will push his own opinions, sometimes to a point of offending.

My father is not easily insulted. But Mom is gentle and kind. I've often felt the need to protect her. She's not as fast-talking, but she's bright as a whip—the one who helped us as children with our homework or any intellectual pursuits. It's not that Mom can't be judgmental. Judgment is part of the Italian way. My mother does not lash back. Instead, she swallows any hurtful comments, tucking them away in a place that none of us have ever reached.

While I do hide some of my feelings, I still have Dad's blood flowing through me. Even if it takes a while, I attempt to deal with my emotions by writing them down or walking them out of my system. Not Mom—she hides her feelings from everyone, maybe even herself.

The glimmer in her eyes, when first mentioning the sitcom, has turned somber, her smile gone. I took a jab at something that excited her. It may not have been a high academic way of learning about the Spanish Steps, *but it was my mother's way.* The more I think about it, the worse I feel.

Mom walks quietly with us in the direction of the *Piazza di'Spagna.* En route, we talk to an American couple who tell us the Spanish Steps are much further than the sign suggests. It's gotten dark, and we have to be up early to catch the train to Sicily. So we turn back and wave down a *tassi* at the *Piazza Rotonda*.

I promise Mom that the Spanish Steps will be a definite part of our sightseeing when we return to Rome at the end of our trip.

6) Train to Messina

Thursday a.m. October 19

The four of us are packed, ready, and down in the lobby by 6:30 a.m. The hotel agreed to store an extra suitcase with books and other paraphernalia in Rome that we won't need in Sicily. They, also, arranged a breakfast bag for each of us, since the *prima colazione* doesn't start until seven.

On the way to *della Stazione di Roma Termini*, Rome's train station, Dad sits in the front seat so that he can tell the driver where we need to go and to answer any questions that might arise. I'm grateful to not have to think in Italian so early in the day.

Many of the people from Rome, and further north, speak or at least understand some English and are appreciative of any foreigner who attempts to converse in their native tongue. In fact, whenever I struggle with the language, most Italians pitch right in, trying to help out with the appropriate words.

The ancient monuments, in the first light of dawn, have a brilliant luminescence that is distinctively different than the golden illumination of the evening spotlights or the sharp radiance from daylight sun.

Once the driver pulls up to the curb at the train station, I watch Mom and Dad as they closely step from the cab. We've been forewarned by a number of people, including Stephanie from the embassy that gypsies and thieves prey on visitors in Rome especially at the *Termini*.

Although I reminded everyone last night not to be fooled by any tactics, this morning I caution Mom—with her exceptionally warm heart for children—that she should not reach out if someone attempts to hand her a baby at the station.

"Keep one hand on your pocketbook and the other on the handle of your roll-around suitcase."

To be sure they all understand the importance of paying attention, I remind them of Stu's incident back in 1996, during the time of his nephew's wedding.

While walking from the Coliseum over toward the entrance of the Metro, Rome's underground train, a bohemian-looking young woman approached Stu. With the edge of a piece of cardboard, she started poking him near his wristwatch. Stu never noticed a second girl coming up from behind. Having been raised as a polite Anglo-Saxon American male, Stu stayed focused on the first girl, asking her in English what it was that she needed.

I knew exactly what the girl needed, better yet wanted. She and her accomplice were after the contents in Stu's pockets. They tried to distract him, but I quickly, and without conscious thought, bellowed out in Italian, *stai attento,* pay attention, then started swinging my purse at those girls like a wolf defending her cub.

I continued screaming in the *dialetto* of my paternal grandfather, *Nonno* Morina. What shocked me was that I didn't realize those words were still fixed in my memory. *Nonno* had been dead for nineteen years! Later when trying to remember exactly what I'd yelled, I couldn't recall most of what came spurting out.

****

When *Nonno* was still alive, some of us grandchildren would go see him. At the end of our visit, my grandfather would insist on walking to the end of his driveway and directing traffic. Whoever drove would start backing up the car. If he wanted you to wait, he held his hand flat up signaling to stop. If it were clear to pull out, *Nonno* would gesture with his hand in a circular motion to keep moving. Once safely on the road, we would wave goodbye to him out the open car windows. *Nonno* would always yell in his deep-set voice, *"Stai attento, ah!"* which meant anything from *"pay attention, to take care of yourselves, to stay on top of things."*

****

Outside Rome's *Termini,* I wrap the handle of my purse across my chest, tuck it under my arm, clutch my green roll-around suitcase and wait as my mother and father step out of the cab and onto the curb. I look out for any potential danger, just as my grandfather used to do at the end of his driveway. I situate myself so that I can keep an eye on my parents.

Dad pulls out *lire* to pay the cab driver and then turns around and looks at the ground, more aware of something that he must have dropped than someone coming up from behind. In spite of his deep-set Italian features, Dad is a dead give-away for a tourist in his old turquoise and purple Charlotte Hornets jacket.

"Pay attention, Dad," I say.

"Look at him," Mom, responds. "Just look at him. All this commotion for a silly paper clip!"

Now both of them are ignoring my request to watch their surroundings. So, I look around to be sure that no stranger is eyeing up either one of my parents. Finally, I try to hustle all of us, including Stu, away from the cabstand and toward the doors of the *Termini*. But Dad keeps looking down, mumbling under his breath about having lost the clip. All Mom can do is carry on and on about Dad's obsession over his "simple paper clip."

I don't want to scoff at his fixation, but I become apprehensive. At the same time, I can't help but feel a bit protective of Dad, worried actually.

"We'll find you another one," I say, and try not to lash out as I often have with him.

Dad will never pay attention if I'm critical, and the train station is definitely not the place to start a possible argument. It would only lead to more distraction. Besides, I feel more compassion than I do anger. If I weren't so focused on taking care of my parents, I might be tearing up over my father's concern over a seemingly insignificant item.

Once inside, I position the four of us in front of offices with large, expansive windows where glass, instead of open space, is at our backs. No one can sneak up from behind this way. The oversized, black and white train schedule hangs above and straight ahead, where we can periodically check our train's arrival time.

Mom stands on my right grumbling, "Can you believe he's going through all this for a paper clip?" she keeps repeating.

Dad, on the other hand, is totally unaware of her comments, carrying on with Stu instead. I take drink orders, walk to a corner kiosk across the way to buy coffee and bottled water, and return to sour faces and distraught looks.

Dad walks directly toward me.

"I'm so upset about losing that clip!"

He prods and pleads for me to call Stefania back at the hotel, since she was the one who arranged for our early morning pick up.

"Ask her to call the cab driver and see if the clip is still in the taxi," Stu says.

Now, I'm really concerned. First, I try to explain to him that I don't think it's worth pursuing. However, Stu intercedes and tells me that it won't hurt for me to just make the call. I look away from Stu and into my father's eyes, wondering if he's really up for the journey to Sicily. This is new behavior for Dad, which I have never seen before. I'm beginning to feel troubled by his mental state.

"Dad," I say in a soft voice, "It's just a paper clip. I'll find more for you."

"NO!" he shouts. "Do you think I'd carry on like this for some stupid paper clip? It was a money clip engraved with my initials that an old customer gave me as a gift. I've had it for years!"

"Thank God, Dad!" I say. "I was starting to worry about you."

My mother stands there innocently, without saying a word, after having taunted me about my father for the last half an hour or more. I know that together the two of them can give me a run for my money.

I call the hotel and ask Stefania if she can try to reach the cab driver and see if he would at least look in the front seat where my father had been sitting. I suggest that if the driver finds the money clip, perhaps he could leave it at the hotel until we return to Rome.

I didn't say anything else to either of my parents, since calling the hotel quieted them both down. I couldn't help thinking that being so focused on anyone or anything outside one's self, like Mom is with Dad, can set up problems.

If she had just let him be when we were at the cab, he may have found what he lost. On the other hand, Dad does expect her to be available for most of his wants. So how was she to know that this was one time he wasn't looking for her help?

At times like this, I feel like a bouncing ball, first thinking Mom's right, then Dad. I spend a great deal of time trying to balance my own split characteristics that I'm sure I've inherited from my parents.

For the most part, I have favored my mother by wanting to please and fulfill whatever needs someone may have, even to the point of interfering. Then there's the other side of me, like Dad, who wants to accomplish my own tasks and concentrate on my own pursuits. Even on this trip, not only have I caught myself being pulled between my parents, but also between parts of myself.

As it turns out, our 8:10 a.m. train departure keeps getting pushed back every ten minutes. Not only could we have spent time looking for Dad's money clip, but we could have eaten a decent breakfast at the hotel. The dry and packaged pastries that the hotel provided are not that appetizing.

I put the thought of my parents and the clip on the back burner, along with the relief of knowing that my father is not in early stages of dementia. I'm thankful, too, that there are no obvious gypsies or thieves eyeing us at the *Termini*.

Once the train from Florence finally arrives, the announcer makes it clear over the loud speaker that *il treno* will not be staying in Rome any longer than necessary. We shuffle quickly down the platform and scramble back and forth in between other passengers, looking for the number on the side of the car where we have reservations.

People are waiting to board the train as they loosely queue up—in what Stu and I often refer to as Italian style—groups of crammed bodies with pieces of luggage, pushing us in and squeezing from each side. Finally, we jump onto the car we think is ours, and Stu stays put in a corner with my parents and the luggage. I walk through the narrow corridors looking until I find our cabin then go back and wave the three of them on.

While people walk by, still looking for a place to sit, we maneuver our belongings in the racks above our seats. Another couple, already sitting by the windows, fills up our compartment of six.

As the train pulls out of Rome two hours late, we meet our German traveling companions, who speak English fluently. They tell us about having taken a sleeper from Bonn to Florence, where they changed for this train to Rome. They also tell us that they are heading further south into Sicily for a holiday with friends in *Siracusa*, the second major city beyond *Messina*, where we'll be getting off.

7) On the Train

Thursday, October 19

From the large train windows, we see groves and orchards of flourishing fruits, fields of vegetables, and flowers. The voluptuous rolling Apennine mountain range rises to our left. To our right, and beyond the horizon, gleams the blue-green hue of the Mediterranean. The people on the train are as much a part of the atmosphere as is the land that my ancestors came from.

Middle-aged men drape sports jackets over their shoulders rather than put their arms into the sleeves. They smoke cigarettes that hang from their fingers held close to their mouths. Young business professionals chatter expressively on cell phones, accentuating the resounding vowels used in the Italian language. Older folks carry bags of bread and salami, cheeses and fruit.

Trains traveling in and out of Rome are usually full. First-class reservations guarantee a cabin with wide-padded seats, head rests, overhead storage for luggage, and air-conditioning that runs most times.

The atmosphere on the train promises a great deal of activity, especially at stops, when some get off and others get on and pass through the corridors, looking for their reserved places. Those without reservations hustle about, hoping to find an empty spot in one of the nicer cars. It's all part of the ambiance of the journey.

This setting is the perfect place for one of my favorite pastimes—eavesdropping on people talking and moving through the corridor, outside our compartment. I also listen to the couple that shares our space, although I don't understand a word of the German they speak.

Growing up Italian has taught me to watch people's faces and expressions, which reveal more than fifty percent of what they say and most of what is not said. As we travel south, I daydream about two particular trips I'd taken to Italy and Sicily.

****

Back in 1983, my sister, Teresa, my cousin, Marisa and I landed in Palermo from New York City and we headed by train to Agrigento, in the southernmost tip of Sicily. We spent almost a month riding from south to north, ending at *Lago di Como,* Lake Como, in the northwestern corner of Italy.

While in Sicily, the three of us stopped in my mother's family's town of Linguaglossa as well as Dad's hometown of Gualtieri Sicaminò, sometimes affectionately referred to as Gualtieri. We tracked down relatives in both villages, an experience that only aroused my appetite.

After that trip, I wanted to return to Italy for three specific reasons: the first was to spend time around Venice and study the luminescent light that Venetian artists used in their paintings; second, I hoped to rent a villa near Siena or Florence, spend time viewing the art and exploring the towns and environs of various saints and mystics from that region; and finally—closest to my heart—I wanted to live in my father's village.

When I returned to the states, I begged my father to travel to his hometown with me. He refused then, as he had done many times before. In 1985, two years after having traveled with my sister and cousin, I was given the chance to make one of my dreams come true. Aunt Mary, Dad's older sister, called me one night from Syracuse.

"Uncle Peter and I are going to Gualtieri this summer. It will probably be our last trip. If you really want to go, you can live there with us."

The next morning, I booked my airline tickets.

My immediate relatives—father, grandparents and two aunts— had moved from Gualtieri Sicaminò in Sicily to upstate New York, back in the 1930s and 40s. My aunt's husband, Uncle Peter, had a brother and sister still living in Sicily. His sister and her family spent most of the time in their city apartment in Messina. They offered Aunt Mary and Uncle Peter their family home in Gualtieri, while my aunt and uncle were there visiting.

That summer of 1985, I flew into Rome by myself, staying at the same *pensione* that Teresa, Marisa and I had stayed, two years earlier. Then I traveled by train to Sicily, where my aunt and uncle picked me up at Messina's *Termini,* late that afternoon. One of Uncle Peter's nephews drove them to the station.

When I stepped from the train, Uncle Peter was smiling and Aunt Mary's face beamed. She hugged me and started to cry. She whispered into my ear that she was happy that someone from her own family was now with her. Although she had lots of cousins there, it wasn't the same for Aunt Mary as it was for Uncle Peter who had siblings, nieces and nephews still living in their hometown.

By the time I arrived in Sicily, both Aunt Mary and Uncle Peter had fallen back into the strict mores of their village. I recognized some of the patterns from my own upbringing that my siblings, cousins and I had rebelled against.

Even though I had not lived in my parents' home for more than twenty-five years, had traveled to Europe several times and was already married, my aunt and uncle watched me as if I were still their adolescent niece, instead of a woman almost forty years old. Aunt Mary and Uncle Peter had heard that some of the townspeople found it disconcerting that a wife would travel alone without her *madito*, or husband. I found the reaction amusing. Their mountain *paese* felt safe. What could possibly happen?

Soon after I arrived, Aunt Mary and Uncle Peter sat me down and told me that it would be improper for me to walk the streets alone. As a married woman, I should never stop and talk to any man, anywhere. That included *un Bar*, where Italians grab a *caffè*, *biscotti* or even a quick shot of *liquore* at the counter. That was exactly where I made my first *faux pas*.

While standing in *un Bar* with Aunt Mary and Uncle Peter, I gave a brief response to some guy who asked me a question. It seemed innocent enough to me, especially with my aunt and uncle right there. I realized later that day, in conversation, they were becoming uneasy. They sat me down and explained that they could not be sure I would follow the appropriate village protocol.

Then Aunt Mary and Uncle Peter begged me to give up my idea of renting a car and traveling alone to my mother's family's town, Linguaglossa, at the foot of Mount Etna. It was only a two and a half hour drive away. It was more than they could handle, while living back in their village. Instead, my aunt and uncle wanted to hire a driver, a trusted older gentleman they knew, to take me there. Initially, I resisted. When I saw how much angst it caused them, I gave in.

Along the way, the driver questioned me, in *dialetto*, asking why I would travel without my husband. He shook his head and wondered aloud how any man would allow his wife to travel without him. My explanation, that I was with my aunt and uncle, didn't satisfy the driver one iota. Since it was difficult enough for me to string together a complete sentence, in either Italian or *dialetto*, I didn't broach the subject that my American marriage was not about a husband that lets me travel.

As the driver continued shaking his head, trying to understand, I attempted to explain, in my limited vocabulary, that the mind of an American male was *differente* from *l'uomo Italiano*, the Italian man. I bit my lip and gave up any further explanations. My feminist leanings made me want to spurt out that it was really none of his or anyone else's business, but he was also struggling with me, *l'Americana*, the American woman.

A less controversial custom I learned, while living in Gualtieri with Aunt Mary and Uncle Peter, during the summer of 1985, was to never turn up empty-handed when visiting someone's home—even for a quick cup of *espresso*. Since my whole intention was to live like the people, I worked hard at following the unwritten rules. Luckily, my aunt and uncle were around as permanent consultants in case I fell off track.

A couple of times, I jarred Aunt Mary into remembering her life back in the states, and how her own very American children, my first cousins, would have responded to restrictions in similar ways.

In rare instances, I encouraged my aunt to take a risk—like the day we left Uncle Peter napping—and walked the narrow streets together, just us two women. I had never remembered seeing my aunt's smile quite that wide. She seemed like a young woman again, laughing and pointing out places, giving me quick accounts of episodes of her life from childhood into her twenties, while she was still living there in Gualtieri.

The day before leaving, I wanted to cash more traveler's checks for my trip back to Rome. I overheard my aunt and uncle in the kitchen and realized they were struggling over who would stop what they were doing and walk me to *la Banca*.

At that point, I didn't care what people had to say. I'd be gone the next day. So I walked downstairs, out the door, up to the *piazza*, into the bank and back again, in less than ten minutes. When my aunt answered the doorbell, she was shocked to see me standing there. Neither she nor my uncle had heard me leave.

"What will your father think when people start talking?" she asked.

"Aunt Mary," I said, looking into her eyes, "I'll be gone tomorrow. You'll be gone in two days. You know my father. He doesn't care what other people think or say."

****

Now the train that Mom, Dad, Stu and I are on stops briefly at the station in Naples. I look over at Dad and wonder what it will be like to be in his village with him, until a couple of locals jump on with large, full satchels hanging from their hips.

"Panini, panini," they call out, while rushing down the corridor, *"l'acqua minerale con gas o senza gas,"*

My father signals to them and buys four salami sandwiches, two with cheese, two without, and a round of mineral water with no carbonation, or *senza gas*. We opt for a quick lunch instead of going to the dining car, and we save our main meal for that evening in Messina.

Oddly, when we begin to eat our *panini*, our German traveling companions immediately stop speaking to each other and look down. Have we come upon a custom that none of us know? From my Italian-American experience, talking at dinner is a way of life. The four of us quiet down, at least until the German couple leaves for the dining car.

After eating our sandwiches, we encourage Mom to tell us what she's been reading so intently in the *Farmer's Almanac*. She lists all the predicted weather forecasts for the upcoming winter in the various cities where my siblings and I now live. Mom hangs onto the almanac as if it's a cell phone and I wonder if it's the almanac that somehow keeps Mom connected to home. Dad seems more attuned to being in Italy. After all, he did come from here. Mom, although of Italian descent, is a visitor like Stu and me.

As the train pulls out of the Naples station, Dad starts telling a childhood story that I never heard before.

"At thirteen years old, I took the bus from my small *paese* of Gualtieri Sicaminò to the larger city of Messina and boarded the train for Naples."

Having done that route with my sister and cousin, I knew it had to have taken him at least eight hours one way. Before having left for our trip, my younger brother, Gerard, told me to be sure and tuck a small journal in my pocket in case sights, sounds or smells of the country trigger stories that Dad had long forgotten.

"Dad," I say, "You got on a train like this one at thirteen years old, boarded a ferry, then continued on the train to Naples by yourself?"

"Well, it wasn't exactly like this one," he says, missing the point. "It was sixty years ago. Trains were different then."

"I know trains were different, Dad. I don't mean the kind of train. I mean *Nonna* let you travel by yourself at thirteen, all the way from Gualtieri to Naples?"

I only mention *Nonna* to Dad because I know his father, *Nonno* Morina, was already in the United States. My grandmother stayed in Sicily with Dad and his two sisters, until the day my grandfather could call for them.

"*Nonna* was home with Aunt Mary and Aunt Sarah," my father says.

"And she let you travel by yourself to Naples?" I question, again.

"Well, I had to apply for my papers," he says, matter-of- factly, flipping his hand in the air, "or I couldn't leave for the United States."

I stop pressing the point about him only being thirteen when he traveled, and listen instead to Dad tell how he had moved to the United States, two years after his trip to Naples.

"I lived with my father in that boarding house in Syracuse run by *Zia* Rosa."

That's how my parents met. *Zia* Rosa, Aunt Rose, was my mother's aunt.

Nonna Morina, Dad's mother, and his two sisters stayed in Sicily longer than expected because World War II had broken out. When I ask my father a quick question about his time in the war, he isn't interested in talking about that part of his life. Right now, he wants to talk about his trip to Naples.

"I arrived in Naples alone, in the middle of the night," Dad says. "Then I took a bus to an address that a friend of the family gave me."

Even though I'm listening to Dad's story, I can't get it out of my mind—about my father only being a thirteen-year-old boy—traveling across the Straits of Messina, and up into the mainland by himself.

"Dad, you were only thirteen and traveled alone?"

Dad is unaffected by my preoccupation with his young age and never addresses my concern.

"I had to get to Naples," he repeats, "and get those papers that I needed to travel to America."

Dad goes on and on, telling more of his stories. The minute he stops, he falls quickly asleep. I take a few video shots of him with his mouth drooped open. At one point or another, we all take a nap, playing catch-up from the two previous busy days—our transatlantic flight, sightseeing around Rome, and the Papal Audience.

It won't be until after we get home from the trip that I discover Stu has captured me on the videotape too. I'm snoozing, while sitting next to Dad.

On that video, my own features and movements parallel my father's, as we sit side by side. It's hard not to notice the similarity— our Roman noses, how our mouths fall open in the exact same way when we sleep—and how even bumps from the train against the tracks startle us both into turning at the same time, repositioning our bodies as if in a water ballet.

In the background of the tape, Mom and Stu's voices chuckle quietly about how much alike we are, Dad and me.

8) Messina Arrival

Thursday p.m. October 19

The train pulls into *Reggio di Calabria*, the last city on the mainland. It takes the workers an hour to disconnect the cars and maneuver each one into the hull of the ferry. Once the large-mouth doors of the hull close, the four of us go upstairs to the deck and watch as the ferry heads toward Messina's harbor. Only a half-mile of sea separates the island of Sicily from the boot of Italy.

Despite my array of questions, both of my parents are quiet. I ask Mom how she feels, seeing her parents' homeland for the first time. I press Dad into recalling some of his experiences as a young boy visiting Messina. Neither of them says much.

Mom pulls her crocheted white sweater around her tightly, shrugs her shoulders, swallows deeply and diverts her eyes. Dad wanders down the deck, staring over at the island. His teal-blue jacket hangs loosely at his sides, the cuffs of his pants just miss scraping the floor. I know in time, Dad will say something. I'm also sure that there is no way my mother will openly express her feelings.

Not long ago, I told Mom on the phone that she was an enigma to me.

Her reply was a gleeful, "Thank you."

After I hung up, I pulled out *Webster's Dictionary* and typed up every description under the word, "enigma."

> **1:** an obscure speech or writing
> **2:** something hard to understand or explain
> **3:** an inscrutable or mysterious person
> **syn** see MYSTERY.

I printed two copies, sent one to her, and posted the other on my clipboard above my desk. I reread it whenever something my mother says puzzles me.

When my father is going through any turmoil, he sits and ponders. His brow furrows, his hand rests against his chin, reminding me of Rodin's sculpture, *The Thinker*. Eventually, Dad will say what's on his mind. If he's dealing with sadness or grief, like when his own mother died, Dad clams up and returns to that image of the sculpture. Not me, I wear my emotions for all to see.

It's no wonder I've often questioned how I came from these two people. Both my parents love to tell how sensitive I was as a child—how I cried even when I dropped my doll—I was sure she felt the sting of falling. Plus, I overreacted, so everyone said, by crying and crying whenever facing any physical pain—scraping my knees after tumbling off my bike, slamming my finger in the car door, or cutting my hand after knocking too hard and smashing a plate-glass window.

When I got into trouble, I would beg my father for a punishment—anything but being hit. Once, Dad actually prepared me for a spanking. While he stood over my bed with his belt, I carried on so that he spent most of his time reassuring me that it wouldn't hurt much.

I've long forgotten the sting of the hit, but not the puzzled look on my father's face as he lightly struck the side of my leg with the strap.

My parents have always seemed thicker-skinned, maybe because their life was tougher—living during the Depression—and raising eight children, with all its ups and downs. Then there's Dad, having left behind his Sicilian roots to find a better place.

But even with my overly sensitive nature, there's no denying, I came from the two of them. All I need to do is look in a mirror and see my parents' features staring back at me—dark-set eyes, a Roman nose, thick eyebrows, lashes and hair. My skin color—a tad of olive like Dad's, mixed in with more of Mom's light pigment.

Even if one or another of my siblings thinks their nose is a bit smaller, their eyes more green than brown, their hair a shade lighter than brunette, we are all obviously products of these two people.

Except for Mom, expressiveness is a family forte. And when it comes to emotional temperament, I'm at the top of the family barometer—not always a comfortable place.

As Stu and I stand beside my parents at the ferry's railing, I observe Dad staring out at the sea. In time, he comments about the slate-gray water rushing through the Straits of Messina. A look of awe—eyes wide, mouth partially open—turns into melancholy. My father sighs and his chest moves up and down. He turns his body away, hides his face and drops his head as if gazing into the deep. After regaining composure, Dad turns back, lifts his arm, gestures and points toward the harbor.

"Look, look for the lady out there," he says.

I look in the direction he's pointing and quickly pull out the camcorder.

"What lady?"

"The lady protecting the harbor, blessing the people of Sicily."

Having spent a good deal of my life interpreting my father's comments, I ask if he means a sculpture or a real live lady.

"A real lady?" he scoffs, as if I were silly. "A sculpture, of course!"

"Of course," I reply, hearing my mother chuckle under her breath.

"Of course," she repeats, teasing my father like she does.

A glutton for punishment, I continue.

"Is it a sculpture of a woman? Or the Blessed Mother?"

"The Blessed Mother," my father says fervently, holding his right hand up to his forehead like a visor.

I strain to see a lady, a sculpture, or Christ's mother. I keep one eye attached to the camcorder's viewfinder, the other on Dad's finger, pointing at something bobbing and shifting in the distance.

Finally, a statue of a woman begins to emerge in the video's zoom lens. The sculpture's clothes flow like the water below, one arm held high as if giving a blessing. There it is—an icon, blessing all those who pass by, standing above the moving water—symbols instilled in my father years ago, here in his motherland of Sicily.

****

We depart the train in Messina at 4:30 in the afternoon. It's the same time I arrived here in 1985, when Aunt Mary and Uncle Peter met me at the *Termini*. Schedules and way of life do not change much in Italy and Sicily. Municipal buildings, homes, businesses and roads have been in the same place for centuries. Counting on that constancy helped me when planning the trip.

Just as I remember, the train station in Messina is much smaller than the ones we passed through earlier in the day—Rome, Naples, Salerno and *Reggio di Calabria*. We pull our luggage from the tracks to the stairway that leads up to the terminal. Stu quickly runs up and down the stairs with the suitcases to save my mother and me from injuring sensitive backs.

Dad grabs hold of his own navy bag and I watch him, shoulders rounded beneath his teal-blue and white Charlotte Hornets' jacket. He climbs the stairs one slow step at a time, placing one foot down, lifting the other. I ask him to wait, but he insists on doing his share and continues his climb. After one more corridor and another set of stairs into the main terminal, Stu and Dad pile the bags onto a luggage carrier and settle Mom and me before leaving in a *tassi* to *Europcar*.

Since English is not spoken as much in the south as in northern Italy, Stu definitely needs Dad to translate at the rental agency.

Mom stays with the bags, while I head for the ticket window to purchase our *biglietti*, or tickets, for the following Saturday's train trip back to Rome. While I attempt to speak Italian, a native moves up from behind me and positions herself so close that her arm touches mine.

Italian inquisitiveness is not unusual. There have been numerous instances of natives prying during my travels through Italy, like the taxi guy from the airport, who questioned when I'd been there before, when we first arrived in Rome.

There was also the driver from Gualtieri who couldn't understand why I was in Sicily without my husband. If my stammering over the language gives a curiosity seeker a thrill at the ticket counter, it seems harmless.

What doesn't feel harmless are the sundry characters walking back and forth in the station, looking over any new person that arrives. I'm reminded what Stephanie from the embassy warned us about. Just like Rome, Messina has its own share of gypsies. I spot some right away.

There is a girl—or it may be a boy—with short dark hair and light beige skin, dressed in a pair of paisley pants and a striped shirt. She's thin, skinny really, a thigh no thicker than my lower calf. There's another person, definitely a woman. Her unblemished, smooth skin matches her coffee-color hair. She's dressed in tight leather, her left breast protruding from her partially zipped jacket. She struts up close to us, passes by and walks out the door.

Mom and I head for the one, lone concrete bench in the lobby. *Un Bar* is down at the far other end of the only place to sit. In between and to the left are the *Ufficio Informazioni*, and the ticket counter that I just left. Across from the Information Office sits the *tabacchi* stand where they sell cigarettes, magazines, books, newspapers and maps—

carte geogràfiche. Even though no one around us smokes, the place reeks of stale air. Italians still smoke heavily.

At the opposite side of the terminal, a couple of elderly men are conversing. In the middle of the lone bench, a scraggly, once-upon-a-time hippie gets there before we do and sits down. He gapes at us sharply, and I surprise myself by sitting on the edge of the bench. I position the luggage rack at an angle to face me. Mom chats, oblivious to what is going on.

It's the gypsy women I keep my eye on, mainly because both of them, at one time or another, have their eyes on us. My antenna stays up, aware of the comings and goings of the various people.

In the meantime, my mother talks about my cousin, Ann Marie, and her husband, actually her ex-husband. Well, they aren't really divorced yet, even though they've been separated for eleven years. Mom is renowned for reliving family circumstances. I've been known to do that too. Sometimes it's interesting to hear a tale or two, but right now it's more important to stay alert to our surroundings.

Once the older men at the other side of the terminal leave, and the hippie sitting at the bench with us disappears, Mom talks about stepping outside to see if Stu and Dad have returned with the car.

My purse strap is already wrapped over one shoulder and running diagonally across my chest. I readjust and pull it closer under my arm. The band from the camcorder case hangs around my neck. At one point, Mom held it loosely in her hand, before I silently took hold of it.

Now, seconds after my mother is out of sight, the first girl in paisley pants rushes up to me and mumbles something.

"*Scusi?*" I say firmly, my inflection at the end suggesting she repeat her statement.

"*Ha mille lire?*"

She asks if I have a thousand *lire*, less than a dollar.

"*No*," I respond sharply, raising my head high as I stare into her face. She turns away and quickly scoots around the terminal like a gadfly.

Within minutes, the other gypsy pushes open the front terminal doors and, seconds later, returns with some guy. He comes over and sits three-quarters of the way down on the lone concrete bench—not at the very end or right next to me, but within reaching distance.

Mom returns and stands facing me, resting her handbag down on the bench, the strap no longer wrapped around her body. Rather than repeat my cautionary speech with this guy so close by, I gently lift her purse strap and wrap it over my right shoulder. Mom seems not to notice and picks up where she left off, talking about my cousin before switching over to something about my brother, Gerard, then my sister, JoAnne.

I wait until she's at the end of a thought before telling her about the woman in paisley, asking for money.

"Where is she?" Mom asks.

"The one moving toward those two women," I say, using my eyes to point left in the direction of two finely dressed, middle-aged ladies, standing halfway down the terminal.

One is on the phone, the other's positioned near her, hugging the wall. When the girl in paisley approaches the two women, they turn their entire bodies sharply away—typically Italian, with no subtle gesturing.

"Mom," I say, "Be careful. There's another one down to the left of you."

Like penned animals, we're being circled by wilder, aggressive foes. The only thing they don't know is how forceful I can be if attacked. After all, it's not only me I have to protect, they are eyeing up my mother. There have been songs written about how Italians feel about their mothers. And I feel as protective of my own, as any mother would be of her child.

A real survival of the fittest game is being played out in this somewhat deserted terminal here in Messina. Preparing to strike if anyone gets too close, I take the strap of the camcorder off my neck and hold the handle of the case tightly in my hands. One whack from the metal encasing inside would send anyone running.

****

One summer, when we were kids, Dad decided to have an assault-attack exercise for the girls. This didn't seem unusual, since he'd been known to schedule fire drills. No one was excluded from either. Even my brothers, Anthony and Gerard, had to sit and watch. We were all expected to gather in the living room at an appointed time after dinner.

The site of the training mission was next to the stairs, leading to the second floor of the house. All of us girls lined up in the order we were born. My older sister, Nicki, went first. I was second. Fran,

Teresa, JoAnne and Bridget were directed to sit on the couch and watch before their turn.

Mom stood at the other end of the room, leaning against the frame of the door that led to the dining room. She was shaking her head.

"I swear your father's imagination gets the best of him from all that gossip he hears at the barbershop," she said.

Dad ignored her, walked up the stairs and hid behind the wall, otherwise tagged as an imaginary bush. Then we heard his voice call out to Nicki to walk by. Predictably, he stopped her and told her to amble more casually and pretend like she hadn't a clue someone was hiding behind a bush. So, Nicki began her stroll, while the rest of us watched intently.

This was serious business to Dad. Those who couldn't control themselves held their hands over their mouths, desperately trying not to snicker. When Nicki got close enough, Dad jumped from the stairway and pounced. She pulled her hands and arms in close to her chest and froze in place, letting out only a quiet scream.

"NO, NO, NICOLINA," my father called out, "FIGHT ME! FIGHT ME! You have to protect yourself. Fight me and scream. Scream at the top of your lungs!"

They went a few more rounds, but Nicki did the same thing again and again until he became exasperated and told her to take a break. He looked over at me and announced that I was next.

Climbing back up those stairs and huddling behind the wall, Dad called out for me to start walking and pretend I didn't know he was there. He jumped and I started swinging, kicking, screaming, punching and digging my long nails into his arm. In the background, I heard laughter. I was determined to fight off this attacker, just as I was told to do.

"STOP! STOP!" Dad yelled, "It's me. It's me your father." He pulled himself away, shocked at my defense. "OUCH," he said, "Those nails of yours are weapons."

****

In the Messina terminal, my hand wrapped around the camcorder case ready to strike back at any stalker, I spot Dad walking through the doors. The white on his Charlotte Hornets' jacket shines like a flashlight. I leap up in relief.

"Stu got a BMW!" Dad calls out proudly, unaware of what's been going on around us.

The energy shifts with Dad's grand entrance, and all those who'd been milling around now scatter.

"They had no map," Dad continues, "I'm going to get one."

He heads straight for the *Tabacchi* shop. Since he has no idea what we've been going through, and the situation seems less threatening, I decide to wait and tell him later what's been going on. I hurry toward the front door, pushing the luggage cart through and out the terminal, but still keeping my antenna up for the two women and one man I hope we're leaving behind.

Stu, on the other side of the door, swiftly approaches and grabs the luggage rack, pulling it close to the curb next to the car. As I try to tell him about the people in the station, the suitcases tumble. He starts scrambling to catch them and seems as tense as I've been. I have no idea why. We've been in two different situations over the last hour. This is not the time to commiserate about our time apart.

"I need to find a men's room," he says, looking toward the terminal.

Maybe that's what's bothering him. But still feeling a bit unsure about the gypsies, I try to encourage Stu to wait until Dad returns. It's a frenzied time of shifting luggage and shifting perspectives.

My husband dashes into the terminal, returns to ask me where the restrooms are, runs back in, then out, until we're all finally together and accounted for, ready to go. Standing by the terminal doors are the people who'd been eyeing Mom and me. They are looking over new arrivals stepping out of a *tassi*. As we pull away from the curb, I feel safe, locked in the rental car, leaving the gypsies behind.

****

Stu snakes the car in and around the parking lot of Messina's *Termini*, then out toward a *piazza* of palm trees.

"This is Messina?" Dad questions, as if in shock, and then repeats himself. "This is Messina? It's not supposed to be crowded like this."

Dad is obviously surprised and seems disillusioned with the busyness of the city he knew growing up. I quickly pull out the tape recorder, wanting to capture my father's reactions now that we're on the island of Sicily. *Darn, the recorder isn't working.* I start fumbling with the batteries, but I don't want to be distracted and miss anything that triggers Dad's memories.

"That's the building I went to take my test," Dad says, pointing to a Neo-Classical structure.

"Your barber test?" I ask.

"No," he replies, "It was the test they gave, for what do we call it now? Junior high school?"

I was way off in years. Dad didn't become a barber until after moving to the United States. I keep listening and realize that he's telling about a teacher who took him to Messina's Municipal building that stands in front of us and on the other side of the *piazza.*

The BMW Stu's maneuvering is sandwiched in between other cars that pull up on both sides and behind us.

Dad continues talking about how his teacher practically gave him the answers so that he'd pass the test. It's not that Dad isn't bright. All my life I've heard how mischievous he was in his youth, always trying to outsmart someone or another. Judging from my own experiences as his daughter, I'm not surprised. Nothing that comes from my father's mouth seems to shock me anymore, though I spent years reacting to many of his comments.

Dad keeps chattering about how astonished he is at the pure number of people moving about Messina. While he talks, Stu manages to get us onto the *Via Panorama* that parallels the Straits of Messina. It's the road that the *Hotel Paradis* is located on.

When my father and I get to the check-in desk, the attendant I talked to on the phone from home isn't on duty. It was easier for me to make our accommodations for Sicily from information I found on the Internet than it was to use our travel agent. Because of my previous experiences traveling on the island, I knew more than she did about the towns and places we'd be visiting.

Our rooms in Messina overlook both the harbor and the busy street below. We take our time settling in, rather than rushing about the city. There will be time for sightseeing next Friday, the day before catching the train back to Rome.

Right now, we want to prepare for the busy week ahead, traveling to my parents' villages. The plan is to be up and out early tomorrow morning. For dinner, we eat in the family-style restaurant downstairs in the hotel.

It's Stu, rather than Dad, who draws attention this time, as the waiter turns around and does a double take while walking past our table. Instead of swirling long strings of spaghetti around his fork, like Italians do, Stu slices up his meal into pieces with a knife and fork, chopping and breaking down the long strands into small mouthfuls.

****

It's 2:30 in the morning. The noise of people and motor scooters rustling about on the streets below has stopped. Stu is sound asleep, has been for a while. I'm sure that Mom and Dad are asleep in their room next door. Except for the sound of the sea breaking, a periodic foghorn from a boat in the bay, or a single honk from a car rushing by, there is hardly a sound. I slip out of bed, pull the white sheer curtains aside and look at the shimmering water of the bay.

The quietness seems unnatural for a country whose people talk and gesture wildly. Just on the other side of the narrow passage of water, no more than ten kilometers away, lies the mainland that separates the boot of Italy from the toe—this island of Sicily, my ancestry.

Northern Italians I've met have often mentioned the differences between their region and the south. I've also heard some claim that those in the south don't work as hard, or else complain that Sicilians go north and take all the jobs. Aren't these obvious contradictions? The separation of the mainland from the island haunts me—its geography is like that of the Great Divide.

I suppose it's how some Americans see our own country. Having lived in North Carolina for over twenty years, I've learned my own lessons about misjudging Southerners, who may appear slow, but work hard and accomplish a great deal. Whether one is American, Italian or any other nationality, we are blinded by our own prejudices.

There are more likenesses than differences between the regions of Italy. One area may use a red *Bolognese,* meat, sauce on their pasta, another a creamy *Carbonara*—but no one would mistake either for anything but Italian cuisine. Despite what northern Italians say about Sicilians, when I travel through the country, it feels like one culture. The Italian way of life is still the Italian way of life.

Past the sheer curtains in front of me lies the Straits of Messina, separating us from the mainland. My interest is not to track differences. I'm in search of the similarities between myself and my origins.

9) From Messina to Gualtieri Sicaminò

Friday a.m. October 20

After breakfast and packing the car, we head away from the hotel and circle around a small *piazza*. Outside the window, I see a statue of Neptune—pitchfork in his left hand, two female figures at his feet. Stu is driving, my father navigating. My mother and I sit in the back seat. Friday morning, and we're heading out of Messina. I ask my father about the sculpture.

"Oh, the Giant," he responds. "Anyone who comes to Messina for the first time has to wash the Giant's... What do you call them, Mary? *Palle?*"

My mother chuckles and whispers, "testicles." I tell my husband that *he'll* have to do the washing.

"And you too," Dad says.

"Oh no," I retort, "I've been here a couple of times before, but this is Mom and Stu's first time in Messina."

Dad looks over at Stu then turns his body around and glances at Mom in the back seat.

"Okay," he says, "You can each wash one."

We all laugh. Dad can be very entertaining, when he's not grumpy or bossy. Mom, in her quiet way, is his perfect straight man—or rather woman. They're a real Burns and Allen team, although Mom is much subtler than Gracie was on TV back in the 1950s. I often think that Dad doesn't really hear Mom's underhanded comments, but that can be part of their act.

As we pass the Neptune sculpture, we're right on schedule, heading toward the *autostrada*. Forty-five minutes later, Dad directs Stu to pull off the highway and follow a sign that says Spadafora.

Our first stop is at the home of Maria, one of Dad's first cousins. My father has numerous cousins, some of whom I did not meet even during my stay with Aunt Mary and Uncle Peter in 1985. Maria is one of them. I knew her brother, Nicola, well. He moved to America in the early 1960s. That was when Dad hired Nicola at the barbershop.

Over the last number of years, Nicola has struggled with various health problems—beginning with diabetes and ending with throat cancer. It put him in and out of the hospital and, in turn, in and out of work at the shop. Two months ago, he died.

His wife asked Dad to stop in Spadafora and deliver videotapes of the funeral to Nicola's sister, Maria. The idea of a videotaped funeral seems surreal to me, like something out of a Fellini movie. I keep these thoughts to myself. Well, not quite to myself. I roll my eyes at Mom, who rolls hers back.

At Maria's, we sit around the dining room table with one of her daughters and two of her granddaughters. We stay for about an hour—not long enough to watch the video, thank God!

We drink *caffè,* eat *dolci* and listen as Dad tells Maria, in their *dialetto,* about the last days of her brother's life. There's a lot of head nodding and sighing, expressive hand gesturing, and some silent moments of obvious reflection. Maria, a quiet woman, sheds a few tears that she wipes with a hand-embroidered handkerchief. Perhaps the video will give Nicola's family a sense of closure after all.

****

Death in melting pot America seems different than in the Italian-American culture I grew up in. I'm used to Italians lingering longer over the passing of a loved one than most Americans would tolerate. Italian women wear black far past the customary one-year grieving period. Some never stop wearing black—suggesting that they remain forever in mourning. Granted, the color black has been in and out of style for years both here and in Italy. This is a different black—no bare arms, knees or cleavage showing. This is a cover-me-up, I'm-dead-too black.

The religion that permeates the culture may preach about a better life to follow, but faith in that afterlife is not necessarily reflected in people's behavior. I've seen some Italians at wakes and funerals, me included, go through emotional turmoil—wailing in some cases. It makes me wonder how confident I, or others, may be in the so-called eternal life.

Maria's restraint is impressive, as she and my father talk quietly about her brother's passing. I recall my father's self-control after his parents died. Perhaps that particular moderation runs in their bloodline. I'm not so sure it's something that I've inherited.

****

When we leave, Maria and her family hug and kiss us good-bye. Stu pulls the car onto the main thoroughfare, and Dad informs us that we'll be making a quick stop in the nearby town of Giammoro, where Maria's youngest daughter lives. She and her husband own a grocery store on the main road. Although I picked up pieces of my father's conversation, I had not realized he arranged for an extra stop.

If I was clueless, I'm sure that my Scandinavian-German-Anglo-American husband had no inkling what my father and Maria had been discussing. The extent of Stu's Italian vocabulary is *buon giorno,* or hello; *ciao*, a friendly good-bye; and *arrivederci*, a more formal goodbye. The latter must have come from the song *Arrivederci Roma*, which Stu has been singing periodically along the way.

It's past noon as we drive through small Sicilian towns toward Giammoro. It's hard to tell when we pass from one town into the next—they all blend together. Shops are closed and streets are fairly empty. Most people have headed home or settled in a *ristorante* for the country's traditional afternoon meal.

Zipping along, I'm startled when Dad shouts, "Stop!" We circle back around and head toward an attractive woman in her early 30s, dressed in black, standing at the edge of the curb, waving. Dad's swift observation is impressive, since he's never met Maria's daughter before.

Once out of the car, there is a quick round of greetings—two kisses on everybody's cheeks—and a visit into what would be considered in the States, an old-fashioned corner store. Wooden shelves are stacked with various pastas, cans of tomatoes, jars of olives and numerous other Italian products along with baskets of vegetables and thick-crusted, semolina bread.

We immediately take photographs of each other. I talk briefly in my broken Italian, but I spend more time listening to my father and mother answer questions about her *Zio* Nicola's death. We are there for a brief time before my father asks for the best route to Milazzo.

Since Gualtieri has no hotels, I'd made reservations on the Internet in the nearby resort town of Milazzo. When I was growing up, my father always talked about this seaport village, fourteen kilometers away from his hometown. Dad would bicycle or ride his father's donkey there as a young boy. It's where he acquired his love for swimming in the ocean, and he passed that love of the sea onto my siblings and me.

Driving toward our hotel through the center of what has become a fashionable tourist town in the northeast corner of Sicily, the streets are barren and only a few places are open. It's well past the regular tourist season.

Because it is Friday, Dad says people will be arriving at the shore for their weekend getaways, and Milazzo will come alive again. Numerous shops and fancy boutiques will open along with *le trattorie, i ristoranti* and a number of *gelato* joints.

Just after two in the afternoon, we check into the Hotel Riviera Lido, which faces the *Golfo di Milazzo,* the Gulf of Milazzo. Our rooms overlook the sea, and we can hear waves brush the sand.

After dropping off our luggage, we rush to the center of town for an afternoon meal before any of *i ristoranti* that are serving close, which is at three. The one place we find open is reluctant to let us in so late. Knowing Italians, I count on them having difficulty turning away anyone who's hungry, as well as anyone with *soldi,* or money. The owner acquiesces on the condition that we order only the *secondo piatto,* or second course.

"No pasta," he tells us. "No time."

****

It's past five o'clock before we unpack our suitcases, freshen up and hop in the car for Gualtieri. Dad says that a quick run through his town would be enough for the day. Driving out of Milazzo, my father's whole demeanor changes. His body twists and turns anxiously in the front seat. He looks swiftly out the windows from one side to the other, taking in all the sights.

Dad seems young again as he talks faster than I've ever heard him speak. He directs Stu down a side street, confident that it will take us where we need to go. It does. We backtrack through the town of Giammoro, and we bypass Spadafora, where we visited with his cousin, Maria. We head toward a road sign that says, "Pace del Mela."

"*Autostrada!*" Dad exclaims, pointing out the blue and white signs. "There was never an *autostrada* here before."

Even though my father hasn't been in Sicily for over thirty years, he knows the roads as if he travels them every day.

"Turn down this narrow lane," Dad says to Stu.

Canopies of clinging vines hang over the car. While Dad talks, the rest of us stay quiet, listening to his burst of directions.

"*Right here… A sharp left by that house… Head that way…*"

We slowly begin our ascent up a mountain. Dad says we're approaching his village from the back. Once through the town of Pace del Mela, my father's storytelling begins—this time about his experience as an American soldier.

"It was 1945, and I had a furlough from Kitzingen, Germany, to Sicily, so that I could visit my mother and two sisters, who were still living in Gualtieri. *Nonno* had already called for me to come to America four years earlier. But he had to wait to bring my mother and my two sisters over to the United States because World War II broke out."

I quickly pull out my black journal and start jotting down notes, trying not to miss a thing. Dad talks more swiftly than my made-up short hand can keep up with.

"At nineteen years old, I received a letter in the mail that said, *Greetings from the President.* I was being drafted. Two friends of mine who came from Italy when I did went for their physicals first, to see if they were fit for service. When they came back, they told me to make believe, like they had, that I didn't speak English. But I wouldn't do that.

"The service was better than a college education. I was sent to Fort McClellan in Alabama for Basic Training. Then I became part of the 79th Infantry Division. A lot of the guys were going to the Pacific, but they wanted me in Europe, because I spoke Italian. Before shipping me off, they sent me home to Syracuse for a leave, then onto Yuma, Arizona.

"While I was there, they called me in front of a judge. I had no idea why. The judge asked me if I wanted to be a United States citizen. I said, *Yes.* When he asked me my name, I said, *Nick Morina*—because that's what everyone called me—instead of my given name, Nicolino. That's why my citizenship papers say *Nick.* If I knew that's what it was about, I would have given him my full name.

"When I had that furlough from Kitzingen in 1945, I arrived in Marseilles, France, before I realized that my papers gave me permission to travel by train only. The only way I could get back here to Sicily from that point was by plane. The guy who checked my papers took a liking to me and wired General Headquarters all the way back in Paris. He got me special permission to fly."

My father's chest rises high, and he smirks. I know he's proud of having talked the guy into helping him out.

"But when I got to Palermo, I discovered my duffel bag was missing. It had been misplaced in a pile of luggage back in Marseilles, and it went to Naples instead."

"Did you have to sit and wait for it?" I ask.

"No way. I was too anxious to get home and see my mother and sisters. I just left."

"You left your luggage there?"

"I picked it up on the way back. You could trust people back then," Dad says as he continues with his tale. "I took the *Littorina*—a special express train—that stopped only in a few major towns and would get me home quickly. On the train there was a man, a *compare* of *Nonno's*."

"What's a *compare*?" Stu asks.

"Ya know," Dad, replies. "It's a Sicilian word for *a friend of the family*, or someone who's a godparent to one of your children. Anyway, I pretended not to know the guy, because I didn't have anything to offer him. I'd at least have given him a pack of cigarettes, but they were back in my duffel bag, somewhere between Naples and Palermo. You know it's our Sicilian tradition not to go somewhere without bringing a gift. I was uncomfortable, so I avoided looking at him. The guy kept staring at me, anyway, until finally he asked me where I was going."

Dad starts to chuckle at himself and then continues.

"I pretended like I didn't speak the language and pointed on the map near Gualtieri. Finally, the guy came right out and asked me if I was *Compare* Tony's son, and if I'd forgotten how to speak my own language after having moved to America only a few years before.

"I was embarrassed, but I admitted to the *compare* that I didn't even have a pack of cigarettes to offer, and was hoping that he hadn't recognized me. At least I was able to persuade the conductor on the train to make an extra stop in Giammoro, and the guy was grateful for that, since we both got off the train there. He headed for Pace del Mela, and I hitched a ride to Gualtieri."

We must be following the same route that Dad took back in 1945, because the closer we drive toward Gualtieri, the faster Dad talks. At various junctures along the way, Stu gently interrupts for directions, but he tries not to interfere with Dad's train of thought.

"The man who picked me up in the car had trouble pulling his vehicle over to drop me off. There was an older woman and two young ladies standing in the way, but they had their backs to the car. So the driver pulled around in front of them, and when I jumped out of the car, I came face to face with my mother and two sisters. They were as surprised to see me, as I was to see them."

"What did they do?" I ask, expecting some kind of esoteric response.

Instead Dad answers, "They dropped their plans to visit a cousin, of course, and headed back home with me."

At that point in my father's story, we begin to round a bend. A town, built into the side of the mountain, appears on our left.

"Gualtieri," Dad announces. "It's my hometown. Pull over there."

Hugging the side of the road, Stu slowly glides the car to the right. He leaves room for other vehicles that periodically flash by. As we get out of the car, Dad, who just seconds before was talking faster than I could hear, doesn't say a word.

"What are you feeling, Dad?" I ask.

He whispers the word, "emotional," and then he turns away, staring into a scene from a Western Civilization book. In front of us lies an aerial view of his old Sicilian village. The buildings appear stacked, as if built into the mountains. Steeples from a handful of churches tower in-between.

Browns, beiges and rusty oranges—hues that have stayed in my mind from my two previous visits—are as vivid as my memory. We all linger there, staring for a while. Eventually, I take out the video camera and ask Dad to talk.

"See that steeple there?" Dad points. "That was where I was baptized."

I don't say a word, even though Dad is pointing at the wrong steeple. I know for sure, and so does he, that he was baptized in *San Nicola di Bari* Church in the main *piazza*. He is pointing to an old stone church called The Assumption. I wait for Dad to recognize his home church. In the meantime, I pan the view with the video camera.

The Assumption Church was where Aunt Mary and I went on August 15, during my visit with her in 1985. That date is the feast day, celebrated by the church as The Assumption of Christ's mother into heaven. The building, which was closed for renovation, was reopened on that day for a short time after the traditional midday meal.

A group of women from one of the church societies invited Aunt Mary and me to join them and pray the rosary. Inside, the church was unkempt. Cobwebs hung between posts, around the altar and from the pitched roof. Most pews were dusty, except for a few, where a handful of people knelt around the statue of the Blessed Virgin Mary.

The figure lay horizontally on a chaise-like lounge, made from metal. Pieces of paint were peeling from the wooden form. I never saw that particular sculpture in any of my art history books or the colorful glossy tourist books of the area. Probably some unknown artist from the region had carved the wooden form, years ago.

"No, no," Dad says, bringing me back from my reveries, "I think this is the church over here. This one here."

He points in the direction of a newer church, a beige-yellow Romanesque structure. From our vantage point, I can see part of the town's main *piazza*.

"That's where I was baptized, that's *San Nicola di Bari*. The other one must be *Assumpto*," Dad says in Italian, referring to The Assumption Church.

No one says a word until I ask Mom, who's been exceptionally quiet, to stand next to Dad so I can take pictures with Gualtieri in the background. Mom holds back.

"It's your *father's* hometown, not mine."

Dad stands in front of the distant landscape, and I take some photos. When finished, my father points behind me to the woods beyond our rental car.

"When I was ten years old, I saw a man up there in the mountains," he says, "a well-dressed guy, standing in the woods."

"What were you doing in the woods?" I ask.

"I was up there to get some fruits," Dad continues, using the "s" on fruit, like he always does.

I chuckle as I usually do when he has a glitch in the language. Dad ignores me and continues telling us about the man in the woods.

When Dad looked up from gathering fruit, he saw the guy holding a chalice and stirring. My father positions his left hand, as if grasping a cup, and pretends to stir with the fingers on his right hand.

"And when the man saw me," Dad says, "he disappeared."

"What happened to him then?" I ask.

"No," he says, his voice lilting slightly up, "he disappeared."

"You mean disappeared, disappeared?" I ask.

"Yeah, he just vanished," Dad says, and throws his hands in the air like a magician.

I can't help but think of how religious my father has always been. I know he inherited that from his mother. The story of this disappearing man with a chalice that Dad saw when he was a boy added a piece to my ever-puzzling father and his past.

"Okay," Dad says, as he turns away from the view of his village.

"What are we going to do?" I ask.

He swings his hand out and points toward Gualtieri.

"Get in the car and go into town. Let's see if..." he says, leaving his line wide open.

"If there's anybody you *know*?" Mom chimes in.

"Let's see if they'll let me *in*," Dad chortles.

A car speeds around the bend, and Stu puts his hand out as if to protect us. We stand still for a brief second until the vehicle passes. Then we head for the rental car on the other side of the road. Mom and Dad look up in unison and point to a blooming plant with reddish-pink, lush-looking oval forms.

"Prickly pears!" they both exclaim.

While climbing into the vehicle, we chat about the fruit we ate when I was growing up. As Mom, Dad and I continue talking, Stu slowly pulls the car away from the curb. In my mind's eye, I remember my young father around his own father's table, sitting with *paesani*—the men that had emigrated from his village. Some ate fresh fruit, while others drank his father's wine or dipped *biscotti* into the deep-red liquid before slurping the sweet into their mouths.

My father always sat to the right of his father, one seat down, but never right next to him. That was the same spot where I sat at our large family table at my parents' home. I am not skillful, like Dad, with the short paring knife. He can gracefully peel back the spotted skin on a purple prickly pear. Lush layers of pink pulp lie underneath. Hidden and embedded deeper in the soft tissue are dark-hard seeds that need chewing.

Finally, I'm in Gualtieri with my father. The wooden planks rattle under the tires as our car rolls over the bridge that leads into the old section of town. We're heading towards *San Nicola di Bari* Church in the main *piazza* and to the area where my father had his beginnings!

Gualtieri Sicaminò, Messina, Sicily

Behind the house where we stay,
a rooster crows. I roll in the sheet,
slip back to sleep. I'm jarred
by distant tapping. My aunt answers
the door to a cousin who asks
if I am awake, before offering
figs from her vineyard.

She lifts her voice in dialect
loud enough for me to hear
about my family having moved
to America leaving her
and others behind. Later,

we stroll through narrow byways,
stop for coffee at Colosi's cafe,
head to the cemetery, uncover
tombstones of great-grandparents
hidden among vines, where I pick
ripe figs, peel away thick green skin,
press my teeth into the purple.

10) Entering Gualtieri

Friday p.m. October 20

The clanging of the wooden bridge echoes over the dry riverbed below as Stu drives the BMW toward the old section. Through his side-view mirror, I see the newly constructed houses that we just passed on the edge of town. Traveling down a small incline, the car hugs a low stonewall. We veer right and enter the main *piazza*.

The Romanesque church of *San Nicola di Bari* is straight ahead. Some of the older men from Gualtieri sit on olive-green, wrought-iron benches, underneath a cluster of evergreens and hardwoods that provide a shady respite. The men's hands move as they talk and smoke cigarettes that hang from their mouths. Fumes dance in the direction of their gestures. Through the open car window, I hear words ringing in the clear air as one of the men's voices rises to emphasize a point he's trying to make.

They all look over toward our car. Most squint, glance among themselves, their mouths turn down, shoulders shrug, heads shake back and forth—as if saying they have no idea who we are. In Gualtieri, everyone knows everyone. Strangers are noticed.

****

The first time I had ever driven into Gualtieri's main *piazza* was on a mid-afternoon in August 1983, seventeen years earlier. I was with my sister, Teresa, and cousin, Marisa. We'd rented a small, cobalt blue Fiat in Messina and took the *autostrada* west into the mountains, toward my father's hometown. The men hanging around the *piazza* that day stared at us, too, before glancing at each other, making similar facial expressions and gestures.

After parking the car, we asked two women walking through the square, where the family house of Dad's cousin, Nicola—where Nicola Morina's mother's house was located. She was our great aunt, *Zia* Antoinetta Morina. Nicola, Dad's first cousin, still alive back then, had made arrangements from Syracuse for us to stay overnight with his mother, or so we thought.

Her house was locked up tight, and after we knocked on her door a few times, a neighbor looked out her window.

Signora Morina was not there and would not be returning for a few days.

She was staying with her daughter in the town of Spadafora. We were baffled. We'd been told that *Zia* would introduce us to relatives who lived there in Gualtieri. Now, not only would we never get to meet family, but we had no idea where we'd spend the night.

Luckily, we'd rented a car in Messina after getting off the train. Our first notion had been to take a bus to Gualtieri. That would have been a disaster, since there were no hotels, or *pensioni,* in the small village, and a return bus to Messina would not arrive until the next day.

Teresa, Marisa and I walked back to the main *piazza* just as a *carabiniere,* a traffic policeman, stopped nearby on his moped. As if rehearsed, we called out in unison our family's name, "Morina."

Marisa, who spoke Italian, rolled the rich-organic vowels off of her tongue: *More-een-ah.* The *carabiniere* turned directly toward my cousin. He waved one hand in the air, called out the family name, "Morina," in recognition, and he nodded his head up and down, rattling out words faster than any of us could understand, including Marisa. She told us that, besides not knowing all of the *dialetto* the guy was using, he talked much too quickly for her to decipher what he was saying.

Il carabiniere kept talking just as swiftly as he hobbled away from the *piazza,* one of his legs shorter than another, motioning with his right hand. We followed, trailing behind him down one of the narrow roads that reached out from the square. The street was lined on both sides with stone houses.

The *carabiniere* continued chattering without taking a breath, and Teresa and I still looked toward Marisa for translation. She smiled at him respectfully, responding with a word or two. I picked up a few remarks—enough to understand the gist of his litany of inquiries about our family back in America.

After having walked the length of a city block, the man stopped and turned right toward a rock stairway between two gray-stone houses. He pointed to a passageway before making circular motions with his hand, indicating we should follow him. He shuffled up an alley of granite steps.

At the top and behind the house on the left, there was a wide space that opened into an outdoor terrace. A middle-aged woman with brown hair, probably in her late fifties and who was a tad taller than me at 5'2", was sitting in the hot Sicilian sun, next to an older woman, easily in her eighties.

I was taken totally by surprise when the middle-aged woman jumped up, ran over and threw her arms around me, kissing both my cheeks and hugging me so tight I could hardly breathe. She cried out the name, "*Sarina, Sarina.*"

Sarina was the tender name they called Marisa's mother, my Aunt Sarah, who was my father's youngest sister.

"You've returned after all these years," the woman said in *dialetto*, simple enough for me to understand.

Tears welled up in my eyes as well as in my sister Teresa's eyes. Marisa, who has an innate ability to remain composed in most situations, seemed stunned, too. Her mouth dropped open, her face flushed pink with emotion. She paused before she spoke.

"*Scusi Signora,*" she said, with the utmost respect. "*Non sono Sarina. Sarina è mia madre. Questa è mia cugina e sua nipote Sarina, chiamata Gilda.*"

The woman hugging me continued to hang on tightly while Marisa was explaining that I was not *Sarina,* and that *Sarina* was her *mother*, my aunt. She told the older woman that we were cousins, and that my name was Gilda. Then pointing toward Teresa, Marisa explained in pure Italian, not in dialect, how we were all related.

It took a number of explanations for my cousin to get the two women to understand that Teresa and I were the children of *Nicolino*, my father, and Marisa was the daughter of Sarina, my father's sister. Marisa repeated herself in different ways until they understood.

Finally, the woman holding onto me shook her head up and down, indicating that she understood. She chimed in to say that my father and Marisa's mother also had an older sister, *Maria*, our Aunt Mary.

Then holding up one hand and pointing to my sister and me, Marisa said my father's name and said that we were two of his eight children. With her other hand, she pointed to herself and said that she was one of *Sarina's* five children.

Aunt Sarah was fourteen years old when she left Sicily, thirty-six years earlier, and she had never returned to her hometown. She married Uncle Victor, whom she met in high school, after they both immigrated to the United States.

Uncle Victor had fared from Compobasso in the northern part of Italy, east of Rome. Since my aunt and uncle spoke pure Italian, not dialect, in the home, Marisa and her older sister spoke both Italian and English, and her younger siblings spoke the language a little, too.

I was thirty-four that summer in Sicily with Teresa and Marisa, who were twenty-five and twenty-six respectively. Aunt Sarah was fifty that year. I must have taken for granted my resemblance to her, only sixteen years older.

Although most of Aunt Sarah's cousins in Gualtieri had not seen her in those thirty-six years she had left, tales and pictures had come back from those who'd visited the United States. Aunt Sarah, who took good care of herself by exercising and eating nutritious food, has always looked younger than people her age. It was no wonder they thought I was her.

After the two women on the terrace understood who we were, the one who'd rushed up to me introduced the older woman, *Zia* Rosalia, as her mother, who was our great-aunt by marriage to my grandfather's brother, *Zio* Giovanni.

Maria, the woman who hugged me, was one of their five children. Now there are many Marias in the family, since customarily, all firstborn daughters are named after their paternal grandmother and all firstborn sons after the grandfather.

As a result, not only are there a slew of Marys and Marias, but there are another handful of Nicks, Nicolas, Nicolinos and Nicolinas. This means that every family has cousins with the same name or some derivative thereof. This particular Maria was the eldest daughter of *Nonno* Morina's brother, *Zio* Giovanni.

The clamor we made on the terrace must have stirred the older man who called down from a small doorway above our heads. He was in the stone house on the right, and I was in awe at the sight of this elderly man. Except for his broader body and squarer face, he resembled my grandfather, *Nonno* Antonio, who'd been dead for four years. It was *Nonno's* brother, my great uncle, *Zio* Giovanni. We all stared as he stood at the top of the long, narrow staircase.

When Maria explained to him in *dialetto* who we were, his eyes lit up, just as *Nonno's* once did when any of us grandchildren entered the room. Both brothers had the same sagging eyelids, mouth, jowls and a smaller refined nose, not very Roman-looking. That larger and more pronounced feature of my family came from my father's mother's side, the Merlinos.

Zio slowly began to descend the stairs, taking each step one at a time while placing his hand on the stone wall for support. I watched him shift from one foot to the other in the same blocked way my grandfather had moved when he got older.

When *Zio* reached the bottom of the stairway, we went up and greeted him respectfully, with the customary two kisses, one on each cheek. I felt his arm tenderly around my shoulders. His scent, a bit musty, with a whiff of wine, smelled like *Nonno* Antonio. I stayed there an extra few seconds, holding back my emotions. For a brief instant, I felt I was back in my grandfather's arms.

Maria invited us inside for a cold drink. The scorching sun had made us terribly thirsty. Then, while Maria stayed back to make a meal, *Zia* Rosalia took us out to visit people and areas of town that she thought we'd be interested in seeing.

One family was Aunt Mary's in-laws, who had lived in Syracuse for about ten years before moving back to Gualtieri. It was refreshing to see their youngest daughter, Nicolina. She was Teresa's age and could speak both English and Italian. What a relief to be able to talk without stammering!

After that stay, we continued strolling through the village, *Zia* and I walking arm in arm, the way women do in Italy. She seemed so comfortable clutching onto me. I was sure she still half-believed I was my Aunt Sarah. She walked us by *San Nicola di Bari* Church, the church where Dad's family attended, where the family was baptized and received their Sacraments.

Teresa, Marisa and I looked at each and frowned when we discovered it was locked. *Zia* shrugged her shoulders nonchalantly and continued walking, introducing us to various people along the way. Two ladies, with the same gray dress speckled with large-muted polka dots, stopped to say that they were distant cousins of my grandmother.

At one point, and out of nowhere, a much older woman came right up to us. Years later, I would discover that she was *Zio* Santo's second wife. *Zio* Santo was my grandfather's half-brother.

Zia subtly but quickly turned us in another direction. There was so much to see that the encounter passed me by at the time. *Zia* held her head high while ambling through the village, as if she had something of value that the others watching did not have.

We returned to the meal that Maria had prepared for us—fresh tomato sauce with basil over pasta, salad, breaded veal cutlets, a large loaf of Italian bread and drinks—wine, soda and beer. We ate in her tiny dining room. Around the outside perimeters of the space were cot-like couches that she said were beds.

Afterwards, Maria and *Zia* walked us down to a red, brick house that we'd passed by with the *carabiniere*. Not too far behind, *Zio* Giovanni sauntered along, smoking a cigarette. He held his head up too, looking around, while the town's people stared.

Via Roma, Numero 19 had been my father's and his sisters' childhood home. Maria pointed out that our grandfather's initials were still present in the wrought-iron over the front door—M. A. for Morina, Antonio, family name first.

It belonged to another family now, since my grandfather had sold the house, having finally moved everyone to the United States after World War II in the late 1940s. We took pictures and spoke to a neighbor, who said Aunt Mary's and Uncle Peter's wedding reception was held in her home. Had *Zia* Rosalia and Maria not been with us, we would never have learned this information, met the people we did or taken in the significant sites of Gualtieri Sicaminò.

Heading back through the main *piazza, Zia* Rosalia saw the side doors of the church now opened. A funeral was underway, and a group of people rushed through the square and into the sanctuary. Grown men held up a wooden box, and women, dressed in black, were crying, holding handkerchiefs to their eyes. We quickly snuck into the back of the church behind them. The mourners didn't stay long, following the men in the group who carried the wooden casket back out the church doors.

The gilded altar, which had been in photos brought over from Sicily, stood straight ahead. As we reached for our cameras, one of three older women who followed us hurried inside and turned on bright-overhead lights above the golden canopy. The other two women approached, but they let the first lady do the talking. When she heard who our family was, she motioned for us to step over to the statue of Our Lady of Mount Carmel and said that our grandmother, *Nonna* Nicolina, had a great devotion to this facet of Christ's mother.

According to the woman, *Nonna* had sent money to the church over the years, in honor of her devotion. The statue of Mary was dressed in brown, a very light-beige veil, draped over her head. I held my breath when I pointed out to my sister and cousin that it was the same color as the dress and veil my grandmother was buried in back in Syracuse, two years earlier.

We dropped *lire* into the collection box of the metal candleholder that held rows of small votives. We each lit a candle and said our own private prayers. Mine were for *Nonna* and *Nonno*.

As Maria and *Zia* continued promenading us back down the street, *Zio* continued to follow behind. We passed by their houses and headed toward the other end of town and to another *piazza*. In a much smaller square, there were no buildings, but there were lots of lush green plants, shrubs and people who were taking their traditional *la passeggiata*, the Sicilian evening walk.

At one point, Maria suggested we head back for the car. *Zio* and *Zia* stayed behind, while the rest of us jumped in. Maria directed me to drive over the wooden bridge to the new section of town. That was where her younger sister now lived. Pasqua was about fifty, Aunt Sarah's age. A number of people came in and out, including Pasqua's husband, daughter and infant grandson.

Pasqua served baseball-size figs, prickly pears, blood oranges and an array of additional local fruit. They made a joke about how I was not able to use a paring knife effectively while cutting fruit the way they do in Italy. I asked Marisa to explain that I was used to just holding and biting a piece of fruit, American style. Pasqua found this mode of eating fruit amusing. I must have appeared more foreign than she expected from her own first cousin's daughter.

Toward the end of the day, Maria asked where we were spending the night. Although we tried to avoid telling her about the mishap with Nicola's mother, Marisa explained the situation. Since information travels instantaneously in Gualtieri, Maria and *Zia* knew she was away. That's when Maria insisted we stay overnight with her and her husband, whom we hadn't yet met.

Maria wanted to give us her bedroom. Their four-room house—a very narrow bath, a kitchen, one bedroom and a combination dining/bedroom—was tight enough for them. Although we knew we were going against the mores of the town's culture, we decided among ourselves in English that we would not put these generous people out of their bed.

We had already showed up unexpectedly. They dropped their life for us, fed us dinner and became our tour guides for five whole hours.

I saw the look of concern on Maria, *Zia* Rosalia, and *Zio* Giovanni's faces, as we climbed back into the rented Fiat. The sun had already set and it was nearly dark. The last thing I heard was my great uncle saying, "*State attenti*," just like my grandfather used to do.

Although I hid my concern about finding lodging at such a late hour, I also mustered the inner faith that maybe my grandparents' spirits would guide us to a safe haven.

Teresa, Marisa and I followed our map toward Milazzo, a town we'd driven through on the way there, and one we knew about from listening to the adults when we were young. As we headed down the main strip, we saw a selection of hotels, lined up on the shore. The first one we stopped at was a modern, Italian-style concrete structure. They had a large room available, with three single beds.

Climbing into bed that night, we gratefully agreed that someone or something had guided us comfortably to a safe haven. And it was also nice to know about lodging close by, in case someone back home might want to visit one day.

****

Within minutes after Stu, Mom, Dad and I drive into the main *piazza*, Dad points in the direction of *Via Roma*. *Via Roma*—the road where the *carabiniere* walked my sister, cousin and me that summer of 1983 toward our great uncle's home.

It's been seventeen years since that trip with Teresa and Marisa. *Zio* Giovanni and his wife, *Zia* Rosalia, have long since died, and I haven't heard a thing about their daughter, Maria, for a while.

Stu slowly drives down the road a short distance, until Dad says, "Pull over here."

We stop just beyond my grandfather's red brick house. The letters "M" on the left and "A" on the right—Morina, Antonio—are still in the ironwork over the front door. There've been no renovations, and the house is even more worn then when I first saw it in 1983.

We step out of the car and hang around the small open area in front of the house. It's a corner place, and to the left of it is one of Gualtieri's narrow passageways. To the right, another house abuts my grandfather's old brick home. There's a place across and set back, leaving space for a *cortile*, a small courtyard, in front of my family's old homestead. Dad tells us that the house on the other side of the open area was another place my grandfather once owned.

"We lived in it while the brick house was being built."

While Dad's talking, a woman in the neighborhood approaches him, wanting to know what he's doing. He points to the brick house and tells her that he used to live there. A young, 30-year-old guy, who's just about to climb into his car, also stops and strikes up a conversation with Dad, as does another lady, standing in a nearby doorway.

The whole atmosphere reminds me of the Northside of Syracuse—the Italian section of town—where I lived until I was four years old. It's where my grandparents, on both sides of the family, lived until they died. Like the homes in Gualtieri, two and three-story dwellings stand close. Neighbors look out for each other in Syracuse, too.

That way of living migrated to other areas as Italian-Americans and other European ethnic nationalities blended into American culture, but the lifestyle didn't appeal to me in my teens and young adulthood. Perhaps that's why I left home for a life with more anonymity, or at least more freedom—to come and go without being under constant surveillance.

In Sicily, constant watch is a way of life. So it doesn't bother my father when the neighborhood people stop to ask him questions. Switching from *dialetto* while talking to the inquisitive neighbors and back to English, Dad explains to us that the garage on the right, sitting at a slight angle, used to be a room. It was where his *Nonna* Merlino, his mother's mother, lived in her old age. Above it now is a veranda.

"That's where I sat and talked to my grandmother," Dad says.

Then he points to a small, three-by-five foot balcony, positioned directly above the front door.

"See that balcony," he says. "Your grandfather threw me up in the air once from there, then he caught me."

"For fun?" I ask.

"Fun?" Dad says, his voice rising. "It wasn't fun. He was mad at me."

I remember that story, but I envisioned my father and grandfather standing on *terraferma*, the ground, not on a second floor balcony. *Nonno* had a reputation for having a tumultuous temper, and it was even more turbulent when my father was a boy.

"You're lucky he didn't drop you," I say to Dad.

"Yeah," he answers, his eyes opening wide, aware of the peril he knew.

Dad turns away and looks at all that surrounds us before I hear him ask the people on the street if they know where Denaro lives.

"Pasqualino Denaro?" Dad repeats.

No one seems to know Pasqualino Denaro. He's a man in his eighties by now, one of Dad's older cousins from the Merlino side of the family. Dad motions for us to follow, and says he can find the house himself. He turns and walks away from *Nonno*'s old brick home, past the house across the square, around to the left side of it and into a narrow alleyway, where old stone homes line a path.

We follow Dad down tight passages and up a number of old granite staircases. The more we climb, the more apparent it is that the town is built into the side of a mountain. Stu jokes that what goes up must come down. And I assume he means us, too.

We trail after Dad, who's talking aloud to himself as much as to anyone else, as he reminisces about his cousin, Pasqualino, or is it his cousin, Pasqua? I listen closely to his meanderings and figure out that he's speaking about both of them under his breath.

"One had moved to the other side of the river, the newer side," my father says.

That's Pasqua. It was her place I went to with Teresa and Marisa and returned two years later, with Aunt Mary and Uncle Peter. We follow Dad up another wider set of stairs. He comments that we should have taken the car instead.

"That would have been challenging," I muse. "How do you think we could have driven that car up the stairs, Dad?"

He keeps climbing, obviously knowing where he's going, even though we don't. We arrive at a road that looks familiar. I'm sure that the old Assumption Church is somewhere nearby. I recognize the street from the day Aunt Mary and I went to say the rosary with the women's church society. Dad stops and holds his hand up to his mouth like he does when he's thinking.

Mom makes a few remarks, suggesting that perhaps he doesn't remember the house where one of his cousins lives. He ignores her comment and takes a left onto the road and around a short bend. Just as I suspected, the *Chiesa dell' Assumpto* appears straight ahead.

We walk on past and stop in a small, rectangular square, left of the church—an area designated for parking. A concrete wall creates a border with an opening for a short incline that leads to the other side of the wall, where another walkway begins. The wall has an iron handrail that people use to support themselves while climbing the incline to a walkway that leads up further into the village.

In the open space next to the church, my father is pacing and looking at all the houses. He hangs close by a particular pink stucco place, with a rusty-orange door, *Via Duca, Numero* 40. It's double the width of most of the adjacent homes. A long second floor balcony, with numerous houseplants, hangs above our heads.

In a house diagonally across the road from the pink stucco home, a woman's voice rings out from a second floor terrace, asking my father in *dialetto* who he's looking for.

"Denaro," he says, "Pasqualino Denaro."

"*Non cen'e,*" I hear the woman say.

He isn't there, and she continues to tell Dad that Pasqualino has gone out for his evening walk—*la passeggiata*. After talking with the woman a bit, my father says that Pasqualino might be at the smaller *piazza* on the other end of town. But the neighbor isn't completely sure.

So my father continues heading in the direction we've been walking, away from The Assumption Church. I'm not clear if Dad is on a mission to find his cousin, Pasqualino, or if he's exploring his old environs. It doesn't matter; we follow wherever he goes.

Half a block away, Dad points to a spot.

"That's where my *Nonna* Merlino once lived before moving in with us."

There's no longer a house there, only an empty corner. I sense my father's longing as he moves through the town he once knew so well. We follow him up and down alleyways, behind other houses and through what appears to be private passages. Dad seems to be looking for something, or many things.

I fight back tears. He knows where he's going, although the rest of us don't. I envision him as a little boy, playing in these narrow passages, like some of the young children we pass along the way.

My father moves over onto a path that parallels the street we're on. A waist-tall wall separates the two roads. At the end of the wall, Dad takes a sharp left and heads down yet another stairway. We're now reversing our direction and heading down, just like Stu said we would.

On the way, we come upon a deserted terrace. In the house, adjacent to the desolate space, a door is boarded. On the left, a steep set of narrow-stone steps lead to another door, also boarded. There's no sign of life, not even a flower or plant breaking through the cracks of the stone.

I'm startled when I realize that this is where Teresa, Marisa and I were first led back to in the summer of 1983. We're at my great-uncle, *Zio* Giovanni's house, next to his daughter, Maria's place. We've approached their homes and terrace from the backside—a different direction from the first time the *carabiniere* walked us here.

This must be a route my father took many times—from his home, up to his cousin's on his mother's side, back down to his uncle's on his father side.

"Dad," I say, excited. "This is your *Zio* Giovanni's house."

He doesn't act surprised and keeps on moving, as if he's been here many times before, which of course, he has.

"Is Maria still here?" I ask.

"She's living in the north, in Torino now, with one of her children," Dad answers as he scoots through and down the steps to the road where his old brick house is located, the same road that leads back to the St. Nicholas *piazza*, the first road I ever walked down when entering his town, years before.

Now I know why I've wanted to be in Gualtieri with Dad—to see the place from his perspective, to follow the steps he took as a young boy. I never realized how intense it would feel trailing my father, now in his late seventies, retracing the paths of his past.

Instead of heading left toward the St. Nicholas *piazza*, Dad takes a right toward the smaller square at the opposite end of town. It was the same route that Maria and *Zia* used when leading Teresa, Marisa and me. I watch Dad looking around at all the different men. I'm sure he's hoping to recognize his cousin. The men look at him, too, and at us as we walk by. But he never sees Pasqualino.

Eventually, we turn around and head back to where the car is parked, near his father's old house. A man walks up to Dad in the street and calls him by his birth name, "*Nicolino*."

It takes a while before Dad realizes it's an old neighbor, two years younger, who lived down the street from him when they were growing up. Another man approaches and introduces himself, and then another. Dad introduces my mother first, his *sposa*, his wife, and then me, his daughter, *sua figlia*, and Stu, his son-in-law, or *suo genero*. As the four men talk, I stand at a short distance away, watching my father in his old world.

One of the men asks about my Aunt Mary, and then Aunt Sarah—referring to my second aunt as the little one, *quella piccola*. They want to know how they are both doing in America. After a brief conversation, Dad looks over at me.

"I'm tired," he says in English. "I need to go back."

My father did say that he wanted to leave by dusk, and it's slightly past sundown. The experience of being back in his village has taken a toll on him. The color in his face is drained, perhaps by the emotion of moving around his hometown.

As we approach the car, I hear him say, as much to himself as to us, "This is where it all began. This is my hometown. It is always a part of me. It will always be in me."

I let him be, hold back my questions, comments and tears. His roots, my roots, our roots pulled, dug up, moved thousands of miles away.

11) Milazzo Nights, Gualtieri Days

Friday Evening, October 20, Saturday, October 21

After Dad grabs a quick catnap, we decide to live like the Sicilians and go out for a late dinner. It's around 9:30 Friday night, and cars are bumper to bumper on the streets. Guys beep at girls walking. Some even pull their motorcycles onto the sidewalk. Families, children and groups of pilgrims stop at the shrine for Padre Pio, a contemporary mystic who I first heard about from my father years ago. Lights illuminate the statue of the saint in a small grotto by the sea.

We drive from our hotel to the other side of the strip and find a *trattoria*. We sit outside. Evenings are still comfortable in Sicily in October. I've brought the little black journal that my brother, Gerard, encouraged me to have on hand. My intention is to get my father to talk about pieces of his life that he began unraveling earlier in the day.

Over dinner, Dad briefly mentions that Pasqualino is the cousin who took him to the boat in Palermo when he emigrated in 1939. That's all he has to say about his life here. He's more interested in talking about his time in the army during World War II, about how he became a barber while in the service and how cutting hair gave him extra money to spend—and still have enough to send home to his father. *Nonno* put that money in the bank.

"I didn't need that money," he says, "I made good money barbering and kept some for myself too. Plus, the army had an automatic deduction for my pay, which was $54 a month. I had it sent directly to my mother and sisters in Sicily. But it wasn't until after the war that the army delivered that money to your grandmother and aunts."

"What did they live on?" I ask.

"They got credit," Dad says. "People knew that after the war, someone would pay for them. *Nonno* would pay or I would pay."

I'm amazed that a whole town of people had such trust in each other. Dad tells how his uncles helped too, specifically mentioning *Zio* Giovanni. Dad also talks about how my grandfather, *Nonno* Antonio, took some of my father's barbering money from the bank and also sent that over to my grandmother here in Sicily.

"Your grandfather preferred to spend my money rather than his own," he adds jokingly.

****

Nonno was a thrifty man, a saver. When I came home after my first two years of teaching art in a school system south of Boston, *Nonno* told me that he was sure I saved at least $10,000. It was 1972, and I only made a little over $13,000 a year.

When I laughed and said, "*Nonno*, I could never save that kind of money," his chest puffed out, the lines around his mouth turning down. He glared at me.

If I didn't know better, I'd have thought he was giving me—his own granddaughter, the Sicilian *malocchio*—the evil eye. My father, sitting at the table, laughed at both my grandfather's response and my reaction.

Nonno threw me off guard. He obviously didn't understand my contemporary-American way of life. Besides the rent on my apartment, food, car, insurance and clothes, I wouldn't have dared to tell him about my single, social life—about renting a cottage on Cape Cod during the summer and ski chalets in the winter. In between, I had a traveling and entertainment fund.

Nonno's retort was that if I'd been living at home with my mother and father, like a good Italian daughter should, I wouldn't have had all these unnecessary expenses. Despite my grandfather's frugal habits, *Nonno*, like my father, was a good provider, not only for his immediate family, but also for relatives and others he left behind in Gualtieri.

I remember how, in the 1950s, he collected clothes, shoes, overcoats and other wearables to send back to Sicily to those still struggling after the war. All of his *paesani* who moved to upstate New York would participate in *Nonno*'s drives. He would accumulate apparel for men, women and children and store it all on the enclosed porch off his living room. Loads of clothes were bailed tightly for shipping.

On certain Sunday afternoons, I watched from the kitchen with my older sister, Nicki, and younger brother, Anthony, as the *paesani* from Gualtieri gathered around my grandparents' long, dining room table. *Nonno* sat at his place at the head, while people came by throughout the day.

My grandmother, *Nonna* Nicolina, and my two aunts, Aunt Mary and Aunt Sarah, set out *biscotti* and other Italian pastries for visitors to eat. Wine was served, along with *caffè* or any spirits someone might want.

Besides clothing and other needed supplies, my grandfather also collected money to send back to his hometown. No matter how much someone brought, *Nonno*, with a stern, take-charge manner, would coax each countryman into pulling more cash from his pocket. In *dialetto*, he spoke in a deep raspy tone about taking care of *their own back home*, just like he did when he was a boy.

Nonno was six years old when his mother died. His father remarried and lived somewhere else in Gualtieri, while *Nonno* lived with his grandparents. Even at his young age, it was *Nonno* Antonio—the oldest of three boys—who looked out for his younger brothers. *Zio* Rosario was shorter than my grandfather, and *Zio* Giovanni was as tall as *Nonno* at six-foot-one. Their thick hair, smaller noses, and lighter-colored skin made them look more alike. As a boy, it was my grandfather who made money for the family, by taking people from one town to another on a donkey that belonged to his grandparents.

When I would ask *Nonno* about his father or any other ancestors, his face would get tight. He clammed up and refused to speak. One day, he insisted that I let those who were dead stay buried. What he also wanted buried was any information about our ancestors. I did learn from my father that *Nonno's* father, my great-grandfather, was a violent man, prone to physical mistreatment—not only toward my grandfather and his brothers, but also with others who riled his emotions in any way.

Rumor has it that when *Nonno's* father was a young man, he was accidentally hit in the head with a rock and was never the same. One of many speculations is that he may have developed migraines that set off uncontrollable rages. His violent actions were not limited to just his boys.

He was also abusive toward his wife, *Nonno's* mother, who died in childbirth. After *Nonno's* father remarried, he was as tough on his second wife, even though she was known to have said that "if a woman treated her husband right, he would never raise a hand to her." She still stayed with him and gave him three more children, two girls and a boy—*Zia* Angela, *Zia* Rosaria, and *Zio* Santo.

My grandfather resented his father's cruelty toward his mother and passed his attitude onto my father, who has always been adamant against physical violence against women. My father never raised his hand to my mother—although in keeping with the culture—he believed in disciplining his children with a strap.

"Spare the rod, spoil the child" was the attitude of that time, though not a comfortable one. I found out years later that my father once decided to talk to a priest about disciplining. It was after that Dad's form of punishment became restrictions and sometimes lengthy lectures.

My brothers were given strict orders to never hit us girls. My father insisted that they figure out a way to verbally stand their ground. If the argument got too hot, they were to walk away, cool down and return at another point to settle the dispute.

My brothers, Anthony and Gerard, continue to treat me with great respect. My father told me once that brothers who are allowed to hit sisters contribute to violence against women. Dad was determined to stop the cycle of abuse before it seeped into future generations, especially when it was related to the mistreatment of females. It's no wonder my interest in women's rights and equality is so strong. How ironic. Could it be through Dad that some of my feminist seeds were planted?

****

At the *trattoria* in Milazzo, we follow the old Catholic tradition of no meat on Friday and order pizzas and fish for dinner. Dad has wine, while Stu orders what he calls American wine—beer. Mom and I drink bottled water. The place where we eat is across the street from the *Golfo di Milazzo* on the Tyrrhenian Sea. A narrow side street separates us from the ocean.

We sit outside, enjoying the night air and the people strolling by. When we leave for our hotel, at around eleven, the place is still packed with patrons sitting around tables, talking and drinking.

In bed that night, all I can think of is Dad running up and down those narrow alleyways in Gualtieri and the story he told on the way there—the one about rushing home from Germany to see *Nonna*, Aunt Mary and Aunt Sarah.

What courage it must have taken for my grandfather to leave his village for a more fruitful life. All the tales Dad told us today—his grandfather's and father's temper, the home they lived in, the cousin he's trying to find—came pouring back. I'm trying to get them down on paper, every last word, so that I can bring the stories home to my siblings.

****

Sabato. Saturday, the following morning, Dad rings the bell at the pink stucco row house at *Via Duca, Numero* 40. Mom, Stu and I wait by the car in the open space next to The Assumption Church. We watch as my father turns the doorknob, pushes in and calls out in *dialetto*, "*Sono io Nicolino*,"—*It's me, Nicolino*.

Within seconds, he turns around and waves us toward him. A woman's voice coming from inside the house gets louder and louder. From the top of a stairway, I can hear the person calling out my father's given name.

"*Nicolino, Nicolino*," her deep, raspy and excited pitched voice cries out.

Stu and I look at each other, shrug and grin. We're not quite sure what to expect. A woman with a slim, seventyish figure, dressed in a straight black skirt with a short wrap-around apron for a blouse, stands at the top of the stairs. Long jet-black hair sticks up and out, held in place by thick, gooey dye at her scalp.

At the sight of seeing my father climbing up the staircase, the woman's bellow is piercing. Her holler flips between laughter of joy and crying when Dad appears at her doorstep. She is caught in the middle of coloring her hair.

I make out the Italian word *capeli*, hair—as it pops into the sentences she rattles out. At the same time, she keeps pointing with her hands toward her head. It's obvious that she is a woman concerned with looks and style. Heavy, thick makeup lines her eyes, her nails are polished scarlet and 18-karat gold jewelry covers her fingers, peeking out from behind the apron she wears on the top of her body.

"It's Maria," my father says to us, "Pasqualino's wife."

Another Maria! I think, hoping to keep them all straight. Initially, Maria keeps apologizing for her looks as she rambles on with animation. I would *never* answer the door in the middle of a dye job. But I'm not surprised that a woman from this culture makes herself available to guests, no matter when they show up. My mother is as equally accessible when anyone appears at her doorstep.

Maria is both hospitable and curious. She asks lots of questions. Some I understand—like how we got there, and when we arrived in Italy, Sicily and Gualtieri Sicaminò. Other inquiries I don't grasp completely, but I recognize the questioning inflection of her voice when it rises at the end of her sentences. As we reach the landing, she bearhugs my father, kisses him repeatedly, and then she gives the rest of us the customary *bace*, the kiss on each cheek.

Dad introduces Maria in *dialetto*, and then apologizes to her for switching into English, before introducing us. He tells her that he's changing languages for his *genero*, son-in-law, who does not understand Italian.

To the left, in another doorway, an older man appears—thin, a tad shorter than Dad, with white-gray hair. Contrasting my father's more rectangular-facial features, this man's face is round, and his glasses repeat the same shape. He does not have the hard-edged nose of the Merlinos, Dad's mother's family, although my grandmother and his mother were sisters. He must take after his father's side, the Denaros.

In a quieter, subtle manner and with fewer words, this elderly gentleman grabs my father's face into both his hands, briefly staring into Dad's eyes, and then he kisses Dad on each cheek, half-whispering, "*Nicolino, Nicolino.*"

We all remain silent. Then these two grown men hug each other tightly. I imagine them saying good-bye in a similar way sixty-five years earlier, when Pasqualino escorted Dad to the boat in Palermo.

Eight years older than Dad, it was Pasqualino, Dad's first cousin, charged with seeing my father off to America to meet up with his father—my grandfather, *Nonno* Antonio. Pasqualino's mother, *Zia* Phillipa, and my grandmother, *Nonna* Nicolina, were sisters.

It takes all the strength I can muster to keep from crying at this reunion, as I watch the affection that this fragile eighty-five-year-old man has for my father. After Dad introduces us to his cousin, Pasqualino says in a serene but cavernous voice, "*Entrate, entrate,*" and he positions his hand out gently, but firmly, while directing us to enter his living room.

In the background, Maria speaks loudly and excitedly about her hair, about "*Nicolino*" being "right here" in their home and about finally meeting the foreign born wife my father married.

****

"Foreign born" were the words one of Dad's cousins used to describe my mother, when I was visiting with Aunt Mary and Uncle Peter in 1985.

"Foreigner? My mother's no foreigner," I said, with indignation to Aunt Mary, the only person sitting around the coffee table who understood English.

My ability to speak the language was too limited to defend my mother in either *dialetto* or *Italiano*. I asked Aunt Mary to translate what I said. She wouldn't.

"Aunt Mary," I insisted, "Why do they keep calling my mother a foreigner? She's as Sicilian as they are."

Aunt Mary tried hard to ignore my question, widening her eyes, moving them right to left as if saying "no" and trying to get me to let it go. I wouldn't. Finally, she broke out of her *dialetto* and told me in English that we'd discuss it later. According to Aunt Mary, even though my father married a woman of Sicilian ancestry, she was born and raised in America.

"But she's an Italian-American," I said to Aunt Mary.

She informed me that the concept of Italian-American didn't exist there. My mother was either *Italiana* or *Americana*. As far as that world was concerned, Dad had married a woman from the United States, and it didn't matter where her parents were born—even if it was a town no more than two hours away. Defending my mother became a moot point not only with my aunt, but also with all of the relatives who lived there.

During that summer of 1985 in Gualtieri, I met more family than I ever knew existed. It seemed like every other person on the street approached me to say how we were related—either on the Morina side, *Nonno* Antonio's family, or the Merlinos, *Nonna* Nicolina's relatives. *Nonna* had been one of five sisters and a brother, and the only one who'd moved out of the country.

Growing up, I never knew about my grandmother's nieces and nephews and their children still living in Sicily. Since *Nonna* Nicolina never spoke English as well as my grandfather, I couldn't understand everything she said. The Morina side was a more present force in our lives—one, because my grandfather was more dominant—and the other, because a number of *Nonno*'s nephews had moved to the United States.

Neither of *Nonno's* two brothers—*Zio* Rosario or *Zio* Giovanni—ever moved to America. But *Nonno's* half-brother, *Zio* Santo, did. He died when I was fifteen. My grandfather kept the story of his life secret. However, I learned in Gualtieri that *Zio* Santo had one wife that he was legally married to, who was still living in their hometown.

Zio also had what Dad referred to as a "second wife." I had not given another thought to the woman who'd approached Teresa, Marisa and me in 1983 in the main *piazza*, when *Zia* Rosalia had whisked us away.

One afternoon in 1985, I walked to the corner store while Aunt Mary and Uncle Peter were napping. A stranger appeared out of nowhere. She walked up and said she was *Zio* Santo's wife. Her hair was a straggly gray. She was a bit on the plump side, had few teeth and looked every bit of eighty or more. I found it intriguing that she didn't appear until I was alone, which happened one more time while I was there that summer.

Since divorce was not recognized in Italy until more recently, this second wife would have been referred to in other places of the world as *Zio's* girlfriend or perhaps his mistress. I knew there were family matters that had been hushed up over the years because of my grandfather's wishes to let the dead and all their secrets be buried.

I also learned that this particular viewpoint was quite prevalent with many other Gualtierians. So, during that summer of 1985, I spoke guardedly. If I asked too many questions, I would never get a soul to tell me about my family's past.

****

Looking around the living room in Pasqualino and Maria's home, something seems familiar. The oversized, antique-gold and red paisley wallpaper—visually bouncing off the ornate-antique furniture—is my first clue. I'm sure that I've seen it before. But how I ever could forget Maria is beyond me. Maria reminds me how I stopped there briefly with Aunt Mary and Uncle Peter for a cup of *caffè*.

The memory of a slim middle-aged woman with a bun in her hair creeps back. Aunt Mary must not have been as close to Pasqualino growing up as Dad obviously was, and still is. Instead, when I was with Aunt Mary, we spent more time with others, including many in Uncle Peter's family. It's when I step into Maria's decorative bathroom with purple and green, painted flowers and leaves on the toilet, sink and bidet, I remember. Having been enamored back then by the floral fixtures, I actually have a picture of this bathroom at home in one of my photo albums.

After Maria finishes dying her hair, she shows us through the house, a custom I grew up expecting. Maria starts by pointing out the living-dining room's paisley paper that was the original in the house, sometime late 18th century. In one-third of the living area, a couch and three easy chairs are arranged closely together so that people can sit and face each other in conversation.

A large coffee table fills the center space. On the opposite side of the extra-large room is an elegant antique dining room set—table, buffet and a tall-ornate hutch. Like most Italian households, the table is the focal point. It's where people spend their time, eating, drinking and conversing, endlessly.

On that same second floor, there's the master bedroom, kitchen, the decorative bathroom that I recognized, and a small hallway leading to the terrace in the back. We follow Maria down the same stairway we came up, around to the right, and we enter a doorway into a whole other floor that appears even larger than the top level.

It's furnished with two more bedrooms, another kitchen, a bath, and a couple of rooms used for storage. It smells musty in places, like the way my grandfather's basement used to smell in Syracuse. He made wine there, and *Nonna* canned tomatoes for sauce as well as various vegetables that they grew in the garden behind their house.

Now the Sicilian custom that my grandparents, parents and other relatives have always followed is to never allow guests to stay in a hotel. There were even times when my parents gave up their own bedroom for a *paesano*. So none of us, except for Stu, are surprised when Maria insists that we check out of the hotel in Milazzo and stay with them in Gualtieri.

We all agreed ahead of time that a hotel with private accommodations would be the only way we'd visit Sicily. Trying to persuade a persistent Maria is not going to be an easy task. On the other hand, I can feel my husband's panic. Coming from a family of only two children and few cousins, he is not used to staying in other relatives' homes.

"You said we'd stay in a hotel," he mutters, "I'd be uncomfortable in someone's home that I didn't know. Please don't let your father agree to stay here."

As Maria continues speaking in *dialetto*, she keeps pointing out the extra rooms and beds. I can tell my father is slowly being swayed by his traditional sense of obligation. I speak to Dad in English, mindful not to show any facial expressions that Maria might pick up on. I know the culture well enough that I go right for the jugular and appeal to my father's sense of guilt.

"Dad, if we move in here, you'll take a chance of offending another cousin."

After we go back upstairs, Dad tells Maria and Pasqualino a little white lie—the hotel rooms are already paid for. Dad knows the Italian mindset too well. Never would they want us to pay for something and not get full value.

Maria and Pasqualino acquiesce with the firm resolve that the next time we come to Gualtieri, we have to stay with them, period. They repeat their intention to each of us individually, including Stu. He barely understands what exactly is being said, but he knows we won't be sleeping there, and that's all that's important to him.

Since we won't be staying with Maria and Pasqualino, they insist that all meals be at their house. Like Christ with the loaves and fishes, Maria's in the kitchen, tripling the beef soup that she had planned on having for their afternoon meal. She adds small round pasta noodles and drags Mom and me over to the stove asking if what she's prepared is enough.

It seems plenty to us, but she pulls out some *braciole* from the freezer—rolled minute steaks, stuffed with bread filling. There are olives and eggplant that she canned, artichoke hearts, Italian bread, wine, soda, water and beer—all for unexpected guests.

We keep apologizing for causing extra work. Pasqualino tells my father that *women's work is not work at all, but a labor of love.* Dad smiles and quickly pulls me into their conversation, insisting that I hear what his cousin has to say about women caring for the home. Dad loves getting my feminist dander stirred. I'm not the only one reacting to the patriarchal sensibility spewing from my father and his cousin's mouth. Maria gets wind of the conversation, comes running out of the kitchen and bellows out some slang at her husband.

Pasqualino changes his tune quickly, and even Dad humbly backs off. Both men stop smiling and practically bow to Maria's reaction. Despite Maria's howling voice and personality, I knew there was something about her that I liked.

We're kindred spirits, when it comes to women's rights, anyway. Unexpected guests might be a different story. I would order subs, pizza, or better yet, suggest a local restaurant, instead of digging through my kitchen cupboards and refrigerator freezer.

Then again, Maria does have a few decades on me. Her infectious roars and outbursts on just about anything that rouses her keeps us all laughing. Even Stu begins to piece together what she's saying through her gestures and expressive waves.

Most of the time Dad, Mom or even I translate for Stu. His lack of comprehension means little to Maria. She takes a liking to my husband and talks loudly—the way some people do, when talking to a foreigner. Stu's been known to do that himself, whenever he meets someone who can't speak English very well. It's as if the louder he talks, the clearer the words become. I smile at him with that understanding husbands and wives have after living together for almost twenty-five years.

"You reap, what you sow," I murmur, smiling.

After lunch, Dad and I step out onto the back terrace of the house. Most Gualtierian homes have terraces off their second floors. Rust-colored, Siena-tile roofs cover the tops of the town. Off to the left, Dad sees a metal roof.

Excited, he calls Stu outside so that he can show him the growth that is taking place in his hometown. Since Stu has recently bought into a metal roof business, there is a round of picture taking of the old tile next to new metal. Even in this ancient village in the mountains of Sicily, progress finds its way.

After lunch, Maria offers to escort us a few blocks away by foot to see Caterina, another cousin of Dad's. Pasqualino says he'll stay back, joking that he's too old to make the trip. Over lunch, we learned that Pasqualino is recuperating from a serious heart operation.

Just two years ago, Dad had his own open-heart surgery. He's always attributed his heart condition to a case of Rheumatic fever when he was a boy. This is the first time I start wondering if there is a genetic disposition to heart problems in the family that no one has known about.

Pasqualino waves to us from the balcony on the second floor of his home, then he leans over boxes that line the railing, picking away the dying flowers. There are a few fresh buds, but most are wilted, as the region moves into late autumn.

After heading out and through the small square in front where our car is parked, we trek up the concrete incline that takes us further into the mountain toward Caterina's house. Hiking further up the paved streets into the hilly terrain, it's obvious that the climb would be too much for Dad's aging cousin.

Caterina's husband, Micio, his nickname for Dominic, meets us at the front door. He dons a beret-like cap and a light brown vest. A rust-colored jacket is flung over, Italian-style, hanging from his broad shoulders over his slender body.

We hear Caterina calling my father's name from the top of her three-story house, which is where most Gualtierians have their kitchens and terraces. Caterina, a quiet, more traditional, robust Italian woman, has leg problems and is unable to move up and down the stairs easily.

When we reach the third floor, Caterina hugs my father tightly and kisses his cheeks repeatedly. She turns away, rubbing tears from her face, and then she takes a few minutes to compose herself. Caterina, a gentle soul, like my mother, remembers me as we kiss.

She's equally as tender meeting my mother and husband. It is Caterina's daughter, Carmella, a few years younger than I am, who took me around in 1985 to visit outlying towns and sites of the area. Carmella is now married and no longer living in Gualtieri, although Maria calls her on the phone right then, so that we can plan a visit.

Caterina's husband, Micio, takes a liking to Stu, acknowledging his lighter features and asks my father in *dialetto* if Stu is of German descent. Once Micio figures that out, he switches from Italian to a broken German. Stu's mouth drops.

We all laugh at the additional confusion with the various languages and dialect now rattling throughout the room. Dad tries to explain that Stu's German ancestors were a few generations removed and that he has an additional mix of Scandinavian, English and a number of other Nordic genes.

Dad also tells him that, although Stu has German in the mix, it doesn't mean that he understands a word of it. Micio keeps talking his version of German, whether anyone understands him or not.

Our brief visit ends with a round of anisette shots, or it may have been some other *liquore*. Mom and I manage to avoid the round, since no one pushes liquor on women. Stu and Dad are not quite so lucky.

For men, it's obligatory to have at least one drink with the man of the house. One jigger turns into two—at least for my husband. Dad manages to avoid any additional shots, claiming his *zucchero*, or diabetes, will not allow it. So Stu fulfills the obligation for both of them by chugging down. At the end, he gets a huge, accepting slap on the back by Micio.

Maybe there's something about in-laws connecting with each other, even distant ones. I heard Maria tell Caterina on the phone before we left her house that my mother speaks the language better than my father. I chuckle inside, knowing that Mom would be delighted with the accolade—especially since Dad always takes center stage.

I mentioned the conversation to Mom on our walk up to Caterina's house. Mom's eyes twinkled and broke out into a large smile. When she briefly mentioned it to Dad, he snickered, shook it off and said he was sure I hadn't understood correctly. Then he questioned Maria. To Dad's surprise, Maria assured all of us that she had in fact said that very thing about Mom.

It's been fascinating watching my father with his cousins. It's equally intriguing to watch my mother quietly watch the man she's been living with for over fifty years, as he moves through his childhood surroundings. Outside of a comment here and there, I can never quite tell what Mom is thinking.

****

Later in the afternoon, Pasqualino takes us for a walk down a much gentler incline, through the second and smaller *piazza* in town, opposite the main square where St. Nicholas Church stands. We head for a garden, a plot of land that had been owned by Pasqualino's mother—*Zia* Phillipa, who was one of *Nonna* Nicolina's four sisters.

As we walk, I review aloud with Dad, then Mom, or whoever's attention I can get, about which side of the family Dad's cousins belong. Pasqualino, Caterina and Dad are first cousins by three different sisters on *Nonna* Nicolina's side—the Merlinos.

Dad mentions the names of other cousins—some I met with Aunt Mary and Uncle Peter, and others I have no clue existed. If I don't get Dad's cousins straight while here in Gualtieri, I'll never remember the family members he left behind.

On our stroll, Dad points to the corner, where his Merlino grandparents' house once stood—the same spot he mentioned the night before. The house was torn down years earlier to make room for a curve in the rather narrow concrete roads that snake through town.

We walk by Uncle Peter's sister's house, where I stayed with him and Aunt Mary in 1985. The wooden blinds that most Sicilians used to keep out the heat are completely closed. The house is locked tight. Uncle Peter's sister is probably in Messina, where she lives most of the year.

Her home, a renovated and sophisticated building in the old part of Gualtieri, has now become only an occasional get away for her and her adult children.

We walk to a vegetable garden, full of lemon and orange trees. The fruit, not quite ripe, is beginning to change into its harvested color. A rooster from the property next door bellows a *cock-a-doodle-do*, in spite of it being late afternoon. I remember a rooster waking me each morning in '85, long before I ever wanted to get up. Our presence this time of day must disturb the rooster's natural order of things.

This is still siesta time, when people of the village are resting and off the streets. Toward the back of the property, Pasqualino unlocks two sheds. Dad continues pointing out things that he remembers, especially the smaller shed on the right. Pasqualino pushes the door wide open, so we can see inside.

"*Nonna* had this built," Dad says, as he approaches the door. "She used to keep chickens in this building, and I used to steal the eggs and sell them," he said, chortling. "Then I gambled the money."

"Dad!" I scold, although I know of his rebellious history as a kid.

That was why I never understood how he could be such a hard-ass when any of us stepped out of line even a smidgen. Maybe it's Dad's own past that called my siblings and me to task before trouble arose.

Dad tells Pasqualino, in *dialetto*, about gambling the money he retrieved from the stolen eggs. His older cousin smiles in recognition of their earlier days. Pasqualino stands at the entrance, proudly showing us the once-upon-a-time chicken coop—now a wine cellar—a place of esteem for Italian men.

After meandering back up the road to Pasqualino and Maria's, Pasqualino plans for us to stop by another of Dad's cousin's house. We also discuss the next day, *domenica,* which is Sunday. We'll be eating the *festa* meal at noon with them. Also, Dad wants to attend Mass at *San Nicola di Bari* Church. When he asks for the schedule, his cousin informs him that he doesn't believe in a monotheistic God.

There's a brief discussion about Pasqualino being an agnostic, or possibly an atheist. I don't quite get the gist of the conversation, but this is probably the first time I see my father back off from being an evangelist for the religion in which he and his cousin were raised.

Even after all these years, Dad obviously respects the birth order that his cultural tradition espouses. Despite his cousin's   lack of participation in church, Pasqualino is sure the bells ring at ten o'clock for the start of Mass the next day. Dinner would be at their place afterwards.

****

Maria drives with us over the wooden bridge that leads away from the old town. She rings the doorbell of another house that I've been to twice before. Pasqua, Dad's cousin from the Morina side, lives in a more contemporary Italian home. Pasqua and Maria know each other, even though they aren't related. Stu and I stand back, while Dad, Mom and Maria wait by the door.

Pasqua greets Maria and then stares back and forth from my father to my mother. In her mid-to-late-sixties, Pasqua is a soft-spoken and calm woman. Stu and I can hardly hear what she's saying from where we stand.

She continues looking from Mom to Dad, and I hear her talking to them and to herself as she tries to decipher whose faces she's seeing. Then, just like Pasqualino and Caterina did, she grabs my father's face and starts kissing him, laughing, smiling and wiping tears from her eyes.

When Pasqua sees me in the distance, she remembers me and says something about my visit with Aunt Mary and Uncle Peter, and before then, with Teresa and Marisa. I remind her, in my broken Italian, how I am the one who couldn't cut and peel fruit with a knife very well. She smiles in recognition and asks how my aunt, uncle, sister and cousin are doing.

We don't stay long at Pasqua's and decline any *caffè*, pastry, soda or water, but Dad promises that we'll return and stay longer. After dropping Maria back at *Via Duca, Numero*. 40, we head to our hotel in Milazzo. Dad, used to napping, is worn out. The day has been an emotional roller coaster for him. I'm surprised at the amount of energy he's maintained—the same energy, I remember, he had when I was young.

I'm also impressed with Stu and how he goes along with whatever happens. This has to be a culture shock, coming from a more reserved, Nordic ancestry. Stu remarks, humorously, that we've been talking and eating and, in his own made-up word, "passajohning" all day.

"It's *passeggiata*!" I say, laughing at the way Stu pronounces the Italian word for walk.

"We're seeing exactly what we came here to see," Stu says to me when we're back in our hotel room alone. "Your father's roots."

I'm so grateful that Stu appreciates my family's heritage. Over the years, Stu's taught me how to become less judgmental and to take pleasure in people as they are. He's also always been an advocate for my mother and father.

I think it's from having lost his parents at a young age. He was thirteen when his mother died of a brain aneurysm— twenty-one when his father passed away in the hospital, from complications of a minor surgery. I suppose Stu could have been a cautious and bitter person, but that's not him. His two mottoes are, "Be happy!" and, "Make it to the next day!"

"Nothing else matters," he says, "if you don't."

Whenever I've struggled with my parents—mostly my father—Stu just listens. If he speaks up, it's usually in defense of my folks. That, of course, hasn't always settled well with me. I secretly must admit that I appreciate how Stu does not participate in my carrying on. After settling down from whatever conflict I'm dealing with—and inevitably I *do* settle down—Stu lets me know how fortunate I am to still have my parents.

****

Dad crashes when he gets back to the hotel. Mom, Stu and I venture out around nine o'clock and find a small, elegant and peaceful restaurant. We don't talk much, after a day of constant chatter and listening. Stu sips an Italian beer, while Mom and I have bottled water, *senza gas*—no bubbles.

They both order veal, and I choose something local— crayfish. It doesn't really suit my taste buds. The crayfish resembles lobster. It's smaller in size, but a lot spinier. I hoped for a little more meat in the shell. The fresh greens in the salad, the Roma tomatoes, balsamic vinegar and deep-green olive oil is enough to satisfy my palate, for tonight anyway.

12) *Domenica*

Sunday, October 22

The clear air of an autumn Mediterranean morning sweeps across the patio at the Hotel Riviera Lido. The array of boats I've seen on previous summer visits no longer dot the horizon. Only a single ferry heads out from Milazzo's wharf, toward the islands. Of the seven Aeolian Islands, I've been to one of them—*Vulcano*.

Angelo Isgro and his nephew—friends from my father's village—included me on one of their day trips to the volcanic island the August I lived with Aunt Mary and Uncle Peter. When my aunt cautioned that it wasn't proper for me to travel as a woman with men outside my family, Angelo quickly dismissed the comment with a wave of his hand.

"She'll be gone in a week. What difference does it make?"

Angelo knew of the wanderlust Americans have for travel and adventure. He and his wife, Giovannina, spend half their year in Gualtieri and the other half in upstate New York. I've known Angelo since childhood. He's my father's age, has a son my age, and he and his wife are close friends with my aunt and uncle. I was safe with him.

The Isle of *Vulcano* is a place where Angelo travels often to sit in warm lava baths and relieve a health problem he's struggled with for years. I assume it's something like arthritis, even though he never talks about what ails him.

It's obviously painful enough for him to leave his son and grandchildren in the United States and regularly visit the volcanic baths. I half-wonder if it's Angelo's body that calls him back to his hometown of Gualtieri Sicaminò. Many who have left yearn to return to their roots. My father is not one of them. My grandfather always said he wanted to die in his hometown. He didn't.

****

Toward the end of *Nonno* Morina's life, he had a series of strokes that caused loss of control over his facial muscles. One of the most difficult symptoms for my proud Sicilian grandfather was that he drooled. He kept a handkerchief near. The right side of his body shaked, and he walked much slower than he once did.

One day, when I went to visit him and my grandmother, *Nonno* was in his bedroom, off the kitchen. I could hear from the other side of the door that he was frustrated about something. *Nonna* Nicolina was standing in the kitchen, grasping the edge of the counter.

In a quiet but futile voice, she told me that she couldn't help him. My grandfather had been shaking so much that he was unable to lift either one of his legs high enough to put on his own pants. According to *Nonna*, he'd been at it a good part of the morning.

I guided *Nonna* over to a kitchen chair and encouraged her to sit down. Then I stepped over by the door of my grandfather's bedroom.

"*Nonno*," I called in, "may I help you?"

At first there was silence. Then I heard my grandfather rustling around anxiously, probably trying again to put on his pants.

"It's okay, *Nonno*. I'm your granddaughter. I want to help," I said.

There was a huge lull before he cracked the door open, ever so slightly.

I waited for him to say, "Come in."

Nonno had on underwear, socks and a dress shirt, that hung mid-thigh. His eyes were drooping, like they did, increasingly, as he aged. Saliva dribbled from his mouth. I lifted his handkerchief from the bed and gently wiped his mouth. It was one thing he allowed me to do.

I asked him to sit on the bed, and he did, without saying a word. I knelt at his feet, lifted his right foot, and I slipped on one pant leg. He tried to help, and I let him. It seemed awkward—me helping this once strong man—but I swallowed any sadness and continued. We did the same with the left pant leg.

After maneuvering the trousers to his knees, *Nonno* stood, and together we finished pulling his pants up to his waist. His hands shaking, he zipped his pants by himself. We both fumbled with his belt for a few seconds, until I left him alone and said I'd wait in the kitchen. After a few minutes, my grandfather stepped out of his room. We fell into conversation, like we always did.

Then *Nonno* walked me from the kitchen, through the dining room and into the living room to show me a statue of *San Nicola di Bari* and other religious paraphernalia that someone had sent from Gualtieri. At that point in my life, Gualtieri Sicaminò was only a series of hand-me-down stories, but I admired the statue, because it meant so much to him.

Nonno was an affectionate grandfather who loved kissing our cheeks when we were young. But he was brusque with others, especially adults. Being such a stern taskmaster, I was cautious about what I said around him.

Yet my siblings and I knew how *Nonno* felt about us by his actions—directing a car safely out of his driveway, handing us dollar bills or shaving his face a second time, when he knew we were coming for a visit.

As we got a little older, some had the courage to tell *Nonno* that his beard was too rough on our faces, and he had to go shave if he expected a kiss. He acted surprised and would always say that he'd just shaved, and I'm sure he had. But *Nonno*'s beard, like his personality, was rough, no matter how often he shaved it off.

After seeing the statue in the living room and walking with *Nonno* back toward the kitchen, I felt this sense of emotion sweep over me, a feeling deep inside, nudging me to tell my grandfather how I felt about him. I'd never in my life planned this moment. The words just blurted out.

"*Nonno*," I said looking into his cavernous eyes, "I love you."

I didn't know how he would respond to this. It wasn't the kind of exchange I'd ever had with *Nonno*. It was long before people in my family told each other they loved them, unless it was a baby or a toddler in someone's arms. But without the skip of a beat, *Nonno* looked directly into my face, his eyes warm and inviting.

"I love you, too," he said.

It had become obvious that it was too difficult for my grandparents to live alone anymore. In 1979, the elders in the Italian culture had not, for the most part, transitioned into nursing homes easily. My father and my two aunts began thinking of alternative living situations, including one of their own homes.

When *Nonno* got wind of this, he told my father that they only had to worry about my grandmother. Within days, *Nonno* suffered another stroke that landed him in the hospital. I wasn't living in Syracuse when *Nonno* died.

The family members who stood vigil by my grandfather's bedside knew he was at the end of his life. It also seemed apparent that this strong-willed man had enough resolve to allow his own body to transition into death. *Nonno* started drifting in and out of consciousness, until he called out the words, "The plane!"

His face lit up and his eyes stared away into a place that only he could enter. Everyone knew what that meant: *In Nonno's mind, the plane had come to take him home to Gualtieri Sicaminò.* Within minutes, he was gone.

****

One August morning in 1985, when I was living with Aunt Mary and Uncle Peter in Gualtieri, I traveled with Angelo and his nephew to the island of *Vulcano*. There were lots of people on the ferry. The air was clean, and the light cerulean sky was bright from the glowing sun. Once on the island, the smell of sulfur from the volcano settled in my nostrils. I felt clammy, sitting in a warm mud bath of ash and seawater.

As the day went on, the sun grew hotter and the smell stronger. When I couldn't handle sitting in mud any longer, I walked over a small hill and dove into the Tyrrhenian Sea, off the northeast coast of Sicily.

According to legend, *Vulcano* is the home of Aeolus, "god of the winds," and who, in *The Odyssey*, gave his hospitality for a month to Odysseus and his crew. It was this god who called for a west wind to carry them home.

There was no wind on the island the day I visited. The only breeze I felt was on the ferry from Milazzo to *Vulcano*, and back again.

****

Autumn feels different in Milazzo—sweater weather in mornings and evenings, a light shirt during comfortable afternoons. We took this trip in October to avoid the normal, blistering Sicilian summer. Dad initially wanted to be in Gualtieri during the St. Nicholas feast on the last Sunday in August.

When word got around that we were going to Sicily for the festival, Aunt Sarah called my father and asked him to reconsider traveling because of the heat. Dad's youngest sister was concerned about his heart, since he had his operation only two years earlier and was back in the hospital for a pacemaker just the year before.

I understood Aunt Sarah's concern. Like her, I'm a believer in preventative care. Plus, I saw how Aunt Mary and Uncle Peter struggled with the heat the August we were there.

Sicily's weather, hotter than Florida in summer months, was difficult for Aunt Mary and Uncle Peter, after having lived in upstate New York for decades. They had become used to a cooler climate. When they returned to Syracuse, they forewarned anyone who might travel to Gualtieri for the festival someday that it is hot there *beyond their wildest memories!*

Having lived in North Carolina for a while, I'd become more tolerant of the high temperatures. I did miss the air conditioning that was not available in most of the homes, including where Aunt Mary, Uncle Peter and I stayed. Walking up and down those hills in the heat of the day was a strain.

Sitting on the patio in Milazzo in October is pleasant, calm and less stressful than it would have been with the crowds of Italians who flock to the shore in August. Because of fewer people this time of year, we've been getting extra attention at the hotel—the kind that Dad not only flourishes in but also demands. The woman who cleans our rooms takes a liking to my father, as most people do. Since there are so few guests this time of year, this same woman doubles as a waitress at the buffet breakfast. She's a young, middle-aged Sicilian, about forty-five. The woman and Dad chat, in *dialetto*, and he fills her in on details about how he comes from this region and how he hasn't been back in over thirty years.

The woman asks Dad lots of questions about himself, about America and why we're visiting Gualtieri Sicaminò in autumn rather than in August, when most who've left return for the feast day. She wants to know where Dad lives in the United States, what he did for work and the names of some of his relatives in Gualtieri. She shakes her head and says she doesn't know any of them. She also marvels at the fact that Dad's still barbering and hasn't retired.

They talk about his health, his pacemaker, and his *zucchero*—the word every Italian I've known uses when referring to diabetes. Dad has been testing his bloodsugar level in the mornings. Since it has been elevated while we've been traveling, Dad's blood count is a topic of discussion at every breakfast.

The woman empathizes with my father and tells her own relatives' tales of *zucchero*. I wonder if people from the region are prone to diabetes and if an adjustment in diet would help. As important as food is in the Italian culture, I'm sure most would choose to die before making any drastic dietary change, like eliminating their pastries or their pasta.

"*Un bicchere di succo d'arancia con un po' di limone,*" the woman suggests to Dad—a glass of orange juice and a sizeable squeeze of lemon for my father—then she goes off to prepare it for him.

She tells my father to take a swig every morning, and that it will keep his *zucchero* under control. Actually, it surprises me that Dad's eating or drinking anything before Sunday Mass, since he still follows the old church rule of "no food before communion."

Somehow we've persuaded him that God will understand if he breaks from some of his devout rituals while traveling, although it isn't the God that I've grown to know who has influenced Dad to follow his strict religious practices.

****

Mass on *domenica*, according to what Pasqualino told Dad, was going to be at ten in the morning. Pasqualino also pointed firmly down with his finger toward his living room floor and said, "*qui,*"—right here. *That* is where we can find him before, after and during Mass.

When we arrive at the *piazza* fifteen minutes early, the church doors are closed and locked tight. The men relaxing on the benches in the square are smoking cigarettes and talking low. There's no Mass schedule posted. One of the men comes up to Dad, asks who we are, and tells him that Mass will be somewhere around 10:00 or 10:30.

That is *definitely* Italian time—a scheduled event that can be one time or another, or somewhere in between.

"I guess if Dad wants to know what time Mass is scheduled," I chuckle under my breath, "an atheist cousin would not be the person to ask."

My remark stirs Mom to add her own amusing comments, imitating the Gualtierians.

"How safe it is here!" she says, "We can go anywhere we want."

Mom pulls her shoulders up close to her ears, giggling and breaking out into a big smile.

"But look—they keep their churches locked."

Mom loves to call Dad on his stuff, and calling his *paesani* on their stuff gives her equal pleasure. I snicker with Mom, knowing full well that when we get to Linguaglossa, Dad will have his own series of commentary about *her* family's town.

I've listened to the two of them throwing verbal shots across the kitchen table about each other's Sicilian villages. They're finally in one of the very spots that they've been toying over for years. After this trip, they'll have concrete experiences to draw from. For now, they still have an audience to play to—Stu and me.

While my mother and my husband sit on one of the green, wrought-iron benches in the center of the *piazza* next to the *San Nicola di Bari* Church, I scan the area with the video camera, trying to capture whatever corner of town I can see from my location. I focus down the road that leads to my grandfather's old brick house, less than a block away.

There's a photograph of that road in Aunt Mary and Uncle Peter's wedding album. As a child, my curiosity peaked about the narrow street in the background, behind the young couple and the people throwing confetti and streamers. Of all their pictures, it's the one I looked at again and again.

When I was four years old, Aunt Mary went back to Gualtieri with my grandfather to get married, and she returned with a new uncle and pictures of a wedding. It never occurred to me that someday I'd get to see the actual road from those photos.

When my relatives spoke of the old country, it felt like a place they'd left behind. It never occurred to me that anyone would go back, least of all me. Even though my grandfather said he wanted to return, we knew he would never leave us.

Nonno and *Nonna* did visit on two different occasions. But for the most part, they settled into a home in Syracuse—almost the same distance from their church as their home in Gualtieri had been.

Church was the place where *Nonna* Nicolina spent most of her time, as she got older. After my grandfather retired—if any of us drove down to the Northside to visit them in the middle of the day, *Nonno* would ask us to go to the church and get *Nonna*.

He complained about how many hours she'd already been there, saying her rosary over and over again and reading prayers from her Italian prayer book, or from the memorial cards that commemorated those who died. I knew *Nonno* was using us as an excuse to bring *Nonna* back home.

****

Around ten o'clock, the bells in the Romanesque steeple of *San Nicola di Bari* begin to toll. They clang so loud that we can't hear each other's voices. The ringing doesn't seem to matter. The doors remain closed and no one approaches the church for Mass. Obviously there's a protocol that is unknown to us, and Pasqualino, naturally.

Dad, who's sitting a seat away from Mom on the bench, talks to another man, who moves toward him in the *piazza* and then asks similar questions to the ones Dad answered the night before.

"Who is your family? Why did you leave? Where did you move? What did you do for work?" Like the woman at the hotel, they're always surprised to hear that, at the age of seventy-seven, Dad still cuts hair.

The American Protestant work ethic is quite different from the Italian culture's work habits. Italians value other things besides work— they cherish home, family, friends, food, get-togethers, relaxation and enjoying their environs. When they reach retirement age, Italians retire, collect their government pensions and appreciate life *outside* of work.

At 10:15 a.m., the doors of the church open and a woman at the entrance tells us that Mass will not begin until *undici*—eleven. While the church is still empty, we dash inside to see it before others show up. I recognize the sanctuary from my previous two trips and from old family photos.

I scan the interior with the camcorder, zooming closer into areas that intrigue me, especially the main altar, laden with baroque-like columns, lavishly adorned in plenty of bronzy-gold. It still surprises me, even though I've seen it twice before.

The gold seems more intense than I remember. What astonishes me even more is that, over the past eight years, I've been drawing lots of angels in my studio at home.

Surrounding the figures are layers of gold leaf that I apply to the background, giving the images a celestial atmospheric appearance. Even though I've been to *San Nicola di Bari* Church twice before, I never realized that I must have absorbed this gilded sensibility. Maybe all that gold I've been using is suggestive of my two previous visits to Gualtieri and the visual phenomena of this church. Or is it possible that this gilded sensibility has been genetically tucked away.

Facing the altar in the left-hand corner of the church, and dressed in a dark-brown robe, beige apron and veil, is the statue of Our Lady of Mount Carmel. It's the statue that my grandmother venerated, the one that my sister, Teresa, my cousin, Marisa, and I learned about from the older women who talked to us the first time we entered this church.

When my grandmother died, Aunt Mary and Aunt Sarah buried her in the brown dress that she wore for her 50th Wedding Anniversary. How ironic that *Nonna* would end up being buried in the same color that symbolizes Our Lady of Mount Carmel!

A vision of my grandmother in the casket flashes in my mind—a shiny, silk brown dress, a lacy, beige mantilla covering her head, and the scar she received when she fell at the end of her life. *Nonna* wished she could have been a *suora*, a nun. Lying dead, she was dressed the way she wanted to live.

I'm distracted from my thoughts when Dad calls my name from the other side of the church. He points to the altar at the left of the front door and says that he always wanted to send money to have it fixed. But it slipped his mind. Directly across from that altar is a statue of *San Filippo Neri*.

"They brought that statue up to Sorcorso once," Dad says, "to give to a church in the small mountain village above us. The legend goes that the next day, the statue was right back here in its original spot."

"How did it get back here?" I ask.

Dad shrugs his shoulders and says it's only a legend, but that the statue supposedly returned by itself. I think of my father's numinous story just before we entered Gualtieri—the man in the woods who appeared to Dad as a young boy and how he held a chalice before disappearing. It's no wonder I'm intrigued with mystical experiences—like the voice that woke me the day before leaving on our trip.

We continue walking the nave of the church, and then we head over toward the left altar. Sitting there is the wooden Madonna, lying on a chaise-like structure. It's the same sculpture from The Assumption Church that Aunt Mary and I saw on the feast day when we went to pray the rosary, August 15, 1985.

The Blessed Virgin Mary's hands are still folded in prayer, and the same painted wooden form is peeking out from under a white robe and lacy mantilla that she now wears. Beneath the clothing, I can still see small segments of paint, peeling from the wooden form, just as it did fifteen years ago. Bits and pieces of my father's family history, unraveling.

****

Dad learns that there's time before Mass starts. He wants to run over to Pasqualino and Maria's to let them know that we'll be later than any of us thought. First, we hurry across the square to a *pasticceria,* the bakery, to pick up some *dolci,* sweets. I notice a large round chocolate dessert marked *Morina*—our name—waiting to be picked up by someone.

Then we drive up to Pasqualino and Maria's and drop off *cannoli, biscotti* and other sweets. They've been waiting for us, thinking we were coming for at least a cup of *caffè* before Mass. Maria has been preparing the traditional Sunday meal. With sauce brewing on the stove, the place smells like *Nonna* Nicolina's house.

Since everything's within walking distance in the old part of town, we leave the car and walk back down the hill to the church, only a block and a half away. People are finally arriving, entering the square from the streets that lead to the main *piazza.* It's how it looked the day of the St. Nicholas Feast that I celebrated with Aunt Mary and Uncle Peter.

****

For years, Dad, his family and their *paesani* talked about the big feast as they sat around my grandfather's table. One summer, they decided to celebrate the event and include all of their relatives—in-laws, children, grandchildren, and even friends—who wanted to attend.

At Green Lake Park in upstate New York, people gathered after Mass, early in the day on the last Sunday in August. Plenty of food covered the tables, including the roasted lamb, which is traditionally served in every home in Gualtieri on that occasion.

In 1985, I saw for myself how the feast day encompassed every niche and crevice of the village. Early in the morning, the bells rang continually, calling all to church. Not all answered.

The building was full of women and children, but only a small number of men. Uncle Peter and a few *Americani*, visiting from the United States, attended Mass with their wives and families. The local men did not. I questioned my uncle's sister-in-law, asking why the men didn't go to church, but she insisted they were there.

"Close *enough*, anyway!" she told me.

After all, they were sitting right outside the door in the *piazza*.

The singing I heard that feast day in church had the same nasal twang I remembered hearing when my father pulled out his mandolin at Christmas time. He played, sang and even taught us the old Italian Christmas carols of his childhood. I always wondered why Dad's twang only came out when he sang those particular songs.

When I heard that same nasal sound the morning of the St. Nicholas Feast, I wished I had a tape recorder to capture the hymns for my parents and siblings as a souvenir, a memory of Christmases past.

****

Now in St. Nicholas's church with camcorder in hand, I'm not only determined to get a picture of the choir singing, but I want to capture the tone of the voices. As I zoom in closer, scanning both the center altar and the priest saying Mass, that nasal twang plays in the background.

Two seats away, Dad shuffles from foot to foot. Mom stands between us.

"Gilda, your father wants you to stop," she says, under her breath, her lips positioned left and pointing at me, while her head faces straight keeping her eyes on the altar.

I don't stop. I'm not going to miss this opportunity. How can I be sure I'll ever have it again?

"*Basta!*" my mother says in Italian, a word she's used with us kids before.

"Enough! Your father's getting mad."

I glance in his direction, seeing that grimacing look of disapproval on his face. By then, I've recorded enough music for my siblings to hear and a piece of the Mass to add to the visual effect.

The service is in Italian, of course, and Stu, the patient Episcopalian, stands and kneels on cue, just like he does when he attends church with me at home.

I cannot say why, but after communion, I feel *Nonno* and *Nonna* Morina's presence in a way that I've not experienced since before their deaths. Right here, in *San Nicola di Bari* Church, they seem to be hovering around me before expanding over toward my mother and father, then up to the altar. Within minutes, the whole area encompasses their energy as it encircles the interior of the church—the smells, the sounds, the feelings I had when I was with my grandparents.

I envision my aunts as young women, kneeling in the same space, and my father as a younger man, even though the older Dad stands only a person away. He is, in my mind's eye, embracing his cousin Pasqualino, imagining them at the boat in Palermo, I see the hugs he gets so tightly from his female cousins, Pasqua and Caterina, and Caterina's husband, Micio.

The sense of family, of ancestry, wells up like the tears that start flowing, as my grandparents' presence engulfs me. My heart could drop from my chest. In this moment, *Nonno* and *Nonna* are here, and I couldn't be more certain of anything else in my life.

I start praying to God—no, *begging* God—to pull back the intense feelings rising to the surface. I want to stop crying, breathe every form of breath I've ever learned, in an attempt to control the passion and bewilderment I feel from my grandparents' presence.

They're in the hymns being sung, the nasal sounds of the voices floating over the music, the memories of being in church with them at Our Lady of Pompeii, back in Syracuse, out in their garden behind their house, and sitting around their kitchen and dining room tables.

I feel their arms around me, their kisses on my cheeks—like the ones they said good-bye with before I walked out their side door. I stare at the statue of St. Nicholas, behind the altar, surrounded with gold, and in my heart, I am with *Nonno* and *Nonna* again, in this life.

13) After Mass

Domenica Afternoon, October 22

My parents don't notice my tears. I count on that. They've tried hard, over the years, to understand the emotion that wells up in me and not in them. Stu shuffles over quietly, trying to get closer, resting his arm gently against mine, sensing that something's going on. He knows that I can't disguise deep feelings.

Although he's told me that he doesn't go to those depths, Stu has learned to stretch when my emotions surface. He hasn't known what to say or do. Nor have I, at times. But my husband's attempts at understanding me have created a strong bond in our marriage.

"Are you all right," he mouths.

I nod my head slightly, trying not to draw attention to myself. I pretend to blow my nose while wiping tears from my eyes.

"I just felt my grandparents around me," I whisper.

Stu's brow does not even crease. From what I can remember, other than Aunt Mary, who cried at weddings, the rest of the Morinas, and many of the Gualtierians I've met, control their public crying. That made me an oddity growing up, although I can count on a few of my sisters to shed some tears.

At a young age, I knew I would need to work at pulling myself together in certain situations. Crying in *San Nicola di Bari* Church in Gualtieri Sicaminò, during an ordinary Sunday Mass, is one of those times. I must compose myself before people in the rows ahead turn around to leave, or before one of my parents look my way.

Luckily after Mass, my mother and father are pulled aside by a couple they met back in Syracuse a few years ago. The couple in Gualtieri actually live in Norwich, New York, a town south of Syracuse, where other *paesani* from Gualtieri settled. Stu is delighted to find someone in town who speaks English, after having spent the last two days immersed in the native language.

The six of us walk down a road that parallels the street where *Nonno*'s old house still stands. This road follows the river that separates the old town from the new. Italian style, the women stroll together, while Dad, Stu and the gentleman from Norwich saunter behind us, chatting. Following a Sicilian custom, we stop by the couple's family home to show respect to her mother.

When we return to Pasqualino and Maria's, the dining room table is set, as if celebrating *la festa*, the feast day. The fine china sparkles in the outside light that shines through the open balcony doors on the front of the house. White lace curtains blow gently in a mild breeze.

Daylight, almost della Francesca-like in its luminescence, makes the whole place seem festive for an ordinary Sunday in October. Maria expresses her pleasure in making a fine meal for us, while apologizing for what she insists was a meager lunch the day before.

"I'm not sure I'd ever be so gracious if someone just showed up on my doorstep unannounced," I say to Stu.

I've become so Americanized that most people call me before they drop by. In Syracuse, company appears at my parents' door all of the time. It's a way of life—people coming and going, coffee on, Mom's cookies always available for just in case.

If it happens to be mealtime—just like Maria and most Italian women I've known—my mother is prepared with a little extra. If not, she too, will whip something out of the freezer, refrigerator or cupboard. Maria is duplicating the same generosity I grew up with.

Nothing is without costs. I've learned that, along with being close and open, comes an enmeshment that can be stifling at times. As an American, I'm more independent than my ancestors would have ever accepted. Right now, in Gualtieri, I take pleasure in the bounty of my heritage. I can tell my husband does, too.

"Get this recipe," Stu mumbles under his breath, as he dives into the pasta Maria made mixed with ricotta, tomatoes and eggplant.

Mom and I tell Maria how much Stu enjoys her pasta. He smiles at her and nods his head up and down, crooning a sound of delight, while chewing his food. When Mom and I ask Maria for the recipe, I'm not surprised that there's no formally written instruction. A description of a little of this and a pinch of that follows.

Creative cooking has always made Stu a little crazy. At home, he pokes his head in the kitchen and says, "Any chance you'll follow a recipe tonight?"

I rarely do. It's more fun to be spontaneous and adventuresome in mixing together food with different spices, herbs and sauces. The challenge comes when I can't repeat the same dish twice.

It usually tastes close enough to the last time I prepared the chicken, meat, pasta, fish or vegetable dish. Besides, Stu's idea of cooking a meal comes from his bachelor days of peanut butter and jelly on a muffin, opening a can of Campbell's Tomato Soup, or his infamous green-olive sandwiches on toast, with a touch of mayo.

It's no wonder he loves every bite of Maria's pasta, which is as appealing as her personality. For the *secondo piatto*, or second course, she serves *bistecca*—steak, a rarity in Italy. Italians don't have grazing land for cows and steers like we do in America. So having beef two days in a row is an indication of a special occasion.

Insalata and *potate arrosto*, salad and roasted potatoes, are served along with olives, bread, homemade pickles and other various *antipasti*. There's coffee and the *dolci* that we brought from the *pasticceria* before Mass. Afterwards, we get up, stretch, and then we sit in the living room and, in Italian style, rest for part of the afternoon.

Somewhere around four, Dad announces it's time to head for the cemetery. Even the mention of the word cemetery wakes Stu up from a drowsy stupor. Death, dying, and especially cemeteries, are not my husband's forte.

****

The time the two of us traveled to northern Italy in 1988, I lured Stu over to the Island of the Dead, in Venice. We took a *vaporetto*, a Venetian boat—Venice's version of a public bus. At first, Stu didn't want to get off the boat, but when I did, he had no choice but to follow, since he was relying on me for the language and directions in and around the city. It was the first time ever in our marriage that Stu was dependent on me for getting us through our travels—a challenge for us both.

Stu literally stood on the edge of the island, refusing to walk into the interior. I went on, knowing that either I'd find him where I left him or he'd soon follow. He followed.

I suppose one might consider that cruel. However, we've led each other into realms that the other has been more reluctant to pursue. Besides, it was a major shift in our relationship.

Until then, I was raised to believe that Stu, being born male, knew more than me. Then mid-life struck and Stu, like other men, was forced to adjust to my coming of age. My father loves to joke with Stu saying, "I don't know what you've done to her. I had her *trained* when she left my house!"

For years, I've found my husband's fast-paced world of racing—including his own go-kart manufacturing company, his interest in NASCAR, Formula One, dirt bikes and every other type of racing imaginable—just as alien as he's found my mystical interests, including death, dying and the afterlife. On a number of occasions, Stu would walk out of a room if anyone began a conversation on death.

****

Now that Stu is bracing himself to visit my ancestor's gravesites, I sense the same anxiety he had when we were in Venice. His eyes widen and his face turns ashen. Stu could stay with Pasqualino, who is staying back like he did yesterday afternoon, but Stu isn't about to leave my side in a foreign country and be with someone where communication is not possible.

So my husband musters up the courage and agrees to drive the five of us, including Maria, in our rented BMW, as Maria's small Fiat will only hold four people comfortably. Stu and Dad take their seats in the front, and we three women sit in the back.

Maria poises herself in the middle and on the edge of the seat so that she can direct Stu along the way. As we head up the mountain toward the cemetery, there are diversions along the way. First, we come face-to-face with a small municipal, light gray, concrete building.

"That's the school I went to," Dad says, and then he asks Maria if the building is still used for a school.

"*Certo*," she replies with expressive animation, as if wondering why anyone would even ask such a question. Things don't change that rapidly in Italy.

"That window over there—" Dad points out, "that window was where my teacher threw out my themes."

I chuckle at his use of the word, "themes." Dad continues about how his teacher would read students' papers, and if he didn't like one of them, he'd just open the window and toss it. Dad snickers. I find it humorous, too, but I'm sure for a different reason.

After having lived through my father's stringent demands for good grades in school, it was an eye-opener to hear how Dad had not always been the poster child for education.

"Which window?" I ask Dad, zooming in with the camcorder. It was the window to the left of the center door.

Dad's quickly distracted. He shifts his attention, pointing out a house to Stu, a house that belonged to yet another relative. Separate conversations go on at once. Dad and Stu, Dad and I—although he's not aware I'm talking to him.

Maria is calling out, in *dialetto*, but Stu has no clue she's giving directions. In between, Mom tries to translate for my husband.

While we sit at the stop sign, facing the school, a few cars come up from behind. They barely stop and beep as a warning before zooming and spinning their wheels, turning left or right in front of us. Stu and I learned on our previous trips that, since there are fewer rules of the road in Italy, Italian drivers are assertive.

Once the street is clear, I jump out with the camcorder to get a better visual angle of the school. I know my siblings will get a kick not only out of the building, but also hearing about Dad's "themes" being thrown out a window.

****

Growing up, education was a priority in our family. Bringing home bad grades was not acceptable. If grades did not meet my father's expectations, the anxiety around the house on report card day was tense.

Mom was equally attentive to education, but she was less a disciplinarian and much more concerned about how Dad would react when he got home from the barbershop. If our grades were low, there would be punishments—no television, no talking on the phone, and no extracurricular activities.

Worse than his final pronouncements, we experienced his inflamed fury and stern lectures about what we had *not* accomplished—making us feel ashamed of ourselves.

From his sons, Dad expected an advanced education, whether it was college, a business school or a trade. But from his daughters, Dad demanded an advanced education.

"I want you girls to always have something to fall back on."

He never wanted us to become so dependent on a man that we couldn't take care of ourselves. A number of my childhood girlfriends from the 1950s and 60s went on to college, but weren't expected to be the breadwinners of their families.

I guess my father instilled a notion more prevalent in a new millennium, where many women raise children alone. Some of us struggled in school more than others, though some did quite well. But we all graduated with four-year-college degrees, and half of us have our Masters.

As it turns out, a number of my sisters have, at one time or another, been the major financial providers for their families. So I have to acknowledge that my father was a visionary of sorts.

I also have to acknowledge that once again, whether Dad realizes it or not, he instilled some of my feminist attitudes that we butt heads about each time I raise a red flag against a rampant patriarchal world.

****

As odd as it may seem, journeying up the mountain to a cemetery becomes a cheerful experience with Maria as guide. She demonstrates to Stu with her hand that we need to go up and around the winding road. Each time we come to a turn, Maria taps Stu on his right shoulder and yells in his ear with an enormous nasal twang, "*Suona, Suona.*" It's her signal for Stu to beep the horn in case another car's coming down from the mountain.

At first, Maria taps Stu's shoulder and bellows at the same time, "*Suona, Suona.*" Then, she skips the tapping and tells us, in *dialetto*, that she believes Stu is beginning to understand the language. We all laugh, including Stu, when we translate what Maria says about him.

"Of course I know what she means," Stu says, "As I take these blind curves, she keeps repeating the same words over and over again. How can I *not* know what she's saying?"

It must be how Stu's been feeling over the last few days—going into one blind curve after another, never sure where we'll be next. Maria continues repeating "*Suona, Suona,*" loudly, at least two dozen times, as we travel further up the mountain.

Circling around and around, we can see Gualtieri Sicaminò below and other small towns dotting the landscape. Dad points beyond the countryside and into the distance.

"*Il mare,*" he says, the sea.

On this clear sunny day, we see bright turquoise water, and land, spotted with rich, fertile growth, and the mountain, still continuing above our heads.

Dad and Maria talk about the Royal Palace, situated at the top of the mountain. Or at least that's what Dad calls the place where a guy whom they call *il Duca* lived. The Duke was a wealthy recluse. I had heard about him when I was last here.

Maria says that the Duke's land has been split into individual villas. When I ask what happened to the Duke, Dad answers, in a very matter-of-fact manner.

"He died." And then Dad points to an open space, overlooking the panorama view. "Pull over," he tells Stu.

We follow my father and Maria across the street toward a tall stone wall and enter through an open door. To our surprise, it's the entrance to the cemetery.

Over toward the left, an entire brick wall houses old stone mausoleums. There are a few empty holes, but most are full. Family names that were carved into rock have been worn over time. Old black and white photos of the deceased are attached and protected behind plastic coverings.

"Up there," Dad says, as he points to the top row, about fifteen feet above our heads. "*That's* where my grandfather and grandmother are buried."

We keep looking, trying to figure out exactly which stone belongs to Dad's grandparents. I even use the zoom lens on the camcorder to see the names of those on the top row. One said Merlino, Antonio.

"That's my grandfather," Dad says, "my mother's father."

"What was your grandmother's maiden name?" I ask.

"Impallamina," he says, spelling it out.

I knew Dad's grandmother's name was Caterina. My grandmother gave birth to two daughters after Dad was born. The first Caterina died as a baby. *Nonna* then named the next child Caterina, and again, after her mother.

Unfortunately, the second Caterina died as a toddler. No one ever knew why, except that there were childhood illnesses and no antibiotics to thwart off serious diseases. When my grandmother gave birth to one more girl, my youngest aunt, *Nonna* gave up on her mother's name and called her Sarah instead.

Directly to the left of the tomb with the name Merlino is a Caterina. It's the only Caterina up there. It reads, "*Isgro, Caterina*," since the women in that town still use their maiden names.

"Are we related to Angelo and Giovannina Isgro?" I ask Dad.

He's sure that we aren't, but I can't find the name, Impallamina. We never resolve the mystery of my great-grandmother's maiden name or her actual burial site, before Maria nudges Dad to keep moving.

We follow her further into the cemetery, away from the mausoleum-like structures and to actual gravesites. Just like in Venice, burial sites are positioned so close to each other that one can hardly get along the path.

There are narrow rows, only wide enough to walk in front of the graves. Knowing how Stu feels about cemeteries, I don't dare look at him and focus instead on tall stones with angels and saints, towering over the sarcophagi-like structures. Maria takes Dad directly to Pasqualino's parents' gravesites.

"*Zia* Phillipa," Dad says.

A woman who looks a lot like my grandmother, *Nonna* Nicolina, is in a round picture frame, next to a man that resembles Pasqualino when he must have been younger.

"What number was *Zia* Phillipa in *Nonna*'s family?" I ask my father.

"Second," he says, "I think she was second."

"Who was first?"

He stands there, his hand to lips, twisting them like he does when he's thinking.

"I think *Zia* Rosa came first."

"Then *Zia* Phillipa…" I nod. "And then who?"

He continues on with *Zia* Maruzza, whose name I recognize. I don't remember who her children are. Later, I learn that, like me, she had no children. Then my grandmother, *Nonna* Nicolina, comes next. Dad thinks that *Nonna*'s brother, Carmello, is the youngest, although he keeps flipping between *Nonna* and her brother. How interesting that my grandmother comes from a family where there were more girls than boys!

In Dad's immediate family, there were two girls, Aunt Mary and Aunt Sarah. Dad fell in the middle. In *my* family, there are six sisters and two brothers. Sisters are big. Even though we don't live near each other anymore, we stay in touch often and do as much as we can for each other. Maybe it was passed down.

I wish I'd understood my grandmother, *Nonna* Nicolina, well enough growing up to have talked to her about her sisters. It wasn't until I came to Italy with Aunt Mary and Uncle Peter that I discovered how important *Nonna*'s sisters were in her life. How hard it must have been for her to leave them in midlife and come to a foreign country, where she could hardly speak the language.

As I've gotten older, it's been harder and harder for me to be geographically separated from my five sisters and two brothers. We work hard at getting together—flying or driving to visit each other on special occasions, summer vacations, or just to be with each other. My grandmother was more than an ocean away, but after she moved to the United States, she only returned to Gualtieri and saw her siblings two more times.

While Dad and I review genealogy from his mother's side, Stu and Mom help Maria adjust a light, attached somehow to a small lantern— as a permanent votive for Pasqualino's parents. Then we meander slowly through the graveyard, heading back toward the entrance. I recognize last names of relatives and *paesani*.

Dad starts telling us about the time his uncle, *Zio* Santo, was left in the cemetery overnight as a boy (*Zio* Santo—*Nonno*'s youngest half-brother, a Morina, and not a Merlino).

Although neither Mom nor I relish the thought of a young boy locked in the cemetery overnight, it's Stu who gasps at the thought. To allay Stu's fears, Dad tries to minimize the event.

"*Zio* Santo didn't want to sleep with the dead, so he broke into the chapel and slept there."

Dad points to a small building at the front of the cemetery.

"How did he get out?" I ask.

"He got out the next morning, when they unlocked the cemetery door," Dad answers, as if it was no big thing to sleep in a graveyard overnight.

Stu's eyes widen. He looks stunned at Dad's nonchalant response. All along, I'm thinking of how unusual it is that a town's burial ground would be totally enclosed behind tall walls. Then again, Venice has an island, all of its own, just for its deceased.

Dad doesn't linger much longer looking for other dead relatives, although he mentions that there are plenty he hasn't tracked down. We follow my father back toward the door at the front gate. There are cups and a spout, with mountain water, standing at the right as we exit. Dad pours himself a drink and speaks of a legend.

"Whoever drinks the water from here will live ten years longer than normal."

Stu, who anxiously reaches the door and slips out before the rest of us, calls back to Dad.

"If that's true, why is it in a cemetery?"

Dad smiles in amusement, and then he looks around, almost content, as he lifts a cup of water to his mouth.

"Didn't do *them* any good!" he says and breathes a sigh after tasting the fresh mountain water of his childhood.

He doesn't say much more about those who've died, although later I realize that he never looked for the gravesites of his grandmother and grandfather Morina, from his father's side.

14) Sunday Evening

Domenica p.m. October 22

After returning from the cemetery, I discover that I lost my sunglasses. Maria says she saw them on my lap before I jumped out of the car at Dad's old school. Preoccupied with videotaping, trying to find names on mausoleums, stacked above my head, and listening to what my father had to say about buried ancestors, distracted me from the sun in my eyes.

From what I can determine, the last place I saw them was near the school where the *maestro* threw Dad's essay out the window. Since most areas in the old section of Gualtieri are in walking distance, Stu and I decide to stroll up to the school to see if we can find my glasses.

Even though the glasses are nowhere on the road or anywhere else nearby, this walk gives us a few minutes alone with each other. The glasses aren't prescription or a name brand, so I've lost nothing of material value.

But those spectacles were worn-in perfectly, stretched enough to fit my extra-large head of dark-thick hair, which I inherited from Dad's side of the family. I decide it's an omen, similar to the three coins I threw in the Fountain of Trevi, back in Rome. If I leave something behind in Gualtieri, it will assure my return again someday.

****

Earlier, Maria called Caterina's daughter, Carmella. We made plans to meet with her and her family around six-thirty in the evening. The first time I met or heard about Carmella was in 1985, with Aunt Mary and Uncle Peter. That summer I spent a considerable amount of time with her.

Since Carmella's mother, Caterina, is Dad's first cousin, Carmella is my father's first cousin, once removed, and in turn my second cousin. Eight years younger than me, Carmella is now in her early forties and closer in age to my sisters, Fran and Teresa.

In 1985, Carmella was in her late twenties, still single and zooming around town. She picked me up in a beat-up blue Fiat. Given that Aunt Mary and Uncle Peter were attentive about me being escorted everywhere, they were grateful that Carmella would take me around.

But the language barrier was a challenge. My Italian was not much better back then, and Carmella didn't understand a word of English.

We greeted each other and had very brief conversations. Frustration set in when we tried to talk about any philosophical, political or ethical issues. From our expressions and gestures, it was clear we both had intense positions about these subjects.

I loved when Aunt Mary was around to translate. That's when we'd lunge into discussions about the existence of God, *il Comunista* government in Sicily and the differences between my American way and her Sicilian lifestyle.

During that summer, Carmella arrived most evenings for the country's pasttime of *la passeggiata*—promenading through the streets. In one of my exchanges with Aunt Mary, she hinted that some of the town's people were disturbed by the way Carmella traveled by herself to different villages and towns. That attitude felt archaic. Besides, whenever I was with Carmella, her behavior was ever so respectful of her culture's mores.

There was a night when Carmella and I drove to the nearby Sicilian town of Barcellona to meet a group of her friends who she went to school with at the University in Messina. Another time, we attended a summer rock concert in a distant village. There was also a late Sunday afternoon, when we headed further up the mountain to get together with an old school chum of Carmela's in an even smaller village, which overlooked Gualtieri Sicaminò. The town, called Sicaminò, was where The Duke lived. He was still alive in 1985.

As we stood near the *piazza*, waiting for Carmella's friend, she pointed up and mentioned *il Duca's* so-called palace, perched on a higher peak. Three men, hanging around the *piazza*, tried to make eye contact, but Carmella grabbed my arm and placed it inside hers—the way Italian women do, walking arm and arm.

My cousin held her head high and firm, avoiding the stares, walking straight away from the center. She was resolute, as she motioned to me with her eyes, indicating that I, too, must look away from their direction.

Having spent that time with Carmella, I attributed the hearsay comments my aunt mentioned simply as smalltown gossip. I was grateful for this newfound female cousin, who gave me insight into the contemporary side of Sicilian life from a woman's perspective.

Carmella represented the best of the old and new Sicily—her respect for the past, with a blend of the present, helped me see how life might have been for me had my family never emigrated.

****

Since I last saw Carmella, fifteen years ago, she's married and has a son who is now almost thirteen years old. She no longer lives in Gualtieri, but in the town of Sorcorso, further up the mountain. Heading up the road and into her small village feels like we're climbing the northern Italian town of Assisi. The road leading into Sorcorso is steep and winding and takes us into the main *piazza,* where we park the car and wait for Carmella, as planned.

There are now two things I know about Sorcorso. One is the legend that Dad told us about earlier in the day—how the black marble sculpture of *San Filippo Neri* was brought up the mountain to this small village—and it returned overnight, in some unknown way. The second thing about Sorcorso is that Dad performed in a band here as a young boy.

"I played my *sexophone,*" Dad says, pronouncing the instrument with his accent, as he walks away from the ridge that overlooks towns below.

"*Sexophone?*" I say, facetiously.

"Saxophone," my mother interjects. "He means *saxophone.* Remember how your father used to play the saxophone?"

****

I never realized that my father had an accent until I was in fifth grade and saw him on television during the local news. Dad had called the TV station that morning, and he told them to send a camera and a reporter, so that they could take footage of how the city plows had failed to clear away mounds of snow, pushed in front of his barbershop.

The snow was not only blocking customers from parking, but heaps had been shoved so far over that it obstructed the sidewalk leading into the building. Dad, never afraid to speak his mind, appeared in living color—actually black and white in those days.

My father made a point of saying on the air that all the snow stacked in front of his place was disrupting his livelihood. That night at the dinner table, Dad said there was a lesson for us to learn about seizing an opportunity. Dad, the consummate businessman, saw this as free advertising for the barbershop.

The following morning in school, one of my classmates, who had his hair cut at the shop, teased me about my father being on television with his thick accent.

"Accent? My father doesn't have an accent," I said, emphatically.

Others standing around insisted that my father definitely had an accent, and they were sure I was pulling their leg by pretending I didn't notice. The truth was I had never noticed.

My father *always* spoke that way, and it seemed perfectly normal to me. After that incident, I became aware that, not only did my father have an accent, but sometimes he used it effectively to get attention or make a point.

****

Dad never flinches when I call him on his "sexophone" comment in Sorcorso. Instead, he ignores me and strolls gracefully away from the ridge, surrounding the town, and heads toward the village's small *piazza*.

Carmella, her husband Nicola, and their teenage son, Carmello, show up within minutes of our arrival. Carmella and I walk swiftly toward each other. With confidence, she pauses a moment, looks at me endearingly, kisses me on both cheeks, and then rushes over and respectfully greets my father, before acknowledging Mom and Stu with smiles, handshakes and kisses.

She introduces her own family in the same loving way. Once formalities are completed, Carmella reaches over and slips her arm into mine, just as we did back in 1985, when strolling *la passeggiata* every night through Gualtieri and other local Sicilian towns.

As if Carmella is the matriarch, everyone else follows behind. We climb a steep incline, heading toward her home. She looks at me kindly and asks how I've been.

"*Bene*," I say, good, and in my broken *dialetto*, I ask her the same.

She smiles, as I'm sure she remembers my language deficiency. Being in her country, I believe it's my responsibility to speak the language.

Carmella is impeccably graceful, warm and caring. She wears a proper dark suit that hits at her knees, a jacket and heels to match. Her hair's cropped close to her head, in a professional business manner. Her style has changed from the jeans and long flowing hair that she wore the last time I saw her.

I want to ask, so much more than my vocabulary will permit, about her life over the last fifteen years. She appears happily married, proud of her husband, son and her present state in life. There's definitely a blood connection with Carmella, but our weak communication clearly interferes with getting down to the core of our lives.

Fortunately, Dad and Mom, like Aunt Mary before them, are there for translation this time around. But that kind of talk is not the intense conversation I'd love to have with Carmella.

She tells us that her husband, Nicola, is a contractor who takes on various entrepreneurial projects—a similarity to my own husband. Nicola had been the general contractor for their contemporary Italian-style home.

Just the year before, Stu did the same for our home back in North Carolina. One of the differences is that Carmella and Nicola follow the Sicilian custom of living above a parent's home. Nicola's father lives in the house below them. His mother passed away years earlier.

The exterior of Carmella and Nicola's house is porcelain-white-colored stucco. On the right, in a spacious entryway, stands a wide, slightly-circular marble staircase. Carmela's childhood home in Gualtieri with her parents, Caterina and Micio, is considerably smaller—three levels with only a small room on each. Carmella's lifestyle has changed significantly.

On the first floor of this home, there is a huge living room, a long hallway, leading to a large master bed and bath, and an extra bedroom, where she says her parents periodically stay. Lush, rich couches and chairs match the white walls. Candelabras, big enough to absorb the extra-size rooms, hang in the living room and master bedroom.

Carmella leads us up the circular stairway to the second floor, where she continues to show us more bedrooms, another bathroom, kitchen and family area. We step onto a grand balcony overlooking the expansive vista of towns and mountains below.

Back inside, there are aperitifs and wonderful Italian cookies—*amaretti*—almond paste, the rainbow Neapolitans and anise cookies. Candied-covered almonds, which I grew up craving, were wrapped individually in different-colored tissue paper. The blue and yellow boxes of *Torrone,* an Italian nougat candy, are positioned next to my favorite chocolate, *Boci*—each with a hazelnut inside. I sit next to my cousin, chewing and savoring the blends of flavors.

Carmella's features have changed. In '85, she was ultra *magro,* or thin. A few pounds make her look more mature. Through Dad and Mom, Carmella and I briefly catch up. She insists that I haven't changed a bit, and then she holds her baby finger up the way Italians do when they say that someone looks skinny. I suppose my weight is still the same—although I wouldn't call myself skinny.

Carmella asks Dad and Mom about themselves and about family back home. I take a round of photos and I even video-tape Dad and Carmella singing *Santa Nicola,* an old song that came from their village. Arms around each other, they sing with that nasal twang, while Carmella motions with her finger, like a conductor keeping the beat going.

At the end, she waves and greets my aunts and uncles back in the states. *Saluti!* she calls out to Aunt Mary and Uncle Peter—*Saluti Maria et Pietro.* Then she does the same for Aunt Sarah and Uncle Victor. *Saluti Sarina et Victorio. Saluti a tutti!* she says, greeting everyone—those she knows and those who she has never met.

****

When I first met Carmella, I was captivated by what she knew about my family and surprised at the deep love and appreciation she had for those who'd left and gone to the United States. That's when I heard the stories about my Morina grandparents, *Nonna* Nicolina and *Nonno* Antonio, and the amount of help they actually gave to those in Gualtieri. Evidently, Carmella's grandmother, *Nonna* Nicolina's sister, Rosa, never let her family forget how my grandparents, especially my grandmother, were there for her after her husband died.

Zia Rosa had to raise her three children alone—Maria, Caterina and Nicola. One of those children was Carmella's mother, Caterina—

Dad's cousin, whom we'd visited. *Nonna* always made sure they had food and more—even when it was difficult for my grandmother to make ends meet during World War II. The stories were kept alive, from our grandparents' generation to our parents' generation, and down to Carmella.

From my side of the Atlantic, I saw my grandparents collecting clothes and money to send to Gualtieri after the war. But I had no way of knowing how it was received, or how much had been done earlier during the war—when my grandmother and two aunts were still living in Gualtieri, fending for themselves on limited resources.

If I hadn't met Carmella that summer I lived in Gualtieri, I would never have known what my soft-spoken grandmother's generosity did for a family. She knew stories about my own grandparents that I didn't even know. Carmella is the vessel that holds the history of the Merlino side of the family. Pieces of the family puzzle are still filling in.

****

I'm not sure where we're going—now that we've left Carmella and Nicola's house, but I think that Mom and Dad know. We've taken two cars—our rental, and one of their vehicles—women in one, guys in the other. We follow signs to Giammoro. My mother finally explains to me that Carmella wants to show us their business before heading to a *ristorante*, where they have made reservations.

After pulling up in front of a clinic and going inside, I figure out that Carmella's husband has also been the general contractor for this facility. She's eager to show what her husband has accomplished. He's equally enthusiastic when he takes us into her office and tells about her position as administrator.

They own the building and provide dialysis for kidney patients, most of whom are subsidized by the Italian government. The large facility is easily five thousand square-feet or more, with specialized rooms and up-to-date equipment. Outside and behind the building, a large area houses compressors and generators.

Carmella pulls me aside when no one else is looking and asks if I remember the boyfriend she had when I was there. Although I never met him, I knew his name was Nicola. She wants to assure me that, although she married someone with the same name, it's not the same person. This Nicola, her husband, is kinder, gentler, industrious and much more successful.

Nicola is sophisticated, bright and humble. He smiles often, listens attentively and speaks in a calm manner. He's obviously done well in business. By the polite and respectful way he communicates, he's also successful in personal relations. Nicola is attentive to my cousin, their son, and to us relatives—strangers really—who show up on his doorstep. He's hospitable and more than welcoming.

It's gratifying to see that one of my own female relatives from the old country has broken through antiquated barriers—especially after having learned about the struggles that Carmella's family endured through the years, back through her grandmother's generation. Granted, Carmella married well, but she has also risen up in business into a position of an administrator.

Carmella and Nicola's marriage and business arrangement appear to be a partnership, and not just a woman tied to her husband's success. It's also satisfying to see that progress in Sicily has advanced, and that the past has made way for new opportunities—not only for those close to my age, but also for family that never left.

On our way to the *ristorante*, my mother sits in front with Carmella. They chat affectionately. It's heartwarming to watch my mother's gentle spirit in action. She's always taking a back seat to everyone else. Her own *dialetto*, although different from the Gualtierians, is close enough for Mom and Carmella to understand each other.

Plus, Mom is familiar with this dialect, having communicated with her own in-laws for years. I wonder if Maria's earlier comment about my mother speaking the language better than my father has given Mom a confidence to speak out.

Carmella chats with Mom, showing respect and thoughtfulness. Sometimes Carmella calls out my name and says something she wants me to know. If I don't totally understand, Mom translates.

At one point, Carmella says the Italian word, *lupo*. She'd used the word *lupo* fifteen years ago, when we drove through these same mountains, again, at nighttime. My small pocket dictionary didn't have the word in it then, and I had no clue what she was saying.

"What is that?" I ask Mom.

"There are wolves in this area," Mom replies.

I laugh, and so does Carmella, when she explains to my mother how she tried to tell me the same thing once before. We keep chattering, and through my mother, I realize how my cousin and I keep remembering the same situations from years earlier. When the two of them talk, I enjoy watching their facial expressions and listening to the musical tones of the Italian language.

It's always been a tradition for the women in my family to sit around the table, talking about women stuff—the house, kids, husbands, menstrual periods, pregnancies or whatever else might be going on in someone's life.

The older women encourage young girls to hang around, ask questions and talk about their own lives—school, boyfriends, hairdos and clothes. My mother, sisters, aunts and I still do that with my nieces and cousins.

It's something I've only had a chance to do a little with this cousin, first through Aunt Mary. Now, with my mother, we're doing women's talk again—just us girls in the car together, talking freely and listening to each other. My head wraps around every word I can possibly understand—wolves, hair and the winding road, taking us further and further to the top of yet another mountain.

Stu is laughing when he pulls himself out of the back seat of the car.

"Whew," he breathes a sign of relief. "That Nicola is some driver. I hung on tight when he took those curves."

Nicola drove our rental. My husband has been involved in racing for the thirty years that I've known him, and he's always been a risk-taker on the road. Nicola must have been doing some wild driving, since speed rarely affects Stu.

We were so involved in our own world inside Carmella's car that we never paid attention to what the guys were doing. Plus, Stu and I have never gotten used to the crazy drivers in Italy.

Nicola quickly parks the rental, jumps out, takes the wheel from Carmella and parks *her* car. The lot is partly an open field, partly an area of trees—where people just stick their cars wherever they can find a spot.

When we walk through the doors of the *ristorante* close to nine o'clock, it's obvious that we're expected. The host seats us at a table by the window. When most Americans would be cleaning up from

Sunday dinner and preparing for the workweek ahead, these Sicilians, like most Italians, are just beginning their evening meal.

Carmella and Nicola had phoned in an order ahead, and in a short time, an assortment of *antipasti* begins to arrive at the table. There are platters of stuffed mushrooms, breaded and fried eggplant, *bruschetta*— pieces of round Italian bread with tomato and pepper, some with tomato and mozzarella. There is a serving of various cheeses and another plate of mixed olives—cured black, Greek kalamata and Sicilian green. There is also *calamari*—fried squid, loaves of Italian bread, *melone e prosciutto*—melon and cured ham.

Such a huge selection of appetizers feels like another full meal, including artichoke hearts, potatoes and roasted, grilled and fried peppers. Bottles of beer, wine, water and soda keep flowing as we keep eating.

Our eyes roll with astonishment at the feast that continues to come our way. As one platter is half finished, another is brought over by a waiter, holding each serving dish high in the air, then swooping it over into the middle of the table.

At one point, I stand up to take a picture of the banquet. Swarms of other people at tables are eating the same amount. At the end, Carmella and Nicola stand up to leave and tell us the bill is already covered. They insist we were their guests.

I hadn't expected such generosity, although my father whispers to me that he knew it would be that way. Earlier, when we were passing out small gifts at their home, Dad gave them each a new American silver dollar that he brought as a memento from the United States. They accepted the coins in the spirit my father offered them.

Carmello, her son, seemed excited to receive a coin from another country. Reflecting on family stories about the hard times the family endured after the war, it was obvious that Carmella's family no longer needed help. Although it's not Carmella who received the assistance back then, there is a part of me that wonders, whether consciously or unconsciously, if we had just received a huge thank you from Carmella and her ancestors through her.

In the parking lot, we say our goodbyes—everyone kissing each other with the customary peck on both cheeks before climbing into our separate cars. We follow them down the hill until they point to the sign that reads, "Giammoro, Milazzo." After rolling down our windows and waving, Carmella throws kisses after kisses. I follow suit.

The dark road that Carmella pointed out to us will lead to Giammoro, where we'll pick up signs to Milazzo and our hotel. I wonder if I'll ever see Carmella again. A part of me imagines us older, meeting later in life after our parents, aunts and uncles are all gone. How will we ever communicate then?

With Stu, Dad and Mom at the Papal Audience

Mom and Dad on train to Sicily

Gualtieri Sicaminò
Dad overlooking his Sicilian hometown

Nonna and Nonno Stagnitta, Nonno and Nonna Morina

Nonna Egidia

Breakfast in Taormina
Mom and Dad in front, Stu and me in the back

With Mom and Dad at ancient ruins in Taormina

With Stu in front of Mount Etna

15) Tindari

Monday Morning, October 23

On our final day in Dad's Province of Messina, my father wants to make a pilgrimage to the Black Madonna before seeing his cousins one more time. Built high on top of the striking Cape Tindari, the cathedral combines both a Neo-Romanesque and Gothic structure with an evocative view of the sea. Tindari is a place where Dad and his family journeyed to visit when he was a child.

We check out of our hotel after an early continental breakfast and head west on the *autostrada*. We pass the town of Barcellona, where I went one evening with Carmella in 1985. We travel past Oliveri, another town where Dad says he went to play the saxophone with his boyhood band.

On our right, the turquoise blue waters of the Tyrennhian Sea peak in and out as we travel. To the left are wide, fertile areas of farmland, small villages and farmhouses, sporadically break into the landscape. Dad reminisces about how the construction of the *autostrada*, from Messina south to the city of *Siracusa*, has drastically changed the island.

"They've really done well in Sicily. I'm proud of my country," Dad muses, while recalling events of the last few days.

During the forty minutes it takes to reach Tindari, I ask my father how he and his family could have possibly traveled this far from Gualtieri without a car.

"We dressed up a horse and buggy and brought them up here," he says. "We got on top of the *carretto,* the cart—about ten of us, and traveled the dirt road."

"How often did you come?" I ask.

"Once a year. When they had their feast."

"You traveled all this way, attended a feast and headed back home all in one day?"

"No," Dad says. "We slept on the ground with blankets and camped out."

There were no paved roads then, and Dad talks about the fun they had while plodding along. His memories seem only joyful. I envision my father and his family, gathering around a camp fire in the countryside, cooking, eating and telling stories of the relatives who went before him.

When we finally arrive at the bottom of the mountain and look up toward the large cathedral looming overhead, I ask Dad how they ever climbed it by foot.

"We were tough when we were kids," he responds, with little expression on his face.

Stu begins the ascent by car, gripping each curve, beeping when approaching blind spots.

"*Suona, Suona*," Mom and I call out amusingly, from the back seat.

As we turn each bend, the ochre-colored basilica on the hill appears, disappears, and then reappears, again.

****

When I traveled here with Carmella fifteen years ago, she took those curves, sharp and biting, with her little blue Fiat. It was a Sunday afternoon in August. The place was packed with Italian tourists. Carmella was anxious to show me the Madonna, having known the great devotion my grandmother had toward Christ's mother.

My cousin told me then how *Nonna* Nicolina sent regular contributions to the new building standing on the site where our ancestors made numerous pilgrimages. There were so many things I never even knew to ask my grandmother until after having met Carmella. By then it was too late.

****

Tindari's parking lot was packed and overflowing in the summer of 1985. But now in October, the lot is scantily filled, peppered with a small number of cars. There are a few tourists' buses, carrying mostly senior citizens. The sunshine and the colorful vendor stands smack of a festive atmosphere, despite the limited number of visitors mulling around.

The area, open and spacious, is much more comfortable without the masses of sightseers rubbing up against everybody else. The slow pace that people now move gives room to meander by the booths and look, as we trek the incline that leads to the basilica.

On the way, there are trinkets, sculptures of the Black Madonna in various sizes, and other religious items—rosary beads, scapulars and a slew of saints' metals. There are a lot of *ceramica*, as Sicily is known for its ceramics industry. Scattered about are replicas of small, decorated and colorfully-painted wooden carts and horses, which hold small figurines of Sicilians, dressed in vibrant native costumes. They remind me of my childhood.

When any relative, or *paesani*, returned from Sicily, they would bring back souvenirs, including one replica of a Sicilian cart for each family. As I grew older and into adolescence, my sisters, brothers, cousins and I would roll our eyes, chuckling among ourselves about the tacky *carretto siciliano*—the Sicilian cart, decorating the mantels in everybody's home. Now here I am, wondering how I can carry back these replicas of carts with horses as gifts for each sibling—seven boxes in my suitcase.

"You can't," Stu says. "There's no room for these and all of the other gifts you intend to buy. You better start thinking flat. Those balsa-wood carts will never make it back in one piece."

Stu's much more practical, and as much as I would like to bring back those nostalgic mementos, my husband's suggestion makes sense. He follows me up the road as I take pictures of the various vendors, laughing while moving the camcorder to the beat of an old Sicilian tune bellowing from one of the booths.

I start singing along with the song about the moon in the middle of the ocean.

C'e la luna in mezzo al mare, mamma mia... la, la, la, la, la...

I can't remember all the words and revert to singing babble at the end of each stanza. Ahead of me, Mom and Dad slowly continue their climb.

Once in front of the basilica, the four of us walk over to the ridge, looking out at the vast sea sparkling with the warm light of mid-morning. A few miles below us lay the narrow piece of land that begins the legend of the Black Madonna. At the end of a long, narrow jetty sticking out into the water is a round, sandy island, no wider than a football field.

"Is that the island?" I ask my father.

"Yeah," he says, "Where they found the baby."

Then he points to a ragged trail that leads from where we stand, at the edge of the *piazza* in front of the cathedral, down to the water below.

"The mother walked down that path to get the child," Dad says, and then he looks around and comments about the landscaping and pruning.

"They must have redone this entire area."

I want the details of the story without my father getting sidetracked.

"Tell me the legend again, Dad."

My father repeats the story he has told numerous times when I was growing up—about the woman with a very sick infant. In her prayers, she promised Our Blessed Mother that if her baby got well, she would travel to Tindari and pay homage to the Madonna. When the baby was healed, that was exactly what the mother did.

"When she got here," Dad responds, and as if he can read my mind, "and I don't know from where or how far away, but she saw the statue and the statue was black. The lady looked at the Madonna and said, 'I came all this way to find somebody darker than me?' In that second, the baby disappeared from the mother's arms. She and everyone with her panicked."

Dad points from high on the ridge to the narrow peninsula of sand extending out from the land and into the sea.

"That was when the mother looked down. She saw the baby playing in the middle of the sand at the end of the jetty. This was the LEGEND!" Dad says, raising his voice an octave to make his point.

"I understand," I say, knowing that the Blessed Mother had been trying to teach the child's mother a lesson.

"Then the mother went and got the baby and walked back over those ridges and returned to this spot," my father says.

I am aware that this is the very spot, where a church was built in honor of the Black Madonna. We are all quiet, standing, staring out at the water. Dad, the first to break the stillness, turns and walks away.

"Okay, let's go in," he says, and heads toward the church.

In the vestibule, a gentleman comes up and quietly tells us, in Italian, that a Mass is going on. He looks at my camera and says we'll have to wait to take photographs. Dad motions to me with his hand toward the inside of the church and mouths that he wants to attend. I wave him on.

He's already given up a number of days with no daily Mass for the sake of the trip. I know it's been a sacrifice for him. I'm also sure that he and his God will somehow work that out between themselves. As Mom starts following Dad down the aisle, she mouths to us that she wants to join him. We wave her on too.

Stu and I go outside to look at more souvenirs that merchants have placed on tables and stands in and out of their stores. We also go in search of the *toilettes,* as well as *l'ufficio postale,* the post office. I don't have enough *francobolli*— stamps for the postcards I've been writing in the hotel at night.

A couple of American men are hanging outside the post office. When we step back out, an older, heavier-set gentleman is holding a small brown paper bag. Both men reach in, pull out and pop, *ceci,* dried-hardened garbanzo beans, into their mouths.

"Want some, Honey," says the older man, with a Brooklyn accent.

"No thanks," I answer, and ask if he's from New York.

"Nah," he says, "Southern Florida. Our wives are inside. Some service is going on in there, but we don't feel like sitting through it. We're waiting out here."

"It's a Mass," I say.

"Oh," he replies, "I'm Jewish."

He does all the talking and tells us that they've been on a cruise in the Mediterranean for two weeks and are touring the island of Sicily today. After chatting a few minutes, he mentions that he's actually met the pope once.

"He's a nice guy," he says.

I chuckle, thinking about calling John Paul II or any pope a nice guy.

"Did you see him in Rome?" I ask.

"Nah," he says, "When he came to Miami, I got to shake his hand and all. Some mafia guy I knew arranged it for me."

I chuckle inside and see Stu's eyes light up, his lips trying to hold in his own quiet snicker. Stu loves macho and entertaining characters like this man who's latched onto us.

"He's going to retire, ya know," the guy says, reaching out with the bag of *ceci,* encouraging us to take some.

"No thanks. I don't eat much in the morning," I reply before remarking on his comment about the pope.

"I don't think that's going to happen—the pope retiring. That's not how it's done"

"Oh, yeah?" he says, "That's what he said in Miami. He's definitely getting ready to retire."

Stu and I humor him and move away slowly toward the church. We tell the guy we're going in to find my parents.

Out of the guy's earshot, Stu asks, "How old do popes have to be when they retire?"

"They don't retire," I say.

"What do they do then?" Stu asks.

"Everyone waits until they die. Then the cardinals pick a new one."

"As frail and as sick as he looks," Stu says, "the pope needs to step down and take a break."

This time I laugh aloud at Stu. It's so funny to hear other's perspectives on the religion that at one time made so much sense to me.

"It'll never happen," I say. "It's just the way it's always been done."

When we walk into the basilica, Mass is over and we find Mom and Dad in the vestibule. I look through the camcorder and scan the contemporary painted murals on the walls. They don't look like frescoes, as the colors are more pastel than the ones I've seen in older churches.

Dad can't remember when the new basilica was actually built, but it was sometime after he moved away. I stare at the art and architecture—the beautiful barrel-vaulted ceiling that runs above the nave of the main aisle, the paintings of saints and scenes from the Bible. Angels decorate the ceiling. The celestial figures appear in a more modern style than those I've seen in Renaissance and Baroque architecture in Rome, Florence, Venice and other Italian churches.

I get a closer view when I zoom in with the camcorder lens. I'm grateful to have it with me because I can now see details I would otherwise miss. When we reach the front of the church, a statue of the Black Madonna, much smaller than I expected, stands behind the main altar, flanked by large bronze angels. I take the 35mm camera from Stu and snap pictures of the seraphim from different angles. Having drawn angels for almost a decade, I want a shot of the images for my reference file back home.

"Come on, come on!" Dad says, moving us quickly toward the side of the front altar. "I found a guy who's going to take us to the old church. We have to wait over here by this gate."

A bronze and wrought-iron gate separates us and all the other tourists from going behind the main altar. From where we stand, I can see that there are even more images of saints and scenes from Bible stories. While I've been preoccupied with the art and architecture out front, Dad has arranged to get us behind the main altar.

After passing through the gate and down the circular hall, I see that the art that I've been eyeing from a distance is made up of small tiny pieces of glass, creating fine and delicate mosaics. I want to linger, but I put my inquisitive nature aside with the hope of catching a better look at the details on the way out. I hurry to keep up with the man who Dad has talked into taking us to the old church. I didn't know it still exists.

"There it is," Dad says, as we head out a door.

Directly across an enclosed courtyard is a more traditional Romanesque building. The exterior is constructed of concrete and a light red stone. The dome rises only slightly from the center of the building, unlike the new basilica's higher and expansive *cupola*.

This church is less than half the size of the newly constructed basilica we just left. Until I can get more information out of Dad, who's sprinting to stay up, I assume this is the church he visited with his family more than sixty years ago.

While everyone else hurries ahead, I hang back and take a photo of the courtyard, the door of the new church we just walked out of and the entrance to the old building. I make it inside in time to hear Dad say, "Here she is."

A Byzantine Black Madonna sits inconspicuously on a right side altar, set back from the center of the church. Although similar in intent to the statue in the larger more contemporary basilica, the Madonna's shape is squarer in form, more primitive and fitting the style of the medieval structure. My parents stop in front of the side altar.

My father directs his eyes at me, and then toward the sculpture.

"Is that the original Black Madonna?" I ask.

"Well, she looks like the original," my father says. "But the original is being kept in a safe place."

Before I have time to ask another question, we're trailing after the man and my father through a narrow door and down another hallway.

While quickly following along, I wonder if we're going to get to see the original Black Madonna. But we stop instead at a series of windows.

The man points out one of them and tells us to look. Below is the jetty that we saw earlier, with its small sand island. In *dialetto*, the guy mentions the baby to my father. My father nods his head in recognition. Dad excitedly looks from window to window and back again. I know it pleases him to see behind the scenes, where most pilgrims are not allowed to enter.

My father has been treated well in his region. He delights in telling people from the area how he was born and raised here, that he's one of them. His countrymen, whether they know him or not, appreciate his return by showering him with extra attention.

On the way back through the building, we go a different route, where additional windows are protected by bars. There is a posted sign that says, *silenzio*. I'm puzzled about why the bars exist at all. We're up so high—it seems impossible that anyone could break in from up here. From the stories I've heard and read, Sicily still struggles with crime, internal wars and the mafia.

"It's like we're in prison," I say, to my father.

"*Silenzio*," he whispers, smiling, as if enjoying the word flowing off his tongue.

My mind begins to wander. A command for silence reminds me of a penitentiary, another metaphor relating to how the church's hierarchy has controlled its faithful— sequestering them with edicts and pronouncements, handed down by the church fathers. I wonder how my father, a bright, inquisitive and rather rebellious sort, can be so loyal to this institution.

I suppose just as I've been devoted to learning about the art and architecture of the buildings themselves, Dad is as dedicated to the dogmas of the Church. There's no need in tormenting my father at this point with what the bars and sign suggest to me.

Instead I marvel along with him over the colorful mosaics we see when we finally enter the new basilica and walk behind the private realm of the main altar.

****

Heading back down the hill past vendors, the smell of roasted nuts permeates the air. Necklaces of strung hazelnuts line the stands.

They're similar to the ones we once bought at the Italian festivals in the Northside of Syracuse. We'd munched on the nuts hanging from our necks while taking in sounds and smells of grilled sausage, peppers, onions and other mouth-watering specialties.

When we first arrived at the basilica, the food vendors of Tindari were not yet open. But now they're calling out to us to purchase their nuts. We attempt to walk on by, but Dad and I run back and buy a bagful of hazelnuts to bring along on our trip.

By the time we get down the hill, away from the basilica, and reach the parking lot, the morning cast is gone and a crystal clear view appears. Facing inland, we can see Mount Etna. We'll be heading there, to my mother's family's region, later today.

But we still have one stop to make in Giammoro before returning to Gualtieri for a final meal with Dad's cousin, Pasqua, and before saying goodbye to his other cousins and to his hometown.

16) After Tindari

Monday Noon, October 23

By noon, we're driving down main street Giammoro and pulling up in front of a store called *Tentazioni Gioielleria*. *Gioielleria* is a jeweler's shop. *Tentazioni* is the name of the owner, who also happens to be Maria's younger sister.

Maria whips her car into place a few parking spots ahead of us. Her ebony hair hangs halfway down her back, pulled tight into a ponytail at the top. She's dressed in a straight black skirt. Her eyes are covered with deep blue eye shadow and lots of heavy, thick mascara, her lips bright red. Dad made arrangements at Pasqualino's the day before to meet Maria and her sister around noon.

Maria greets us loudly, tells us again that she feels guilty about our having slept in a hotel rather than at her house. She continues about not cooking for us today. On and on she goes. Dad nods his head up, down and sideways, as if expressing both understanding and gratitude for her generous spirit. He shrugs his shoulders and stretches his arms and hands, explaining that he didn't want to offend his cousin, Pasqua, who asked to have us over for a meal, too.

Once Dad says that, Maria stops, nods her head and maintains that she really does understand how Dad would also like to spend some time with his cousin on the other side of the family. The stay in the hotel, however, is another matter.

My guess is that Maria needs to be sure that we know we're wanted at her home. Eventually, she changes the subject and asks about our visit with Carmella last night and the trip to Tindari this morning.

In Italy, entering a jewelry store is like entering a bank vault. One or two customers stand inside an enclosed glass entry and wait until the outside door closes and locks. Once someone is securely inside the compartment and identified, a button is pushed, and the revolving door opens on the inside. Maria goes first, and then we follow two at a time.

After a round of introductions, Maria's sister walks us toward the back of the store, where a waist-high showcase separates customers from a walk-in vault. Maria's sister disappears inside and returns with large, leather album portfolios that she rests on top of the glass showcase. Red velvet fabric is pulled back, exposing layers of fine jewelry.

This is Mom's time, as she begins her search for 18-karat gold that she and my father will be bringing home for each of their children, their children's spouses, including Stu and me, plus eighteen *nipotini*, grandchildren.

Maria's sister's eyes sparkle when she hears the sheer number of pieces my parents plan on purchasing—thirty-four altogether. Seeing as we're scheduled to be at Pasqua's house by one-thirty for our afternoon meal, Mom has slightly over an hour to make her decisions.

****

Eighteen karat gold jewelry is something that my family has valued over the years. On one of my Italy trips, I purchased round-looped gold earrings in a store near the *Ponte Vecchio* Bridge in Florence. My maternal grandmother, *Nonna* Egidia, was still alive then. When I wore them at home, she turned her nose up and said in very broken English,

"No eighteen *care-ott.*"

"Oh yes," I insisted, "That's what the guy in *Firenze* told me."

She reached up to her right ear, took off one of her own very yellow gold dangling earrings and directed me to do the same with my new looped ones. Then she said the word yellow—pronouncing it *yaylow*—and pointed to her jewelry, indicating that hers was much deeper in color than mine.

Nonna would have noticed. All of her jewelry was 18-karat gold— the wedding band that she wore when she first arrived in America plus the additional pieces of jewelry my grandfather, Stagnitta, brought back to her each time he went to Sicily to visit his relatives in Linguaglossa. *Nonno* Stagnitta always returned with jewelry for his children, and grandchildren too.

I treasure the jewelry that *Nonno* gave me and wear it often— always at family occasions. In fact, I now own the *yaylow* earrings that *Nonna* so poignantly took off and pointed to that day.

Being the first granddaughter to be named after my grandmother, my mother and her brothers gave me those 18-karat gold dangling earrings when *Nonna* Egidia died.

****

Passing down the tradition that my mother's family started, Mom is now about to buy 18-karat gold for her own family. My mother, like me, does not make decisions quickly. I've attributed that to our Sicilian ancestry, where the man—father, husband, brother, son—has been deferred to when making most decisions.

Being brought up that way taught me to stuff down my own desires, making it difficult at times to have known exactly what it was I really liked or didn't like. Dad supported that dependency when he used to say that, if I wasn't sure what to do in a situation, I could count on him to give me the right answer.

Not having married until my late twenties and not having married an Italian man has helped me learn how to make my own choices. But it's not always been that easy. Stu and Dad have a running joke. When I have an opinion that challenges the male status quo, and I often do, Stu threatens to send me back to Syracuse on a one-way plane ticket. Dad laughs and says he'll return me the same way. I don't know who would be more challenged—my father or me.

Dad still has a great deal of influence on my mother. When she starts to look through the jewelry, Dad shows little interest. Mom tries to draw me into helping her decide what jewelry to buy, but I feel uncomfortable.

I don't know how much money my parents want to spend. And Stu—who always urges me to stay out of the middle between my parents, siblings and friends—is standing nearby.

I draw back and look at other items in the store. From the nervous exchanges I overhear between my mother and father, I sense that Mom is pulling away from Dad's resistance and focusing on the jewelry in front of her. I'm not sure that Dad is as invested as Mom is in purchasing all that jewelry. Ultimately, my father jumps back into the game and together they narrow down and make a decision—necklaces for everyone.

At that point, Mom solicits my advice on designs and lengths for guys, girls and younger children. It takes time, but Mom selects thirty-four lovely gold necklaces. Throughout the process, she continues mumbling to me, under her breath, that she isn't quite sure she's making the absolute right choices. I'm used to second-guessing. I do it myself.

While Mom frets, Maria's sister drapes the necklaces together in a couple of groupings. She wraps each pile in tissue and places them in those decorative marbleized bags, found in fine-Italian stores. Then she tells my mother to stick them down her bra rather than declaring the jewelry at customs when leaving the country. My father vehemently disagrees, but Maria and her sister start haggling with Dad and encourage my mother to do it anyway.

While Stu thinks everyone else is busy with business, he whispers to me that he wants to get me a piece of jewelry.

"A reminder of our trip," he says, ever so quietly.

Maria, who we think is preoccupied—and has insisted all along that she and Stu really understand each other—immediately jumps in. She points to some extra-large, looped earrings, and her sister takes the pair and holds them up to my ears. *The bigger, the better, the more money to be made.* They're much too hefty for my size. I don't like large, loopy earrings hanging from my head. I'm too short and prefer subtlety. So I select a more delicate pair of round-shaped, incised gold forms on posts.

Just before cashing out, Dad starts picking out silver and gold-plated platters. Without consulting my mother, he selects gifts to give to Maria, his cousin, Pasqua, where we're going for lunch, and for his other cousin, Caterina.

How can I not notice the contradiction? My mother defers to my father when making choices, while he independently does what he feels like doing. My mother's attention has been on choosing gifts for her present day family, while my father is centered on people from his past.

As we drive out of Giammoro toward Gualtieri for the last time, we tail Maria's car, retracing the back mountain road that we drove on when we first arrived. Dad talks about his cousins, about how close they are, even after all these years.

"Gosh Dad, we're close to our cousins too," I say, thinking that we must have learned how to be close with cousins from Dad.

"This isn't about *you!*" he lashes back.

His abrupt comment is like a blow to my stomach, where I've carried most of my sensitivity. I'm trying to point out how he's continued that tradition into the next generation. But his sudden response seems odd and hurtful, after the places we've been with each other.

Within seconds, my mother, who's sitting directly behind my father, whacks him on the back of his head and says his name firmly.

"Nick!"

Dad has gone a little too far, even for Mom. She tells me to ignore him, that he's too involved with his own thoughts and isn't making the connection.

By then, Maria's taking the final curve down into Gualtieri. She waves us on and heads home over the wooden planks of the bridge, toward the old part of town. Stu turns left into the newer section, and Dad directs him toward Pasqua's house.

****

Before we left the states, my sister, Teresa, reminded me of what had taken place in Gualtieri on the day I was there with her and our cousin, Marisa. Teresa remembered how clumsy I'd been at Pasqua's when I tried to cut, peel and eat fruit with a knife, all in one movement. It's a knack that I've observed Sicilians do gracefully. In our family, the littlest tales, not the hidden secrets, get repeated over and over again.

Teresa also reminded me that Pasqua had a grandson named Antonio. In 1983, Antonio was a one-year-old and would now be eighteen, a year older than Teresa's eldest son, Nicholas, born the summer after our trip (and named after my father). My sister asked me to find out more about Antonio, and if the two-distant cousins resemble each other in anyway.

****

When we walk upstairs into Pasqua's house, Antonio happens to be there. He has just returned on his scooter, with a bag of groceries for his grandmother. Scooters are the way young people there get around.

It appears that Antonio will be joining us for the afternoon meal, so I'll be able to give Teresa a first-hand account of the young boy she's curious about. I'm also surprised to see how much he does remind me of Teresa's son, Nicholas—tall with dark brown eyes and hair, a long, Roman-style nose, a touch of olive skin.

With my mother as interpreter, I explain to Pasqua that Teresa gave birth to a son one year after we visited, a boy only a year younger than Antonio, and that Teresa asked me to inquire about her grandson. Of all her grandchildren, what a coincidence that it's Antonio who's there sharing a meal with us. Who knows? Maybe the two boys will meet some day.

Pasqua makes me feel comfortable. She looks like my Aunt Mary on the Morina side of the family. She keeps a meticulous home, like my two aunts have always done. Her mannerisms are gentle and the tone of her voice is soft.

It was Pasqua's sister, Maria, who had mistaken me for Aunt Sarah when she cried out seventeen years ago.

"*Sarina, Sarina*, you've returned after all these years!"

Pasqua is close in age to Aunt Sarah, probably now in their mid-to-late-sixties. Often Pasqua looks over at me, and some of her comments make me feel that she's thinking of my youngest aunt. Despite the mistaken identity, Pasqua treats me as if I am the long lost cousin she grew up with more than half a century ago.

Pasqua's kitchen is large, sunny and contemporary. Her husband had been a general contractor for many new homes in Gualtieri, including their own. A few years ago, he died unexpectedly, in his early sixties. Pasqua asks my father, in their *dialetto*, if we visited her husband's gravesite at the cemetery yesterday.

Very apologetic, Dad excuses himself for not having done so, explaining that there was no way for him to know where her *marito* was buried. After all, my father told her, he was with Maria, who was from the Merlino side of the family.

"He was right *there!*" Pasqua says, motioning with her hands to the right side of her body and explaining how he was buried close to the other relatives, who she was sure my father had stopped to see.

But Dad admits that he didn't see many of the Morina burial spots, wishing aloud now in English that he looked further. Dad starts listing a litany of people's gravesites that he missed and wanted to see. I ask if he wants to return. He says no. Pasqua sighs.

Once we get beyond talking about the cemetery and the dead, Pasqua's mood lifts as she and my father continue chatting about other affairs. My mother is pulled into the conversation, too, and so are Stu and I, via my parents. The whole experience feels like an event in an Italian foreign movie.

While Pasqua puts pasta into boiling water, we eat *antipasti*— *prosciutto e melone*, Italian ham with cantaloupe. There are other selections on platters in the middle of the table—a variety of olives, canned peppers and other homemade canned vegetables from Pasqua's garden.

For the *primo piatto*, Pasqua serves a light tomato sauce with peas, over *spaghettini*. The second course consists of both veal and beef cutlets, each the size of our plates. There are green beans, salad, roasted potatoes and plenty of hard-crusted Italian bread.

Stu leans over and asks me to get the recipe for this meal too. He wants me to cook it for an Italian dinner we'll be hosting next month for some of his business associates. When Mom tells Pasqua what Stu just said, Pasqua tells me how easy it is to make the sauce. She cuts up and sautés a small onion with garlic, adds fresh tomatoes with basil and cooks it all for a short time before adding peas.

Mom translates the instructions, and in the oral tradition, another recipe is handed down from woman to woman.

Mix breadcrumbs with a little of this, a little of that, put in a quarter handful of parsley, a pinch of salt and pepper to taste.

Stu rolls his eyes. Maybe he'll finally give up asking why I don't follow recipes to the "t."

Antonio helps his grandmother with drinks and bread and other incidentals that she needs. When he takes out the fruit after dinner, Pasqua jokes about how poorly I cut and eat fruit with a knife. Some stories die hard, or not at all, and I tell Dad's cousin that Teresa reminded me of that too.

After *dolci* and *caffè*, Pasqua disappears, returning laden down with gifts for us to take home: a platter of Sicilian *ceramica*, for each of our homes; homemade doilies, that she's crocheted; and large pieces of painted fabric from the region. She has presents for Teresa, Marisa, my aunts and others. After going back into her bedroom and returning with her apron off and a fresh dress on, she grabs her purse. It's time for us to go one more place.

It must have something to do with what Pasqua and Dad commiserated over earlier. Every family has their secrets, and the Morinas have always maintained a certain level of confidentiality about their family's history. That's why, when I began writing family stories, both of my aunts expressed concern. My father, on the other hand, only hopes that he will be mentioned and not forgotten.

"Fat chance!" my mother has said, knowing that there are no family stories without Dad in the center. Now my grandfather, who vowed to carry secrets to his grave, would roll over if he knew I've tried to get as much information as anyone would give.

It so happens that we are going off to see my great uncle, *Zio* Santo's, wife and daughter. *Zio* was part of the fabric of my childhood. He was *Nonno* Morina's half-brother, one of the children born to his father's second wife.

****

Zio lived with my grandparents for a short time, until the Sunday my grandfather got mad and kicked him out. I don't know why, and even my father—who has been willing to tell me most anything, has refused to share that piece of his family's story.

As a child, it never dawned on me to question why *Zio* Santo had no wife or children. He was my great uncle, part of a group of elders. But back in Sicily, *Zio* Santo actually had *two* wives.

The second wife, who my father told me was his common-law wife, was the woman who approached me in the streets in Gualtieri on two different occasions. The first occasion was on my initial visit, with Teresa and Marisa, when *Zia* Rosalia was walking us proudly through the town. She quickly turned us around into another direction when a particular woman approached.

The second time always stuck more vividly in my mind. It was in 1985, when staying with Aunt Mary and Uncle Peter, *Zio*'s common-law wife approached me in the street when I was alone. She must have been waiting for me to be by myself, since that happened only twice that I could remember.

The woman who came up to me was old—her hips and body had spread considerably, her hair was a stringy gray-white and her front teeth were missing. She kept saying my great uncle's name, *Santo, Santo,* and then she pointed to herself.

Later, Aunt Mary revealed that the woman and *Zio* had a daughter together. But my aunt would not say anything more.

****

Now in Gualtieri with Dad, we're off to visit another woman that he and Pasqua refer to as *Zia*. I have not met this woman or her daughter, my uncle's first child. Dad says we're going to visit *Zio* Santo's first wife, and according to him, *Zio's* true love.

17. Zio Santo & Our Good Byes

Monday, p.m. October 23

In January of 1964, Dad came home from his yearly men's retreat to a frantic phone call from *Nonno*. My grandfather needed to see Dad right away. The police had contacted him after a tenant in *Zio*'s apartment house suspected something wasn't right in my great-uncle's flat.

An unusual odor was seeping through the walls. The police needed a relative present when they broke down *Zio*'s door, and my grandfather wanted Dad to be there with him. I still remember the repulsive look on my father's face as he later explained to my mother how my grandfather got violently sick after seeing his brother's decomposing body.

Zio Santo was not murdered, but he was found naked in bed, dead of a heart attack. He was only fifty-three at the time. Since my grandfather's understanding of the American legal system was limited, as was his English, my father took on the responsibilities of executor.

Dad used some of my great uncle's money for the wake, funeral, burial plot and gravestone. The rest was sent, via the Bank of Sicily, to *Zio*'s youngest daughter, the child born from his common-law wife. *Zio* left nothing to the daughter of his first wife.

Zio Santo had told my father that, if he were ever to die unexpectedly, he wanted any remaining assets to go to his youngest child in Gualtieri. *Zio* Santo knew that his first daughter was an attractive woman, already married to a man who could take good care of her.

He thought that his second daughter, who was not as attractive, would have a difficult time finding a suitor. Besides her looks, Dad said that she was someone, in this day and age, who would be considered learning disabled. *Zio*'s intention was to leave his youngest daughter with a dowry that might lure a potential spouse.

Now if that doesn't rub every bone in my feminist body, I don't know what would. However, instead of reacting, I make myself consider the Italian mindset of the mid-1900s. Besides, any criticism I make might discourage even my father from disclosing more family history. Dowries, common-law wives, half-sisters and brothers are not what I was used to while growing up.

Yet, these are my family's origins, and I want to uncover as much of the past as my father or anyone else from Gualtieri is willing to divulge.

****

Zio Santo's story continues to unfold here in Gualtieri, leaving me with more questions than answers. Why had *Zio* Santo taken a second wife, when he was still in love with the first? Why had he never returned to Sicily to see either of his wives or daughters? Why had a third woman, a stranger no one recognized, stood at a distance in the cemetery during his burial in Syracuse? My father can only speculate from his own understanding of his culture and the times.

Dad says that no one ever learned about the identity of the stranger at the cemetery. Dad does know *Zio*'s history from Gualtieri. His uncle's first wife had gotten involved with another man while *Zio* was serving in World War II.

Even though *Zio* still loved his wife and was willing to take her back, my father says, "The custom would not allow it." His uncle would have been labeled a cuckold man, something no full-blooded Italian male would have ever wanted. My father also says that there might have even been a child by this other man, since *Zio* returned from the war to find his wife pregnant.

"Who knows," Dad says, "maybe *Zio's* wife thought he died in the war."

When I ask what happened to the child, Dad's either unsure or unwilling to say. But what Dad is sure of is that *Zio*'s first wife has a daughter born from his "uncle's seed."

Zio's daughter, Peppina, is Dad's first cousin.

****

Peppina never forgave Dad for sending the remainder of her father's money to her half-sister. She told him so the last time they met in 1968, four years after her father's death. Dad tells me that he tried, during that visit, to explain her father's way of thinking, but according to Dad, "Peppina wouldn't listen to reason."

Peppina's anger and disappointment makes sense to me. How does anyone get over being forgotten by a parent? I keep those thoughts to myself and decide to watch and listen. When Peppina found out that my father was in town, thirty-two years after their last meeting, she asked Pasqua if there was any chance she could see him.

That is why the five of us are heading over to Peppina's place. Pasqua takes my arm and tucks it under hers. I'm surprised it's my arm and not my mother's. I'm sure, like her sister, Maria, back in 1985, she still half-believes that I'm her cousin, my Aunt Sarah.

Pasqua walks in a direction behind her house that leads to a more concealed area of town. She tells me this is not a surprise visit. We're expected at Peppina's home, where *Zio* Santo's first wife also lives. We walk around the block, down a street or two, and cross kitty corner toward a tall apartment building.

Around back, we sidestep numerous cats mulling about and climb a set of stairs to an apartment on the third floor. A woman who is younger than my father—perhaps in her early-to-mid-60s—answers the door.

She comes close to bowing at my father's feet, and Dad, who's now fairly quiet, seems relieved but puzzled, as his brow furls. My father and Peppina, *Zio* Santo's first daughter, offer each other the customary kiss on both cheeks. Pasqua follows suit before introducing my mother, Dad's *sposa*, me, his *figlia*, and Stu, his *genero*.

Peppina is an attractive woman with dark, blonde hair, petite facial features and a medium-thin build. Speaking in a soft, gracious tone, she thanks us for taking the time to stop by. She continues expressing her gratitude, almost in a curtsy, which makes me feel uncomfortable for her.

This same woman, who thirty-two years earlier was furious with Dad's decision to send her father's remaining assets to her half-sister, is almost in adulation of my father. Dad remains painfully silent, his shoulders more rounded than usual, his head hanging.

We follow Peppina down a short narrow hallway and are led to a small sitting room on the left, with a few elegantly upholstered armchairs and a fine wooden table. A small bed is pushed up against the right wall.

With seven people in the room, it feels tight. Besides Pasqua, Peppina and the four of us, there is a woman, easily in her nineties, sitting on a single bed, rocking back and forth.

In Italian she says, "*Sono io!*"—It's me!

She continues speaking out in a simple almost childlike fashion using the *dialetto*.

"It's me, it's just me."

Stretching out her arms, she turns her mouth down and repeats something in her language that sounds like,

"This is all I am or I'm just here. There's nothing more of me, just this."

Then she looks down at herself, as if she has nothing to offer anyone.

Antonia, *Zio* Santo's first wife, must have been a beautiful young woman, a Marlena Dietrick of her day. At ninety, her appearance is still quite refined, with a slim, diminutive figure. Her long white hair, pulled back in a stylish fashion, shows off her delicate nose and facial features.

She's dressed in a gray skirt, with a matching cashmere sweater. Her hands are like a china doll's, except more veined. Her legs and feet dangle off the side of the bed. This elderly woman sits, staring into space, her voice melodic, as she repeats the same phrases while rocking herself over and over again.

Peppina's daughter comes into the room. She's probably in her late twenties or early thirties, but I can only guess—since she, her mother and her grandmother do not show their age. The young woman seems embarrassed and attempts to get her grandmother's attention, giggling nervously when the older woman does not respond. The granddaughter sits down on one side of her grandmother.

Pasqua, on the other side of the older woman, wraps her arm into hers and talks softly. Out of respect, Pasqua calls her *Zia*. She tries to tell *Zia* Antonia who she is, who my father is, who all of us are that have entered her private haven. *Zia* Antonia doesn't recognize a soul, not Pasqua or my father, not even her own granddaughter.

Everyone and everything appears to be a mystery to her. When she tries to lie down, her granddaughter won't allow it and tells her that she has company from America and needs to sit up and greet us properly.

The scene seems to continue indefinitely, with *Zia* Antonia as the focus. Peppina, who's been running in and out offering drinks, *dolci*, and a box of rich Italian chocolates, prods us to have something to eat in her home. To show respect, I take a chocolate. Stu and Mom follow. Dad begs to be forgiven because of his *zucchero*.

Shortly after we arrive, my father asks Peppina if they can talk in private. They go off together, while we continue to watch my once-great-aunt sitting and staring into space, speaking only a phrase or two of nonsensical gibberish. I'm grateful for Pasqua's presence, comforting this beautiful old woman, lost in dementia.

****

Walking away from the apartment, Pasqua takes my arm. Her touch feels more relaxed, and the lines on her brow have disappeared. She thanks us for taking the time to visit. Pasqua points up into the mountains, and my mother translates this one for me.

An apartment only blocks away, but further set up into a hill, is where the other woman and second daughter of *Zio* Santo live. All are within eyeshot of each other's lives. One man, gone for almost forty years, yet those left behind still live out the drama.

I look over at my father, trying to get an indication of what he might be thinking. Whatever he and his cousin talked about behind closed doors left him quiet and hesitant. Before we left, Peppina reappeared, calm and centered, from their private conversation. I wonder if Dad's visit was a gesture toward mending old family wounds.

On the walk back, I move up next to Dad and ask in English if he gave Peppina some money to patch things up. He didn't. What he did was explain again her father's rationale for wanting his remaining assets to go to her half-sister.

"Peppina accepted my explanation this time," Dad says.

I tell my father that it was courageous to meet with her alone.

"You did something big, Dad." I say. "Some type of healing just took place, and you were part of that. You need to give yourself credit."

Dad shrugs his shoulders and says nothing. Maybe forgiveness has occurred in my father's generation and in the generation before him. A healing from a wound that started before I was even born. I've read that, when you heal something within yourself, you heal seven generations before and seven generations after.

Could my yearning to return to my family's origins be part of an unconscious need to understand the past before I existed? I've always wondered what we genetically carry with us, knowingly or unknowingly. If our eyes, nose and color of hair are passed down from generation to generation, then our ways of thinking and feeling must too.

Fears, resentments, uncertainties, as well as love and caring, must be harbored in our unconscious minds and bodies. If these feelings are being released from my father and his cousin, then perhaps challenges that have held me down will be expelled someday too.

We stand outside of Pasqua's house for a few minutes and talk about what we just experienced at Peppina's apartment. Then we begin our farewells. Pasqua starts crying, asking Dad to come back again soon.

Hugging him tightly around the neck, she sobs, in their *dialetto*.

"I'll never see you, again, Nicolino," and then she covers her face, wiping her tears at the same time.

I was not prepared for her remark. Dad's younger cousin, a rather young and healthy looking woman in her 60s, is saying good-bye to her older cousin. Granted, Dad has aged considerably over the years, but I'm not ready for these mortality issues that are playing out in my father's hometown.

From our car window, we wave to Pasqua. I work hard at holding back my own tears. I don't look up at Dad, sitting in the front seat next to Stu. Tires from the car rattle the old wooden bridge below as we cross over, heading back into the old part of town to say goodbye to Dad's cousins on the Merlino side.

****

After seeing Pasqua's reaction, I better brace myself for our remaining farewells. We leave our car in front of *Numero 40, Via Duca,* Maria and Pasqualino's home. Maria escorts us again by foot to Caterina's. Dad gives her one of the dishes he bought earlier at the *Gioielleria,* the jewelry store. Caterina's husband, Micio, has a round or two of shots ready for the guys as he sends them on their way.

Before drinking, Dad hands Micio one of the commemorative silver dollars that he brought from the United States. Micio turns his body away from Dad and tells him that they don't need money anymore. My father walks around Micio and stands face-to-face with him and says that it's simply a souvenir, not for spending.

He assures his cousin's husband that he knows the old days of poverty in Gualtieri are gone, but Micio looks straight into my father's eyes, his brow furrowed, his mouth held firm and stiff.

"Look how successful your daughter, Carmella, and son-in-law, Nicola, have been," Dad says, in *dialetto*. "Nicola and your grandson, Carmello, didn't need the money either. But they took the coin, as a souvenir from America."

Micio listens, his head half-tilted, his brow less wrinkled. He carefully reaches out and accepts the coin that my father is holding between his finger and thumb. Then Micio changes the subject and points out Stu's light features and square jaw, again.

The mood lightens as Dad and Stu joke with Micio about talking to Stu in German. Even though my husband insists that he doesn't understand, which he doesn't, Micio flips between Italian and German, leaving Stu totally in the dark.

Dad teases Stu in English, warning him that he better pucker up. After having observed the Italian men for the last three days, Stu is fully aware that Micio will be kissing him on both cheeks before he walks out the door.

It's a light note compared to the coin incident and will ultimately become another sad goodbye. The scene with Dad and Caterina is similar to the one he had with Pasqua.

At Pasqualino and Maria's, they load us with gifts too. Dad gives them the plate he picked out earlier that day. Before we leave, Maria wants to walk us through the upstairs once more, where they spend all of their time.

She takes us into their master bedroom and shows us her closet, her clothes and all her fine jewelry. It must be another way of letting my father know that life turned out all right for those who remained in Gualtieri.

As we head down the stairway, both Pasqualino and Maria follow, insisting that we return the following August for the St. Nicholas Feast. Dad says he'll try and will even attempt to bring his oldest son, my brother Anthony, who was named after *Nonno* Antonio, Dad's father.

"*Stai qui*," Maria yells out, and Pasqualino repeats her demand that we stay there next time.

Then Pasqualino turns to Stu and me and says, in *dialetto*, that we are both still young and can get around and don't have to wait for Dad to visit their hometown. Then he tells Dad to translate his exact words.

"Don't wait too long," Dad repeats in English, "I'm an old man. I won't be around forever."

Pasqualino laughs and we smile at his wit. Then it's time to really say goodbye. Maria and Pasqualino kiss Stu and me first on both cheeks. We walk slowly toward our rental car, leaving Dad alone to say goodbye to his cousin. We lean against the car and wait. Two old, grown men are in each other's arms, hugging tightly, thin skin covering their frail bones. The words are never said, but left unspoken is the feeling that they are saying goodbye to each other for the last time. Mom and Maria stand nearby.

All of us look away. I can't help but envision the two men as young boys—Dad at fifteen—and Pasqualino only nineteen years old, sending his younger cousin off on a ship alone, miles away from the only home they both knew.

Once my father and his cousin separate, he and Mom walk toward us and climb into the car. As we drive away, everyone waves to each other in a bittersweet moment. With his plaid flannel shirtsleeve, Pasqualino lifts his arm and wipes the tears from his eyes in the same manner that Dad's female cousin, Pasqua, did earlier.

I cannot see my father's face, now turned away from me. He sits, quiet and meek, in the navigator seat as we drive down *Via Duca*, through the St. Nicholas *piazza* and over the old wooden bridge. We take a right onto the main road that leads out of town.

18) Arrival In Taormina

Monday & Tuesday, October 23 & 24

Above the *autostrada*, brilliant lights shimmer against an indigo sky. We take the Taormina exit and begin our climb up *Monte Tauro*. The twists and turns of the hilly terrain feel similar to the drive taken earlier this morning toward Tindari.

This is the same road I traveled another dark night in 1983, when Teresa, Marisa and I traveled all day by train from Sicily's most southern region, Agrigento. Back then, a cab driver drove us up the mountain to a *pensione* in the middle of town.

Taormina had been a quaint village, where bohemian types walked the streets—magazines, books and journals tucked under their arms. A number of artists and writers have made sojourns to this mountain village, hovering over the Ionian Sea that lay between Sicily and Greece.

Since my last visit, I learned that D.H. Lawrence once lived in a villa, located south of Taormina's eastern town gate. The writer stayed for three years in a pink and cream-colored building, now a private residence. I hope to find the house while we're here.

It's past ten when we drive through the main gate of the walled medieval town. We head up *Via Bagnoli Croce*. How foolish of me to think that any Italian town would be quiet this time of night! Taormina bustles with people on the street out in droves for their evening jaunt.

Afternoon siestas must give Italians that extra boost of energy that keeps them going late into the night. Streets are packed with residents and tourists. Stu steers our rental around and in between people, bikes, cars and scooters.

This is the one place where I had not booked a room before leaving home. The person who'd taken my reservation at the hotel in Milazzo had told me that they could call ahead for us, once we arrived in Sicily. That's exactly what they did a few days ago.

Now, according to the map, *Villa San Michele*, the small hotel where we're staying, is located near the *Piazza Sant' Antonio*. Just beyond the main entrance of the walled city, we stop at a *Farmacia*, a pharmacy, for directions. Dad comes in with me to help with the language, although it turns out that the Italian woman behind the counter speaks English.

After giving us directions, she wants to know where we come from in America. Excited to hear that my father is from somewhere in New York, she hurries out from behind the counter and eagerly starts talking about her first visit to New York City, a year ago.

Dad and I listen, each with a foot aimed toward the door. The woman continues on about a taxi that she and her husband flagged down to take them in and around Manhattan and through the "burbs." Dad and I make eye contact, suspicious that she was taken advantage of by some cab driver. After more conversation, it's obvious that it was her way of getting to see the various facets of the city.

"I love your country," she says, smiling. "I love New York!"

Dad curtly but politely gets us out of there, excusing himself, gently grabbing my arm and pulling me out the door.

The *Piazza Sant'Antonio* and the *Villa San Michele* are located at the opposite side of town. The directions send us on a road carved higher into the mountain, paralleling the main thoroughfare, which is a pedestrian only street.

Once on the other side of Taormina, Stu maneuvers the rental car down the narrow lanes behind the *Duomo*, the main Cathedral, toward the *Piazza Sant'Antonio*. It would be challenging enough during the day to drive on the town's tight roads, but at night it's even trickier. We snake through small tapered alleyways looking for our destination.

Since Italian drivers steer quickly and impatiently around slow moving vehicles, Stu tries his best to keep from being pushed off the road. But after being cut off, we miss the most important left hand turn and end up down a lane so narrow that the outside mirrors come within millimeters of scraping the buildings.

I've never seen Stu tense behind a wheel. In his previous life— BG, or *Before Gilda*—Stu raced go-karts. So I'm always confident that he can get us through any tight pinch. Besides, there is an undersized garbage truck in front of us on the same road. If it squeezes through, I'm sure the BMW can make it too.

Dad and I encourage Stu onward with each maneuver. Mom stays quiet, grasping her top lip with her bottom teeth, like she does when she's nervous, either for herself or someone else. It's the first time I ever see Stu break out in a sweat behind the wheel of a moving vehicle.

"I'm going to scrape this BMW against these buildings," Stu says aloud, while Dad prods him along.

"You're a great driver, Stu," Dad says with high regard.

Dad has always complimented Stu's abilities not only in his driving, but in his ease in handling life in general, including the entrepreneurial ventures that Stu's undertaken over the years. After all, Dad and Stu are both fine businessmen.

Most importantly, Dad appreciates the laid back manner in which Stu handle's me, a hot-blooded Italian. Mom loved Stu from the minute he drove into Syracuse in a blustering snowstorm one Christmas night, back in the mid 1970's.

I've married a combination of the best of both parents—the industrious businessman, blessed with a calm and even-tempered personality. Often I've accused Mom and Stu of having their own mutual admiration society, especially when the two of them look at each other, smile and shake their heads about either Dad's reactive behavior, or mine.

Here in Taormina, I watch as Stu finally gets to the end of the narrow alleyway he's been navigating. After a small sigh, he's resolute that everyone needs to be attentive and keep their eyes open for road signs.

He drives the car up and around the town again, and then back behind the *Duomo*. We all sit upright, looking for the sign that appears on our right, pointing to a street on the left. Stu turns down the road that takes us into another narrow area of town, leading to the *Villa San Michele*.

A single lane street is crammed with cars and other vehicles parked mostly on the sidewalk, but spilling onto the road. Stu drops Dad and me off, while he and Mom look for a place to park.

Before we even step away from the car, Dad looks at me and says, "This place is going to be a dump."

My heart sinks. How can he possibly figure that out? We aren't even close to the building. I'm hoping that this is not another one of those intuitive feelings that my father and I claim to have had over the years. From a more practical perspective, maybe Dad remembers his homeland so well that he can tell from the surroundings that we aren't booked in the best of places.

A dump is not where I want to bring my parents, nor do I want to stay in run-down quarters myself for the next four days and nights. Our plan, after visiting Mom's cousins in Linguaglossa, is to take time relaxing and shopping here in Taormina. We all need a decent place to settle into for a few days.

As we walk toward a dark canopy full of greenery, the building ahead seems old. But old is normal for Italy. Our hotel in Rome was an old, medieval monastery, and we loved those accommodations.

Dad and I end up turning sideways to squeeze through layers of parked cars before we even get close to the hotel. Overgrown trees and brush hide a previously stylish but unkempt patio. We follow cracked and broken Italian *ceramica* that leads to the front door.

By now, I'm squirming inside. Dad's impressions are more accurate than I want to believe. Since the description we were given was one of a view overlooking the exquisite sea—*il mare*, we made an assumption that the exquisite *il mare* also meant there would be fine, polished living quarters.

The hallways in the hotel are narrow and dingy and need a fresh coat of paint. The rooms are adequate, and the toilets initially do not flush. When Stu finally gets them to work, they won't stop running. As for the view, we can see the bay nicely from a small attached patio outside of Mom and Dad's room.

Our room, on the other hand, is located on the side of the building, with only a medium-size double window and a very narrow balcony with no access, unless we want to climb on a chair and squeeze through the casement. If we twist our necks, we at least see a side view of water, glistening from the moon overhead.

It's close to midnight, and despite the disappointment of our accommodations, we are much too tired from a long intense and emotional day to do anything but sleep.

At breakfast, workmen are tearing down a small section of the hotel's dining area, and the waitress makes it a point to say that the future will offer a newer facility. That's not going to help us now. After a bite of *biscotti* and a little sip of *caffè*, we're back in our room, calling around for other lodging in town. We head out through the *Piazza Sant' Antonio*, past the *Duomo*.

Dad is drawn by the presence of the cathedral and says he wants to stay there. He's starting to get grumpy and turning back into the demanding father I'm more familiar with. I try not to react, knowing that it was difficult for him to leave his hometown the night before. He mentioned on the drive to Taormina that he wished we could have stayed longer. But the plan was that we'd visit *both* regions, and now it's Mom's turn.

We leave Dad in the *Duomo*, praying and hoping that there'll be a Mass for him to attend. Mom, Stu and I take off in the direction of one of the many stairways that lead up into the hilly town, toward the places we contacted by phone.

The first few are *pensioni*, which are boarding houses. They're a bit too bohemian for the combination of our foursome. High on top of a hill, we find a large, contemporary place called *Hôtel Méditerranée*, and by 11:00 a.m., we're relocated in first-class accommodations, with large, expansive bedrooms and twin beds.

Stu and I push ours together for the three nights we'll be staying. The furniture is dark antique wood, and there's even a large, Victorian mahogany pull-down desk, where I can write out postcards. Both rooms, adjacent to each other, reach out into spacious, connected patios, which are at least forty-feet by twenty-feet wide.

Our section of the veranda is actually wider and wraps around the building. There, we can see Taormina from various angles and a more glorious view of the sea, with all of its moored boats, a large cruise ship and the daylight sun sparkling off the water of the bay. To add to the setting is the magnificent presence of snow-covered Mount Etna in the distance.

Linguaglossa, my mother's origins, lies in the region below that volcano. Before we head to Linguaglossa, about 50 kilometers away, Mom wants to make contact with her two first cousins, whom she's never met. I met Salvatore—her mother's *nipote*, or nephew, and Gaetano—her father's, when I traveled there with my sister and cousin.

****

Teresa, Marisa and I rented a little Fiat in Taormina, and I drove us up into the piedmont region. My grandmother, *Nonna* Egidia, still alive in 1983, wrote ahead to her nephew, Salvatore, telling him that we would be stopping to meet him and see their hometown.

The second time I visited Linguaglossa was in 1985, when I was living with Aunt Mary and Uncle Peter. I wanted to rent a car, but they insisted on hiring a driver from Gualtieri to bring me to Linguaglossa and to pick me up.

On that trip, I stayed a few nights with Salvatore and his wife, Marianna. Like Stu and me, they were childless. While living with them, I discovered that Marianna also wrote poetry—something that I started doing in my late thirties.

I wanted to understand Marianna better because she seemed like a progressive Italian woman of her era. She told me how she read her poetry in one of the *piazze*. But with no one to help in translation, I never quite picked up all the nuances of her conversations.

Last year, I learned that Marianna had died. Mom's youngest brother, Uncle Alex and his wife, Aunt Barbara, took a side trip to Linguaglossa on their first tour through Italy. My uncle returned home with a bound book of poetry, written by Marianna.

It's in Italian, of course, so I miss the subtleties of poetry in its native tongue. On this trip, I hope to get my own copy and ask a friend back home to help me with translation.

Salvatore, Mom's first cousin, was older than his wife, Marianna. He must carry the Vecchio gene of longevity. Vecchio is my grandmother's maiden name. *Nonna* Egidia and a number of her siblings lived into their nineties. Dad always told me, growing up, that I was a lot like her and would live a long life too.

Having spent a lot more time with *Nonna* Egidia, my maternal grandmother, I grew up understanding Mom's side of the family better than Dad's. My parents lived in a flat above my Stagnitta grandparents on the Northside of Syracuse, where I lived until I was two and a half years old.

Even after we moved into another place on the Northside, we spent a lot of time at *Nonna* Egidia's. I followed my grandmother around, trying to imitate her ways—making meatballs together, rolling homemade macaroni, drying the dishes she washed, picking vegetables in the garden and helping her and Mom can tomatoes.

I'm looking forward to returning to Linguaglossa with my mother. Since Mom's a more guarded person, it's hard to know what she's thinking or feeling. In spite of her initial reluctance to travel outside of the United States, I can't help but think that, at seventy-three years old, my mother must be eager to be so close to the town where her family originated.

19) Taormina

Tuesday Afternoon, October 24

Right away, Dad starts giving us a hard time about visiting Mom's cousins. He announces that he wants to relax and take a nap. He flips on the TV set, sits back against the headboard and delights in finding his favorite sitcom, *Walker, Texas Ranger*, dubbed in Italian.

"I don't feel like going to Linguaglossa today," Dad says.

I can feel myself pulled right back into my old game of defending Mom. She won't say a thing unless she's at her boiling point—like the volcano looming overhead. But I've been known to react long before lava appears. I didn't come all the way to Sicily to watch *Walker, Texas Ranger* in Italian.

"Dad, you got to spend time in your hometown. It is *Mom's* turn now. Don't start."

He hears me, but my warning will not discourage him from pressuring my mother when I'm not in their room. He grumbles something under his breath. My fear is that, now that Dad has had the opportunity to see both the pope and his cousins in Gualtieri, he will revert to his old ways—doing what he wants to do, when he wants to do it. That includes taking numerous naps like he does in Syracuse, when he's not at the barbershop.

At home, Mom complains that he rarely goes out and rarely does anything that interests her, like going to the movies, which they did before they were married. Nor will Dad go on any short day-trips, either by themselves or with the senior citizen group at church. Despite my determination not to start bickering with Dad again, I'm afraid that if he decides to dig his heels in and stay put, we'll head down an old path.

There have been times I've needed to back off. Sometimes, I've even wondered if Mom and Dad's wrangling is for show. I've walked into a room when my parents didn't know I was there and found them talking warmly to each other. Besides, I'm reluctant to say much in front of Stu.

He insists that my parents do fine at home without me and prods me to mind my own business and let them work things out their own way. But when I hear them squabbling, it's tough not to get pulled in. Enmeshment is an Italian way of life.

I decide to leave them alone and walk back to my room via the patio. Mom comes over and tells me that she tried to call her cousin, Salvatore. Mom and Dad have either resolved their differences about going into Linguaglossa or he's sound asleep and she made the call on her own.

Unfortunately, Salvatore's phone has been disconnected. Mom wants to check the number with the one I have in my address book. When we discover our numbers are the same, she asks me to come back to her room and stand by while she attempts to phone her other cousin.

I know she's reached Gaetano as soon as I hear her talking in her own family's *dialetto*. The inflections remind me of the phone conversations she had with her mother, when *Nonna* Egidia was still alive. Like my father, *Nonna* was bigger than life. I'm sure her spirit is hovering around us, watching as she once did with her sideways glance, checking to see how we maneuver in and out of her region.

While listening to Mom's conversation with Gaetano, I gather we'll be stopping in for a quick visit after supper. She tells her cousin we can return tomorrow to Linguaglossa for a longer stay.

After Mom hangs up, she says that Gaetano will track down Salvatore and let him know we're coming. Gaetano has no idea why Salvatore's phone's been disconnected. He still lives in the same place no more than two and a half blocks away.

Even though they live in the same area of town, they do not associate with each other. Salvatore comes from my grandmother's side, the Vecchios. Gaetano is *Nonno* Stagnitta's nephew.

****

With plans for Linguaglossa now arranged, Stu and I spend time in our room, unpacking and settling in. I assume my parents are doing the same next door. After awhile, I walk out onto the patio and over to their room. Dad's just sitting up and stretching from a quick snooze he took. I ask where Mom is.

"She's gone home," he says, flipping out of his pre-nap grumpiness back into his funny self. "I need a nap."

"You've been sleeping for more than forty-five minutes."

"I have?" he questions, yawning and trying to wake himself up.

Mom comes walking out of the bathroom, asking Dad about some *paesano* that she wants to remember to ask about when she sees her cousin.

"Your father's looking for the hole," she says to me.

"The hole?" I question.

"Yeah, he's looking for the hole in the mountain," she says, snickering under her breath.

"Oh, the volcano," I say, thankful that we're back in a lighthearted place and hopeful that they've resolved our trip to Linguaglossa.

"Guess what I'm going to do, Dad, if I find that hole in the volcano?"

Dad sits there unaffected, rubbing his hands together, still trying to wake himself. Just an hour earlier, when he was standing at the edge of the patio and trying to put off going into Linguaglossa, I told him half-joking, half-irritated that if we get to the peak of the volcano, he can either jump or be pushed in—by me.

Now that Dad's mood has lightened up from his rest, I rejoin.

"The volcano or the balcony, Dad. Pick one or the other. Your choice."

He smiles, and I back off.

"Come on—let's go to lunch," I say.

This was Mom, Stu's and my second walk down the hill—Dad's first. There are stairs and more hills before we finally meander through the barrel-arch in the rear of the walled city. I'm always amazed at how each Italian and Sicilian town is unique. Taormina is full of shops and people swaying through the main street closed to most vehicles. The road is at least two-car widths wide—not like the tight narrow alleyway we experienced last night. Buildings of various sizes line either side, interrupted periodically by a *piazza* or an open area that looks out at the volcano in the distance and the sea far below.

Between the buildings, more staircases lead up or down to restaurants, boarding houses, hotels, roads, banks and various municipal buildings. People's homes are tucked behind stores.

Taormina reminds me of an Italian Provincetown on Cape Cod in Massachusetts. We vacationed for many years at the Cape, making periodic trips into Provincetown for dinner or shopping. Both Provincetown and Taormina have boutiques with unusual wares, artsy people, and although not as visible as P-town, my guess is there's also a gay community here in Taormina.

We find a little garden restaurant down a narrow walk, overlooking the side of the mountain. It faces Etna. The *maître d'* reminds me of one of my mother's Vecchio cousins back home.

He laughs and jostles about, with sharp language and small cackling sounds, like Mom's male relatives. It must be the way men from this region express themselves if something seems funny. The *maître d'* gives us free desserts with our coffee, welcoming us to his province.

We need time to get our bearings in this new town, learn the lay of the land for future shopping, and find a bank and an Internet store. I spotted two Internet stores this morning when we were looking for a place to stay. I promised my sister, Teresa, that we'd e-mail her when we got into Taormina and send her the name of the hotel where we're staying.

Teresa is the keeper of the itinerary for our travels, our one contact back home. Teresa's life is the most affected by Mom and Dad being away.

It has become obvious that, with Teresa living close to my folks and organizing family events, she's destined to become the matriarch of the family. Besides, knowing how the computer and the Internet has been a challenge for me, there's no way I'm going to e-mail all seven of my siblings. One is enough to contact.

I enter the Internet store before the others. In my strongest Italian yet, I ask the young girl working if she'll be able to help me. She replies, "Yes," in English, making it clear to me that she speaks and understands our language well. But when the time comes, she's preoccupied chatting with someone else on the Internet, like my own teenage nieces and nephews do.

I find myself getting anxious, not only because dealing with the computer can easily put me in that mood, but also because I'm paying by fifteen-minute intervals and I am not able to find the "@" for the e-mail address on the Italian keyboard.

I'm being a bit reactive when I start complaining about the cost. It's only an extra dollar or two. But I cannot find that "@" key, and the sheer presence of technology makes me borderline crazy.

If I'm in the dark ages because of my weak skills, there's no way Stu, Mom or Dad, hovering over my shoulder, will be of help. None of them have given much time to the computer. As bizarre as it may seem, I'm the expert in this group.

"What are you doing?" Dad asks, as he watches me trying to find my AOL account so that I can fill in my e-mail address, and my sister's too.

"I'm trying to type in Teresa's address," I answer, "It won't even take mine. I can't get the '@' to work."

"I know Teresa's address," my mother says, peering closely over my right shoulder. "It's 175 Home…"

"No, Mom," I interrupt," I'm talking about her *e-mail address*, not her home address."

"But that *is* her address," she says.

"E-MAIL, E-MAIL!" I say, raising my voice.

It doesn't take long at a computer for my hot-blooded Italian nature to rise. I've been known to stuff down feelings of just about anything before they resurge in a verbal eruption. I ask Stu to go and get the girl so she can help, but he shies away from disturbing her.

"I'm paying for this, and she said she'd help," I insist, "Say something to her."

Stu, not at all aggressive during my emotional flare-ups, backs off. The more he withdraws, the more aggravated I become, until an American woman sitting close by stops typing and leans over to show me what key needs to be hit.

A small piece of paper, taped on the computer, states what key I need to use to complete my sister's e-mail address, but with the English syntax off, I don't realize that's what the note is trying to convey. By the time we walk out of the place, my blood is hot, and I am spurting like Etna.

"Stu," I lash out. "Why didn't you say something to that girl?"

Admittedly, he's reluctant to speak—not knowing the language. It always happens that way. As my blood rises, Stu's reserve sets in. I can see his eyes glaze over as he pulls back from any confrontation.

"I *told* you she spoke English, and I asked you to get her!"

"I would have said something," Dad speaks up, "if I knew what it was I was supposed to say."

I walk on ahead, needing space for myself. After getting my bearings on the main street in Taormina, and as I chug back up the stairs toward our hotel, I realize that I'm probably just as tired as Dad admitted to being.

I hate wasting a minute of this trip resting, as I yearn instead to take in every detail of this island. Even worse, I hate that Dad might be right about being worn out—that we need to take a break, and put our feet up. Since we won't be going to Linguaglossa until after dinner, we take the afternoon and kick back, like the natives have sense to do. Everyone takes a siesta, including me.

In Rugged Terrain

Nonna and Zia take a step off
the porch into the backyard,
grab chickens, snap necks dead
against their hips.

They hustle to the kitchen, plunge fowl
into boiling water, pull them out,
place them on the kitchen table, begin
talk about childhood in Linguaglossa,
while plucking feathers from dripping hens.

Nonna starts about goats raised,
Zia, tomatoes grown behind
the stone house. Both sigh
when Nonna mentions black
umbrellas carried to keep away
ash erupting from Etna, as spewed
lava smothered everything
that summer their mother died.

20) Entering Linguaglossa

Tuesday Evening, October 24

Dad refuses to budge from his nap, so Mom, Stu and I decide to grab a light dinner before heading out to Linguaglossa. It's the third time today the three of us will be hiking up and down the hills of Taormina.

It reminds me of the time that Stu and I were in Assisi. We walked straight downhill for about three miles to see St. Francis's hermitage outside of town. When we were ready to return, we asked a young monk where the bus stop was located.

"You *walk*," he said, in simple English with a French accent.

"Are there any cabs that come here?" I asked.

"No," he said smiling, "You walk."

"Is there any other way back up the hill?" Stu questioned further.

"Sorry," he said, "You walk."

It appears that walking is going to be our only mode of transportation in Taormina as well—with steep inclines, the pedestrian-only street, and no buses or cabs that we can see. Fortunately, the distances are short.

We eat small, individual pizzas and a dinner salad at a garden restaurant, located on a stairway off the main thoroughfare. Outside, tables and chairs are sandwiched between each other and layered from step to step. We're quiet and tired, but we are attempting to muster energy for our evening venture into Linguaglossa.

When we walk back to the hotel to rally Dad and get the car, I notice that Mom starts huffing and puffing. It's so bad, I'm afraid she's going to have a heart attack. At seventy-three, she's not accustomed to the three treks we've taken up and down the town's steep inclines.

Even though I warned my mother beforehand that we'd be on foot a lot in Italy, her return to walking, two months before our trip, is obviously not enough for the likes of Taormina's hilly terrain.

"Mom, are you all right?" I ask.

"I'm fine, I'm fine," she insists, "I'm just not used to these hills. I'll be okay."

I am totally unprepared for my emotions—anger, worry, fear. Anxiety builds inside my chest. I try to brush away my angst, but to no avail. Had Mom's lack of exercise and healthy eating gotten the best of her?

I want to cry out and ask her why she hasn't been more conscientious. Does she not know how important she is to me, my sisters, brothers, cousins and all of her grandchildren who think she walks on air?

She's so attentive to everyone else's needs. I want her to be equally attentive to her own. My feelings swell. I am not only afraid for her, but for myself. I don't want my mother to die. Not here on the streets of Sicily. Not ever!

****

Once when I was at home, I decided to phone my mother in Syracuse and ask about her pasta with chickpea recipe. It's not that I don't have all of her recipes written down or memorized. It was my excuse to call her again that week, trying to stay connected for as long as life will allow. Cooking has been one of my doors.

"Mom," I said, holding back tears, "It will be so awful when you won't be there for me to call."

"Where am I going?" she replied, in that matter-of-fact manner she uses when trying to avoid the emotional realm. She quickly changed the subject and began rattling off ingredients and instructions for what she affectionately refers to as *Pasta & Ceci*.

****

Now on the streets of Taormina, I watch my mother as if my eyes could take her pulse. My siblings come to mind. *If Mom keels over right here, I may as well go with her. My sisters and brothers will flip!* I can hear one or more of them saying, "How stupid were you, letting her climb up and down those hills—not only once, but three times in a day! What were you thinking? Obviously you weren't." My imagination begins to get the best of me, and I could regurgitate the pizza, the salad and the bread.

My panic continues after we get back to the hotel and go to our separate rooms. I can't stop talking to Stu about Mom's breathing. Even though he's listening, I can also see the look of fear in his eyes. I don't think he's worried about my mother, but about me. When I get frantic, he doesn't always know what to say to calm me down. It's no wonder that, over the years, Stu's referred to me as Sarah Bernhardt, the old French drama actress from the early 1900s.

Thirty minutes later, after climbing into the car to leave for Linguaglossa, Mom's breathing is still heavy. Listening to her every gulp of air, I chastise myself for dragging her up and down those hills. Now I'm paying as much attention to her as I've been doing with Dad, who is sitting calmly in the front seat.

I wonder if, when my mother and father were alone in their room, Mom confessed to Dad about gasping for breath on those steep inclines. I wonder if he even noticed her breath had changed. I wonder if I keep praying and praying for Mom's breathing to relax, nothing bad will happen.

****

A half an hour later, there's a sign that reads, "*Benvenuti a Linguaglossa.*" Although dusk is setting in, there's enough light for me to recognize a few key landmarks. I'm as shocked by Linguaglossa as I was in Taormina. There seems to be more buildings, more people, more cars and more traffic than the last time I was here, fifteen years earlier. The distraction of getting my bearings and finding the way takes the focus off my mother.

The main street looks wider than what I remember. The same gray-black buildings, resembling lava ash, have been here for decades—some even centuries. But there are new buildings too. We have no written directions, but I didn't have any when I first entered Linguaglossa with Teresa and Marisa.

Back in 1983, I asked my grandmother, *Nonna* Egidia, how to find her nephew. She told me it was a small town and everybody knew everybody else.

"*Just-a stop-a* and *ask-a* somebody on the street. *Somebody-a tell-a* you.*"

This time, I'm navigating strictly from memory or intuition, or perhaps genetics. I lean over Stu's shoulder and direct him to stay on the road and circle around the first *piazza* that we approach. It's bustling with young people, meandering in and out of the square, listening to music, laughing and talking. Off to the side, older folks are performing their evening Italian ritual of walking—*la passeggiata*. I tell Stu to continue driving straight.

"Are you sure you know where you're going?" Dad asks, almost at the same time that I see the sign that points to Mount Etna.

"Turn left here," I say.

The road leading to Etna appears more spacious. I hardly recognize it. Shops seem closer to the street, and the sidewalk looks like it was recently poured—fresh cement. Before crossing the railroad tracks, I see that the old ticket station's been renovated.

"Take a right here before that railroad crossing sign," I say.

After he pulls into an open area in front of the station, I direct Stu to take the next quick right, a few yards away. He swings the car around and heads in that direction. We're entering the part of town where my mother's parents were raised. We pass *Via Due Dante* on our left, the narrow road where Salvatore lives—last house on the right. Of course I remember it—after all, I stayed with Salvatore and Marianna in 1985.

We continue straight, passing the house of my great Aunt Rose's sister. I've been in that house too, in 1983, with Teresa and Marisa. Grazia, *Zia* Rosa's sister, had died since the trip with my sister and cousin. So had *Zia* and that whole generation of my family.

Like *Nonna* Egidia, her best friend, *Zia* Rosa, was one of the women in my family who I looked up to and admired. *Zia* was married to *Nonna*'s oldest brother, *Zio* Joe. Both women were hard workers, intent on keeping the family together. Although *Zia* Rosa was Mom's aunt by marriage, my father also had a special relationship with her.

Zia was like a second mother to Dad. When he immigrated to the United States in 1939, he and his father lived at *Zia* Rosa's boarding house in Syracuse. *Zia* took in men from the old country, in America, without their families, like my father and grandfather. It was through *Zia* that my parents met.

****

Now the tertiary road where *Zia's* sister once lived does not seem as familiar. I swear that Gaetano's house was always visible from halfway up that street, running perpendicular to the road we're on. But this street is now tapered, and I can't see Gaetano's home. I begin to wonder if I've forgotten a turn somewhere.

We continue until we come almost to the end, when I see a new house on the right that was never there before. It's actually obstructing the view of both Gaetano's place and my grandfather, Stagnitta's, old family homestead that stands to the left of Gaetano's home. The gray and black ash building that belongs to *Nonno* Stagnitta's family appears.

The stone house, probably built in the late 1800s, is speckled with indentations from mortar shells embedded in its surface. Gaetano told me during one of my trips that the pockmarks were from attacks the building sustained during World War II. Right next door, contrasting the old with the new, is Gaetano's contemporary one-level stucco residence.

Relieved, I say to Mom, "There's your cousin's house."

We take a left at the end of the road we've been on and park the car on the street, a few yards down. At the turn of the 20th century, *Nonna*, her four siblings and their father lived in that very location, now a one-car garage.

****

Nonna's mother died when Nonna was five years old and her youngest brother, my great uncle, *Zio* Sam, was only three. Their oldest sister, Barbera, took care of the children while their father worked as a sharecropper behind the knee-high lava walls for the various landowners of the village.

Nonno Francesco, my grandfather Stagnitta, lived only a stone's throw away from *Nonna*'s family. He fell in love with my grandmother at a time when it was against social mores to marry below his class status. I never knew about that part of their life until visiting Linguaglossa for the first time. *Zia* Rosa's sister, Grazia, told me then that my grandfather couldn't help himself.

"He just fell in love with her," she said, and in the *dialetto* of their town, told me that my grandparents' marriage was made from a real love relationship—*l'amore*.

After having heard the story, I was surprised that my grandmother never spoke of the class system that existed in Linguaglossa, about how my grandfather took her away from it and how her marriage was uniquely different from most of the arranged marriages in her village.

Situations from my past began to make more sense. Once, when I was a child, we drove over to visit my grandparents, as we often did.

My older sister, Nicki, my brother, Anthony, and I were walking behind my mother into *Nonna* and *Nonno*'s doorway.

"*Ma*," my mother called out firmly, "*i ragazzi.*"

"The kids," Mom was saying, as I peeked around her and caught a glimpse of *Nonna* Egidia, taking a leap off of my grandfather's lap. Strands of gray and white hair were hanging out from the bun she always pinned to the back of her head. She was rushing to button the top of her dress.

Later, even into her nineties, *Nonna* talked about passion and attraction. One day, nearly fifteen years after my grandfather's death, when just us girls were sitting around talking on the eve of one of my cousin's weddings, *Nonna* physically pulled her arms around herself, demonstrating and talking about being embraced by a lover. She'd not forgotten those feelings she had toward my grandfather.

I've periodically thought that this is one of many ways I emulate *Nonna*. My marriage to Stu has been a real love relationship too.

It's not that Stu and I haven't had our troubles. But even after almost twenty-five years of marriage, we both get excited when each other walks in the door. Like my grandmother and grandfather, Stu and I maintain a real passion for each other.

I don't know if it was a fear of traveling or if *Nonna* chose to leave behind the past and the judgments once made about her marriage to my grandfather. But after *Nonna* moved to America, she never showed any interest in returning to her hometown.

When in 1983 I told *Nonna* that I wanted to visit Linguaglossa, she was not thrilled.

"*Why-a* you *want-a* go there. *Nothing-a* there," she said, throwing her right hand in the air, shaking her head and laughing nervously.

When it was obvious that I was going anyway, *Nonna* offered to write her nephew, Salvatore. She even wrote a second letter to my grandfather's nephew, Gaetano, also letting him know that my sister, Teresa, and I would be passing through.

My grandfather, *Nonno* Stagnitta, who was dead for thirteen years by the time I made that first trip, was different than *Nonna*. He returned to Linguaglossa a few times to see his sisters, brothers, nieces and nephews. Gaetano, a nephew who he was close to, was one of those relatives he went to see.

****

Gaetano answers the door. His smile at my mother is broad and genuine. He's obviously delighted to be seeing his cousin for the first time and greets her with the customary kiss on each cheek. Then he holds her out by her shoulders, looks into her face and pulls her back toward him in a big bear hug. He says, in their *dialetto*, that she looks just like their grandmother Stagnitta, on *Nonno*'s side. Since Mom is the first daughter born in her family, she was named after this paternal grandmother—Maria.

Gaetano reaches over and hugs me, acknowledging that he's glad to see me again. He introduces his wife, Rosina, to Mom, and Mom introduces everyone else to each other. Kisses all around—Gaetano kisses Dad and Stu on each cheek.

Dad scrunches up his nose for only us to see. I try not to laugh. I can see Stu holding back from expressing his own amusement over Dad's reaction. After all, Dad's male cousins kissed Stu, and payback is only fair.

"*Entrate, entrate*," Gaetano says, motioning for us to enter his home.

He escorts us into the living room, first room on the left. It's elegant and simply decorated with more traditional Italian furniture than the exterior contemporary structure would suggest. Gaetano tells Mom right away that Salvatore waited for us there all afternoon.

My mother asks why, since our plans were to stop by after dinner. Gaetano shrugs his shoulders as his brow creases. He says that, with Salvatore's hearing loss, it's not always easy for him to understand. Mom also questions why Salvatore's phone was disconnected. Gaetano learned that, since Salvatore is usually out and about, with his old *paesani* and hardly ever home, he had his landline disconnected and bought himself a mobile phone.

We're stunned when Gaetano jumps up quickly and dashes out, saying that he'll go and get Salvatore. He returns shortly, turning his index finger around on the side of his head, as if demonstrating a strange mind.

Even though Salvatore's dog kept barking, he never answered the door. Gaetano points to his own ears and tells Mom that Salvatore has probably turned off his hearing aide. He's also sure it doesn't work that well anyway.

Salvatore talked very loud during the occasions when I met him before. And at night, when I stayed there and the television was on, he turned the volume up so high that I couldn't always hear what he was saying. Since his hearing was poor fifteen years ago, I cannot imagine what it's like now.

Gaetano and Rosina offer us coffee and serve a plate of fresh cookies from one of those wonderfully-decadent bakeries that Italy and Sicily have, scattered throughout each village and town. We've become used to this custom, although Dad continues to refuse, explaining his concern over his diabetes.

Gaetano and Rosina's youngest daughter, whom I met twice before, steps into the room to greet us. Stephania, now in her mid-twenties and dressed in jeans and a sweater, is a student at the college in the larger nearby city of Catania. Her light makeup and a medium long hairdo remind me of my young nieces back in America. She acknowledges me with a warm smile and says she remembers my previous visits.

I was invited for dinner during my trip in 85. That's when I met Stephania and one of her two sisters. How intrigued a young Stephania had been, when I looked up and caught her watching my every move—the way I struggled over navigating the head of a prawn on my plate, how I twirled my spaghetti in a large spoon, my weak use of the Italian language—despite my constant prattle.

In the back of my head, I stashed away the thought that someday, when Stephania was older, she may have an interest in relatives living in the United States, akin to the same curiosity that drew me to Sicily.

Although Stephania didn't speak much English in 1985, it was clear that she continued her study of the language and now understands more than she did the last time I saw her. She says "Hello" in English when we first see her, and when she heads out the door to go off with a friend who is beeping her horn outside, Stephania stops in the living room and says, "Good-bye, it is good to see you again."

After she leaves, Mom asks Gaetano and Rosina about their other two daughters. Both live in Catania, the main city of this region, where many young professionals stay after attending the university.

Gaetano and Rosina's middle child is an attorney, while the oldest daughter, a gymnastics teacher, is married to a lawyer who works in the same firm with her sister. We heard about them from Uncle Alex when he and Aunt Barbara detoured from a tour they were on last year.

Uncle Alex, Mom's youngest brother, and his wife, Aunt Barbara, left their group for a day once they arrived in Taormina, so that they could see Linguaglossa and meet the cousins. Like my mother, it was the first time my uncle had been to Italy, Sicily and his parent's hometown. Gaetano offered to pick up Uncle Alex and Aunt Barbara at their hotel in Taormina and drive them back to his home.

While there, my aunt and uncle had dinner with all of Gaetano's family, including his three daughters and one son-in-law. Sometime during the meal, someone asked Uncle Alex about signing over property that still belonged to my grandfather.

There was no way Uncle Alex was about to give away any property. Besides, no one in the family even realized there was still property in Sicily. Well maybe I did, but I had long forgotten.

****

In 1983, on the trip with Teresa and Marisa, Salvatore asked me to remind my grandmother that she still owned property in Linguaglossa and needed to do something about it. When I told her, she laughed and threw her hands up in the air.

"*Lan-da.* What kind-a *lan-da* over there? *Noth-ing-a* over there," *Nonna* said in a dismissing manner, as if this so-called property might be a shed for a donkey.

Since I thought that the one-car garage characterized the wealth of her family, I let it go. Obviously that was exactly what she did, too. It didn't dawn on me that the property might have come from my grandfather's family's assets. If I ever mentioned the property again, *Nonna* would wave her hand in the air, brushing the whole thought away. She would never discuss it, and I forgot the property existed.

****

Uncle Alex returned from Italy the year before and told us that someone had asked him to sign over property. Since my mother knew the details from last year, she told me that she had no intention of getting into a discussion about turning over any property. In fact, before we left home she said it would be up to her brothers, Uncle Alex, and especially, Uncle Joe, the eldest of her siblings.

Mom's plan was to turn over any land or money decisions to her brothers, just like she always did with Dad. Although that was not the way her mother operated. Despite the Italian patriarchal system, my grandmother, *Nonna* Egidia, was a woman in control of every aspect of her family's life, especially involving money-making decisions.

Mom's forte, although not commerce and money related, is as peacemaker and bearer of gifts. So she gives Gaetano and Rosina the presents that she brought from home. She asks which daughter is her father's godchild.

It turns out to be the eldest, the gymnastics teacher, married to an attorney. Mom hands an extra piece of Oneida silver, a soup ladle, to Rosina and asks her to give it to her daughter, acknowledging the special relationship between godparent and godchild in the Sicilian culture.

We talk for a while, and I am impressed at how my mother carries herself graciously with her own *famiglia*. Even Dad takes a back seat to her now, letting her lead and responding only when he's addressed.

Mom and her cousin talk about who was who in the family and what they remember about my grandfather, grandmother and others. Gaetano remarks to me how delighted he is to meet my husband.

We each have moments of participating in the conversation, but the fascination lies in listening to these two cousins, who've never met before, piece together parts of their family's heritage.

Mom and Gaetano make arrangements for the next day's visit, where we'll be driving to the foot of the volcano. Gaetano mentions that, along the way, he wants Mom to see the property that belongs to her and her brothers.

She happily accepts the invitation to the volcano. I pretty much know that if anything is mentioned about signing papers, Mom will be doing some fast talking, since she has no plans on getting involved.

She stays focused on her own aspiration and tells both Rosina and Gaetano that we want to take them and Salvatore out for the afternoon meal. No cooking, she insists.

"I did not come to make extra work for you," she says, in *dialetto*.

They seem a little uncomfortable, squirming in their chairs and looking at each other in a questioning manner. After all, taking them out to dinner is not customary. They eventually do accept Mom's invitation and say that they also want to show us other areas of Linguaglossa.

My mother is cheerful, her eyes sparkling, her mannerisms gentle and assured as she moves her arms and hands around, falling comfortably into the language she grew up speaking with her parents.

Since my father has always been the decision maker in our home, I rarely see my mother in charge. But when I do, like now here in Linguaglossa, I feel her power.

21) Linguaglossa

Tuesday Night & Wednesday, October 24 & 25

Once on the outskirts of Linguaglossa, Dad starts complaining about how tired he is, about not seeing the need to return the next day and about having to be kissed by Mom's male cousin. I remind him about how patient Mom had been in Gualtieri.

"Not only patient," I say, firmly, "Mom showed genuine interest. Besides, do you really think that Stu wanted to be kissed by *your* male cousins?"

Dad stares out the window, his face expressionless. He appears totally unaffected. I hold back from telling him what I really feel, which is that *everything is not always about him*. When my father's acted like this before, I flip between rage and concern. My first thoughts are that he's self-centered.

After a few minutes of driving, I begin to worry that perhaps his behavior has something to do with aging. I don't think he has the propensity for Alzheimer's. His father never had it, but his mother showed signs of disorientation long before she reached my father's present age.

And Dad's older sister, Aunt Mary, is beginning to show signs of dementia. Since my father is still quite sharp, his self-absorption can still get to me. When we return to our separate rooms in the hotel and start getting undressed for bed, I vent to Stu.

"I can't believe that my father can be so selfish. Mom was totally involved in his town when we were in Gualtieri!"

Stu never says a word, but he just listens as I continue.

"I know he's going to give us a hard time about going back tomorrow!"

My husband has listened to me carry on about comments my father has made over the years. I used to be angry that all Stu did was listen and not agree. It took a while for me to realize that my husband takes *pleasure* in my father's remarks.

In spite of my need to vent, over time I've begun to value Stu's refusal to participate in any criticism about my parents, no matter what I say. Since Stu was young when his parents passed away, not often, but enough times for me to quiet down, he's pointed out that I'm lucky to still have my folks.

After I carry on awhile, Stu has his own story to tell. But once he starts, he can't stop laughing. He chokes on his words. His eyes fill with tears. When he opens his mouth to relay what Dad said, his laugh turns into a snort. He tries not to roar aloud so that my parents won't hear him on the other side of the wall. He doubles over in hysteria and sits down at the edge of the bed to contain himself. By then he has me giggling, too. But I have no clue why.

"Your father…" Stu finally says, unable to finish his sentence. "Your father… he's so funny."

I've often wondered if my husband understands Dad because they're men or because he's married to me, and I've been accused of being like my father.

Stu can keep the straightest face when Dad makes a remark that I swear comes from a self-centered teenager. He lets Dad expound with no interruption. Sometimes, Stu responds with something so humorous that anyone who's around can't help but chuckle—including Dad, including me.

With Stu's uncontrollable laughter, he'll never spit out what antic Dad pulled. But eventually, he tells me that when we were in Linguaglossa, my father said under his breath, "I don't want to kiss any of those men, and if you don't Stu, I won't have to either."

"As if it was you who invented the darn custom to begin with," I say.

Here's my husband, a very American male, accommodating my father's Sicilian culture. I'm sure Stu's never kissed another man in his life, even if only on the cheek. Instead of Stu trying to back step from the tradition, it's Dad.

Finally, Stu spills out what's making him laugh so hard. While Dad and Stu were following behind Mom and me as we walked up Gaetano's front steps, Dad says,

"Tell him you have a cold. If you don't have to kiss him, I won't have to kiss him."

Although the comment wasn't all that funny, we are both now hysterically laughing.

"Did Dad give you a clue as to how you were going to *say* that, since you can't speak the language?"

Stu guffaws even harder.

"He told me to sneeze in a handkerchief or point to my nose and shake my head."

Between venting and giggling, my rage at Dad subsides. Stu and I laugh so hard that we fall back into the twin beds that we'd pushed together earlier. Despite my own psychological fluctuations, Stu is having a grand time. He reaches over and touches my cheek with his right hand and kisses me. Moisture from his tears falls onto my face.

With his left hand, he reaches underneath my pajama top and starts fondling my breasts. We make love for the first time since we left home. My parents, right next door, are sleeping—I hope. Silence finally settles in our room. As we rest warmly in each other's arms, I hear the moaning of my parents' television set through the adjoining wall.

****

The metal screen door on Mom and Dad's room is still down when I step out onto the patio to take more video shots of Mount Etna. The air is clear and fresh, the sky a bright periwinkle. Small patches of billowing smoke rise above the far off volcano. I'm surprised that my parents aren't up before I am.

My mother appears first, giving the rope on the door one quick tug. A metal screen is what Italians use to keep out bugs, while still letting in fresh air. Mom is short enough to easily duck underneath without pulling the screen all the way to the top.

Mom is dressed in an ice-blue blouse and sweater, the color accenting her silver-gray hair. When I was young, Mom's hair was so black that shades of blue flashed through. It was always sharper in tone than my chestnut-brown hair, closer in color to Dad's.

Three of my sisters—Nicki, Teresa and Bridget—have hair that was as black as Mom's. She gave up dyeing long before Dad ever did. He'd say he needed to keep the image up for business, but we all know it had a lot more to do with Dad's vanity.

I'm passed the age that my mother was when she let her hair go natural, but I haven't caught up to the age when Dad finally succumbed to gray. Mom's silver sparkles. I'm sure that my gray would be duller and not shimmer like my mother's hair.

Stu and my sister Fran hound me to keep it brown, swearing I look younger and say they aren't ready for me to let it go gray yet. I've used them both as an excuse. My hairdresser says that it's me who isn't ready. She knows me too well.

"Your father's driving me crazy," my mother says, walking towards me with something in her hand. "He insists that these brown socks are not the same color."

Mom's head is down as she keeps looking and flipping the two socks over and over again. With the camcorder still on from having taken video shots of the volcano, I look down through the zoom lens.

The bright sunlight hits the socks—one a tad darker brown than the other, the ribs slightly varied in shape. I hear my father as he starts coming out from their room, kvetching about the two different socks she pulled out for him to wear.

"They don't even match," he says, then he whacks his head on top of the metal door that Mom had not lifted high enough for him to walk under.

"Dad, be careful!" I say, "You need coffee."

My mother continues to fumble with the socks, and I am not about to say who is right or wrong.

"Your father asks me to find him white socks!"

"Then what are you two arguing about? Brown socks?" I ask.

"I couldn't find his white ones," she says, "I know they're in there somewhere."

Stu, who happens to walk out in time to hear Mom, speaks up.

"I brought some white socks and they're brand new. You can have a pair, Dad."

"My mother *has* all those white socks she brought for her cousins," I say. "Mom, give Dad a pair of those."

But both Mom and Dad insist we look at the brown socks and tell them if they match or not. I stand back and let Stu handle this one.

"Well, they really don't quite match," he says, in his diplomatic way. "Look here, Mom, the color is off just a little."

"Ah, what difference does it make?" she says, "They're close enough."

Then she looks into the lens of the camcorder, still running.

"Oh, he's a pain in the . . ." and just like Mom, who's always refused to say the word ass aloud, she mouths the word instead and starts chuckling.

There was a time when my mother wouldn't even use the word, "darn." As she got older—sometime past my college years—she began to mouth words like "damn" or "ass," never anything more offensive. But she wouldn't say the words aloud. She would smile proudly, acknowledging the courage it took to speak out. Then she'd follow with a giggle.

When my siblings and I were growing up, my father was unwavering about vulgarity. Even words that suggested vulgarity, such as "darn" for "damn," were unacceptable. It's not that he ever washed our mouths out with soap. That would have been too easy. He guilted us into Saturday afternoon confessions, or worse yet, Saturday night confessions with him.

I never do look to see what socks my father finally wears for our trip into Linguaglossa. While everyone manages to get ready after breakfast, I take a few more shots of the view and then the town below. Just before leaving, I overhear my father, talking to Stu about the World Series. Dad has made arrangements at the front desk for an American paper.

"They've had three games already," Dad says, "and I have no idea what the score is for any of them."

I know that my husband is trying to appease my father when he speaks.

"Why don't we wait for the paper?"

"No way," I step in, before Dad has an opportunity to agree. "It will be here when we get back."

I didn't come all the way to Sicily to sit in a hotel room, waiting for some American paper to find out a baseball score that we can't do anything about anyway. Surprised that Dad did not find the score on TV last night, Mom informs me that they were watching more reruns of *Walker, Texas Ranger.*

"After your father fell asleep, I watched *The Price Is Right* in Italian," she says, delighted with her find.

It makes me wonder if they heard us making love. But I won't be that blatant and blurt out the question to my mother. Instead, I skirt around the issue, having learned that approach from her.

"Did you hear Stu laughing last night?"

"No," Mom says, with a blank expression on her face, giving no clue as to whether she really heard us or not.

It's hard to know with Mom. She's always been shy about sexuality—never as open as her mother, *Nonna* Egidia. The day that *Nonna* wrapped her arms around her body, talking about a lover's embrace, Mom got up and walked to the other side of the room, seemingly embarrassed. My sisters, cousin and I teased her about it.

Even if Mom *did* hear Stu and me last night, she won't let on that she did. And she probably would be the only one to have heard us. Even at home, when Dad's sitting on his chair and the grandchildren are running around the room in circles, he's impervious, unless they get between him and his television program.

Fortunately, Mom discourages Dad from turning on the television before we leave for Linguaglossa. While he and Stu lock up the rooms, Mom and I head toward the elevator.

"What was Stu laughing about?" Mom asks.

Since she's bringing it up again, she may have heard more than she's letting on, but I don't pursue that line of questioning. Instead, I tell her how Dad tried to conspire with Stu into not getting kissed by her male cousins in the hopes that he too, could avoid being kissed.

"Oh, your father!" she says, with a twinkle in her eye.

****

When we arrive in Linguaglossa, I direct Stu to turn left down *Via Due Dante*, toward Salvatore's home. My mother wants to go there first, so that she won't offend her cousin who waited all those hours for us at Gaetano's last night. We stop in front of the last house on the right. Just beyond it is his garden. The narrow alleyway, which at one time ended at his property, now continues and connects to a street beyond.

In the past, any car that journeyed down this narrow way had to strategically turn around in a rather tight space. I remember watching Salvatore directing more than one driver on how to make a three-point turn in front of his house.

Salvatore answers the door right away and calls out loudly.

"*Maria. Come stai, Maria,*" he says, to my mother, throwing his hands in the air, asking how she is.

He laughs a prattling laugh and points to me in recognition before quickly giving out his round of kisses, starting with Mom. I don't even look at Stu and Dad. They're on their own.

The way Salvatore talks to Mom, in *dialetto*, sounds like he's known her all of his life. There's something about blood relations and how we relate to each other energetically, whether we've met before or not. The two of them talk with such familiarity—it's as if Mom is conversing with one of her brothers, and Salvatore, with a sister.

Although his voice is thunderous, it isn't as piercing as I remember. He's now wearing thick, brown-framed glasses, which he didn't wear before. Initially, he flips them up and down, from his eyes to the top of his head, until he pulls them off to show us a pair of hearing aids, attached to the end of the frames. He demonstrates how the positioning of his glasses allows the devices to get closer or further away from his ears.

Salvatore is a true Vecchio, my grandmother's family name. He looks exactly like *Nonna* Egidia's younger brother, *Zio* Sam, who's been dead for at least ten years. His voice sounds like my great-uncle Sam's too, with the same cackling chortle.

"*Entrate, entrate,*" Salvatore insists, and we enter into the hallway of his home.

It's hard not to notice the stench of dog. I try not to react. A quick peek to the left, and I see the room where I slept in 1985, when I came from Gualtieri to visit. Crimson red, satin spreads still cover the bed and divan in a rather large parlor-like room. Lying on top are gift boxes, yellowed over time. Black and white pictures sprawl from the open packages. The room looks dingy now.

As we follow Salvatore down the long hallway, we pass the living room, on the right. We're heading in the direction of the dining room and kitchen. The disgusting odor of dog and stale food becomes even more intense. My father holds his nose and covers his mouth. The expression on his face turns to nausea.

****

When Teresa, Marisa and I were here for the first time in 1983, Marianna and Salvatore insisted that we have a meal with them. I remember my cousin, Marisa's, reluctance to eat. They didn't have a dog or cat, and there was no apparent odor. But flying around Marianna's kitchen was a small owl.

"*Gufo, Gufo,*" Marianna sang out affectionately to her pet owl.

It was so tiny that I hadn't realized the bird perched itself over the large pot of brewing tomato sauce while Marianna stirred the soupy ingredients. Later, Marisa told Teresa and me how she noticed the bird hovering over the stove. It definitely shed light on why Marisa did not eat much of the pasta and meatballs that Marianna prepared.

It was a busy day that summer in '83, full of excitement as we ran from home to home, meeting people that Teresa and I only briefly heard about. Since Marisa was our cousin from Dad's side, the people we were meeting had no family connection to her.

Despite the different dialect, it was Marisa who did the translating. The *dialetto* sounded so much like my Stagnitta grandparents that I actually understood some of what was said, and I even spoke a line or two.

When I got ready to return to Sicily two years later with Aunt Mary and Uncle Peter, Marisa expressed her concern about my staying at Salvatore and Marianna's house.

"You're going to have to eat there," she said, her forehead wrinkling.

She had a point, but I was also on a mission to learn my ancestry, and there were places in the world more unusual than Salvatore and Marianna's kitchen. Fortunately, when I returned that summer, Marianna's *Gufo* had died and there were no other animals living in or around their house, except for the native birds that Marianna took me out to see in her garden.

Salvatore must be lonely, now that Marianna is dead. Maybe that's why he has a dog, whose loud bark is coming from the back of the house. As we maneuver ourselves in that direction, there are also cats skittering about. The odor from the animals is more than Dad can handle.

22) Salvatore & *Nonna*

Wednesday a.m. October 25

By the time we get to the end of the hallway and take a right into the dining room, Dad's missing. Stu goes back to find him. In the meantime, I listen to Salvatore and Mom converse about their family. Salvatore is much chattier, while Mom's attentive to everything he says. She's so absorbed in their conversation that she doesn't notice that Dad has disappeared

My mother asks Salvatore if he'd go out to eat in a restaurant as our guest for the afternoon meal. He doesn't respond. Mom doesn't push, but she continues talking with her cousin about family matters— their mothers, siblings and relatives who moved to South America, whom I know little about.

While Mom asks questions, Salvatore hands her old photographs, newspaper exposes and articles that he has lying on the dining room table. He must have dug them out before we arrived. Mom inquires about a picture of their grandmother, Vecchio, their mothers' mother. Edges of his mouth turn down as he raises his shoulders up toward his ears and shakes his head back and forth. I've seen that Italian expression many times from other family members.

Mom isn't ready to give up on finding a photo of her maternal grandmother. She persists and asks Salvatore if any of his siblings or any other relatives might have at least one small picture of their grandmother, who died when *Nonna*, Mom's mother, was only five years old. No matter how much she and Salvatore talk round and round about a possible picture, he still doesn't know of any that exist.

He hands my mother more photos, explaining the different people. Mom glances at the faces. Soon, I see her eyes look past the people in the photos, her top teeth grab the side of her bottom lip as her brow slightly wrinkles. I know Mom's wondering how she'll ever find a picture of her mother's mother.

"*Guarda*," Salvatore says, asking my mother and me to look at the holy cards and then the small statuettes.

Both are replicas of St. Egidio, the Patron Saint of Linguaglossa. Of course I recognize the image of the saint. When I was growing up, *Nonna* Egidia would pass out the same holy cards and statuettes on

September 1st, St. Egidio's Feast Day. She must have had them sent to her from Linguaglossa.

Nonna's name was the female derivative of Egidio. So is mine, since I was named after her. At the time, my mother thought that Gilda was the derivative of Egidia, or at least close enough.

****

Over the years, I heard and reheard the story of the day I was born. Mom announced that my name would be Gilda. Her younger brother, my Uncle Alex, informed her that Egidia and Gilda were not the same name. Giles, the actual English source, has no female offshoot. From what I've gathered, a certain amount of mayhem took place in the hospital that day over the Sicilian cultural practice of naming the first four children born in a family after the grandparents.

My sister Nicki, short for Nicolina—*first child, first daughter*—was named after my father's mother, *Nonna* Nicolina. It was father's family first, then mother's family second. Since my parents held out for a boy to name after my father's father, and I was the second child, second girl, they were expected to name me after my grandmother on my mother's side, Egidia.

Fortunately, my brother, Anthony, came eighteen months after my birth and was named after my father's father, *Nonno* Antonio. The only one left who needed to have someone named after them was my mother's father, *Nonno* Stagnitta, whose first name was Francesco. My sister Fran, or Francine, the fourth living child, was given a female version of my grandfather's name.

I say living, because my mother lost a baby between Anthony and Fran, who died shortly after birth. A healthy normal infant, she was strangled by the umbilical cord. My parents, at least my father, held the physician responsible for the mishap, since the doctor arrived late for the delivery. I suspect my parents have blamed themselves too. They changed doctors during Mom's pregnancy so that she could go to someone closer to home.

It was difficult for the whole family. But it was definitely painful for my mother. Anytime the subject of "the baby" comes up, Mom tears up and walks out of the room, unable to express her grief in front of anyone. Dad has said it was one of the crosses in life that they had to bear, and that their faith in God got them through.

They named the baby Mary, after Christ's mother, and I always assumed, after my own mother. Mary's death has been one of those shadows that linger in our family. After Fran was born, my mother seemed joyful again.

When the next four babies arrived, my parents were able to select names of their own choosing, asking for input from us older kids—Teresa, Gerard, JoAnne and Bridget. Only saint's names were even considered.

Back on the day I was born, when my uncle announced that Gilda was not a derivative of my maternal grandmother's name, it was my grandfather, Antonio, on my father's side, not my mother's father, who insisted that my parents honor *Nonna* Egidia by properly following the Sicilian tradition to the letter of the unwritten law.

Mom wrote "Egidia Ann" on my birth certificate, but always called me Gilda. In fact, she signed me up for kindergarten using Gilda Ann. It wasn't until I graduated from college and moved from New York State to teach in Massachusetts that the state certification office wanted proof that Gilda and Egidia was the same person. So my mother signed a notarized statement that said Egidia Ann Morina and Gilda Ann Morina are one and the same.

Eventually, I had my name legally changed. The day I returned from the lawyer's office, I stopped by *Nonna* Egidia's house before going home. She knew where I'd been and told me that she understood the difficulty with my name over the years. Nonna was a realist, having taken care of all her family's paper work—bills, tenant agreements, insurances, contracts, and any other official legal document.

My grandmother wanted to assure me that she would have done the same thing if it made life easier. I knew she was trying to make me feel better. I unfolded the document that I signed at the lawyer's office and showed her that my name had been changed to Egidia Gilda, leaving the Egidia and adding the Gilda. *Nonna's* face lit up as she tried to hold back a wide smile.

"Oh, you *din-a have-ta keep-a* Egidia. Too hard, too hard!" she said, but I knew she loved the gesture as much as I loved her.

My husband, the jokester, and my sister, Nicki, his counterpart, love to tell the story about my numerous names. I see it coming every time they bring up my long drawn out name, including the one I took for Confirmation—Egidia Gilda Ann Bernadette Morina Syverson.

"And guess what part of this name she eliminated?" Stu always exclaims.

Both smile, look at each other and Nicki, with a twinkle in her eye, exclaims gleefully, "Ann."

"It didn't *happen* that way!" I say, defending myself foolishly, as they laugh and carry on.

Over the years, when September 1st came around, both my grandmother and I were acknowledged for St. Egidio's Feast Day. That was when *Nonna* would give out the holy cards and small statuettes of her patron saint, the same icons Salvatore is handing to my mother and me.

****

When Stu walks back into the dining room, he mouths, for only me to see, that Dad can't stand the smell in the house. Since I'm in the middle of a conversation with Salvatore and my mother—when they aren't looking, I mouth back to Stu, "Tell him I said to come back in here."

Within a few minutes, both Dad and Stu pass through the threshold of the dining room door. My father comes up to me with his hand hovering over his nose.

"I can't stand the smell," he says.

"Offer it up," I whisper back to him, an expression he always used when any of us insisted that we couldn't stomach something.

"Offer it up" means to sacrifice anguish or pain to God or Christ for the poor souls in Purgatory, struggling to get to heaven. At least that's what Dad and the Catholic religion has taught. My father knows exactly what I'm getting at. He needs to suffer through the smell and live what he's preached.

Within a short time, Dad and Stu have their noses in some framed award, with Salvatore's name written on it. As a young man, Salvatore won a gold medal in Alpine skiing. It wasn't an Olympic medal, but an honor that he received for his country, Italy.

Dad and Stu investigate the framed paper, turning it around, looking at the medal, attached on the back. Salvatore has one eye on them and another on Mom, who's asking her cousin about a letter she received when he was taken as an Italian prisoner by the United States army during World War II and held somewhere in Arizona. It turns out it was not Salvatore, but his brother, Alexander, who was held as a detainee. Alexander must be dead, since there's no talk about where he now lives.

Salvatore disappears through French-glass doors that lead from the dining room onto what I refer to as a patio. Once my mother takes a peek outside, she tells me that she wouldn't call what she's looking at a patio. Strewn about everywhere, under a covered outdoor area, are stacks of containers on top of and below tables, where fruits and vegetables were laid down to dry.

There is a well for water, with a large cover that takes up a chunk of space. There are piles of dried dirt in various spots. From somewhere behind a mound of boxes, Salvatore pulls out the old, wooden skis that he used to win the gold medal. In the background, the dog, whose offensive odor is barely tolerable, barks in a menacing way from his cage at the edge of the patio.

Salvatore points around and calls out names of various objects, in his *dialetto*. My mother nods her head in recognition—*pomodori*, tomatoes, *l'acqua dell pozzo*, the well, *uva*, grape and *mustada*.

"Ah, *mustada!*" my mother says, her voice lifting with delight, as she and her first cousin acknowledge something that seems totally foreign to me.

"What's *mustada?*" I ask, before looking over at Stu, who looks equally as puzzled at this dark, thick slab of jelly-like maroon, covered in gray.

"*Mustada* is a boiled-down, red grape that's prepared in ash and water," Mom says.

She continues to explain how the substance of the grapes settles to the bottom of the pot. Everything else is discarded, and the *mustada*, the hardened grapes, are taken out in the form of a one-inch slab, a slight grayish white film, coating one side. Once the *mustada* dries, it's cut into narrow pie-like sections and eaten like a dry fig or any other kind of dry fruit.

****

Like a memory filed away for decades, I'm on *Nonna*'s enclosed back porch. On the white Formica table behind the door lay pieces of newspaper, with a deep-red substance sitting on top.

"What is this, *Nonna?*" I asked.

She shook her head saying, "*Neva-da mine-da.* You *no-a* like it."

I didn't argue. Whatever it was didn't look appealing to me anyway. In the recesses of my mind sits the dark flimsy, almost rubber-like substance. There were other unusual things around *Nonna's* house that I took for granted and never questioned. As much as I listened and absorbed, there are still so many things that disappeared once *Nonna* died.

I loved all of my grandparents, but I was closest to *Nonna* Egidia. She demanded closeness from all of her children and grandchildren. The second youngest of five, *Nonna* was only five years old when her mother died. Her father and older sister, Barbera, Salvatore's mother, raised her. The death of her own mother affected everything about her life, making it vitally important to her that the people she loved remain close.

Nonna's losses mounted. Her sister, Barbera, the only sibling not to have immigrated to the United States, was left behind in Sicily. Much later, *Zia* Barbera moved to Venezuela to live with one of her daughters. Although they wrote often, *Nonna* never saw her again.

Then there was the death of *Nonna's* daughter. My Aunt Josie was *Nonna's* third child out of four, and Mom's younger sister. She died of Lupus when she was only thirty-three. *Nonna* nursed her during the long illness. I was thirteen at the time. My aunt's death was difficult for everyone, but *Nonna's* grief was unrelenting. I remember her sobbing at the funeral home, calling out the affectionate name a mother once gave to her child.

"*Josina, Josina!*"

Afterwards, *Nonna* wore black for years and refused to have any dancing or music played at family parties. When my grandfather died—in spite of her sadness, she told me that she had few tears left, having used them up on Aunt Josie. It was no wonder *Nonna* hung on so tightly to those she loved.

Nonna was equally as important to those of us who loved her. During my childhood, after our family moved away from *Nonna's* house on the Northside—my sister Nicki, brother Anthony and I would return there every summer for a few weeks' vacation—even though it was only ten minutes from our house in Eastwood.

We spent many weekends with her too. *Nonna* let us stay up late and told us stories about the old country and tales about the new that none of the other adults wanted us to hear. She took us proudly around to various *paesani* homes, to Italian weddings and to my grandfather's company picnic. *Nonna*, along with my mother, aunts and great aunts, put together family parties and gatherings.

Nonna often came to our home to lend my mother a hand, especially when my younger siblings were born. She would even stay overnight, help Mom with household chores—cooking, ironing and cleaning—and she paid extra attention to us older ones. When there were no newborns to care for, she took the James Street bus from the Northside to Eastwood.

She and Mom would can tomato sauce and freeze *finocchio*, a rice and fennel dish that I still love. *Nonna* taught my sister, Nicki, and me how to crochet, knit and make various Italian meals. I may never have eaten her *mustada,* but there were other meals she fed us that were nurturing.

All of it homemade—chicken soup, Sicilian bread, sausages, macaroni—that she rolled by hand at Christmas, even when she grew older and her hands were twisted and pained from arthritis. It's impossible to put into words how much *Nonna* meant to all of my siblings, cousins, aunts, uncles, parents and me.

Nonna's energy still lingers. Working in my studio on the sixth anniversary of her death, I had forgotten the date, even though it was written on my calendar—July 26, 1986. There was no window open in my studio, no breeze anywhere. Obsessively working and reworking an angel drawing with colored pencils, I was startled when something flew off the top shelf.

I stepped from my stool to pick it up. It was the photo folder that held the poem that my sister, Nicki, wrote about *Nonna.* On the opposite side, facing the poem, was an old picture of my grandmother when she was in her fifties, still robust and smiling, her hands resting on top of her stomach. I looked around.

"*Nonna*," I said. "You're here, aren't you?"

I scanned the open space of my studio and *Nonna*'s spirit was there. Whenever I sit and write about her, I feel her standing over my shoulder, suggesting things to say. She's in my kitchen as I cook her meatballs, chicken soup, *zuccadadi,* her Italian biscuit, or homemade macaroni. *Nonna* was the female, like my father—the male, who was bigger than life for me.

That summer in my studio, I didn't return to my drawing. It felt more important to take time out, sit in the rocking chair by the window, and reread the poem that my sister, Nicki, wrote after *Nonna's* death.

Nonna's Hands
by Nicki Morina Richards

Those busy hands: cute round fingers, never stopping,
strong and agile, doing the work of women.
Women's work: keeping the daily flow.
Shiny gold rings catch the eye, not adorning
these hands, not stopping to be admired...
Remembered in flight,
The flight and busyness of women's work.
Women's work: for her, the work needing to be done.
Those full round hands: held a fork for turning meatballs,
or a Delmonico steak.
Picked up marinated tuna, dished out tripe,
Breaded cutlets, spread pizza dough
Rolled homemade macaroni, spooned out ricotta
Those hands: peeled tomatoes, wrenched chicken necks,
scooped out innards, weeded gardens, dug up dandelions,
carried serving dishes to the family table, kneaded bread
dough, curved S's and O's,
Stuffed honey and nuts for cookies
The rough working hands softened to hold babies, touch
faces, lift bodies, wipe tears,
They gave away gum, money, candy, ceci beans, first
tastes of wine, anisette, lollipops,
They irrigated catheters, washed backs, turned medicine
tops.
Those small great hands stirred pots of bubbling
tomato sauce and homemade soup,
They held hands of little children en route to a newly-
built church, the candy store, farmer's market, the bank.
Those rapidly moving hands spoke stories, feelings,
affections, laughter, anger, vengeance,
They stretched handmade lace, crocheted tablecloths,
handkerchiefs, sewed buttons, aprons, drapes.
The hands that gripped a telephone or banister,

pressed an iron, stuffed clothes in a wringer,
held fast to pocketbooks.
These quiet hands opened a change purse, caressed coins,
gave away love.
Those hands held on dearly to everyone… one and all, so
they would not go away as her mother, sisters, daughter,
husband.
Those hands held on tightly, for they knew loss—
the void left by loved ones.
They held no illusions—those hands were here to work.
Thus they found their own way, with moving lips
These folded hands held missal with rosary… and prayed.

As those hands grew older, the lines and marks deepened,
Broken bones healed… in their own direction, the
tautness disappeared,
Pale, thin skin, blue veins, old age marks, fell loosely
round old bones,
Injured nails and scars told of happenings.
These hands reached up, releasing hair from its bun,
brushed long thin flowing white strands…
Until one day
These hands reached out to those visiting at bedside,
gripping tightly, to say she was still there, somewhere.
By and by, her spirit released, lifted beyond… then,
These sweet fine hands cradled themselves in their final
rest.

23) Zia Rosa

Wednesday a.m. Continued, October 25

Outside his crimson-colored concrete house, Salvatore demonstrates with his hands how to make a U-turn on his narrow street. He points and suggests that Stu drive to Gaetano's place by going straight on the newly-paved road. But Stu, standing by the car and looking in both directions, wants to turn around and drive back down the way we came.

The first time I walked down *Via Due Dante* with Teresa and Marisa, a fruit and vegetable truck was parked a few doors away. It was a modern version of the old Sicilian *cartolino,* like the replica we saw in Tindari. But the road, now barren, except for our rental car, has plenty of space for Stu to turn around.

I look about and see that Dad's missing again. In the back seat, tucked as far away as he can position himself, my father sits, unreachable, unless someone climbs in and moves over next to him.

"I know what you're doing," I call into the car.

Dad keeps his head down, ignoring me and hoping, I'm sure, that he won't have to kiss Mom's cousin. Salvatore, unaware of Dad's antics, busily points and demonstrates the U-turn specifically to Stu.

Then, and with no forewarning, Salvatore jumps into the front seat. I don't look in at Dad, knowing he didn't expect Mom's cousin to be coming along. It's all I can do not to laugh out loud.

The route to Gaetano's house is clear and simple, and I could get us there. But Salvatore insists that he deliver us safely. My mother smiles and gracefully accepts as she and I climb into the back with Dad. Besides, what could Mom do? Salvatore placed himself in the navigator's seat before anyone could say a word.

After Stu turns the car around and heads down the street, he takes a left, following the same road we took to Gaetano's the night before. I point out Grazia's house, *Zia* Rosa's sister, and start up the camcorder to record the site for *Zia's* family back home.

With the house now boarded up, I wonder what happened to the granddaughter who lived with Grazia. Her own daughter died a few months before Teresa, Marisa and I had arrived in 1983.

****

Zia Rosa, like *Nonna*, was still alive. *Zia*, my great aunt through marriage, was thrilled that we'd be seeing her younger sister. Even though they corresponded, they hadn't seen each other for years. Like *Nonna* did with her nephews, *Zia* sent Grazia a letter, letting her know we were coming.

Grazia reached up to hug and kiss each of us, asking lots of questions about *Zia* Rosa and the rest of her family. Marisa did most of the translating by speaking pure Italian to Grazia's teenage granddaughter, who in turn translated into *dialetto* for her grandmother.

That summer afternoon, there was plenty of talking and interpreting over *caffè* and *dolci*. Grazia showed us lots of family pictures, including ones that *Zia* had sent.

Zia Rosa and *Nonna* Egidia remained lifelong friends, from their childhood in Linguaglossa through to their lives in Syracuse. As they got older, the two talked on the phone to each other three or four times a day. One of their running conversations was about who would outlive the other.

Zia married *Nonna*'s oldest brother, my great uncle, *Zio* Joe. They immigrated to the United States in the 1920s, before *Nonna* arrived. That's when *Zia* opened the boarding house, where my father and his father lived and where my parents met.

Zio Joe died when I was only two, but I still have an abiding memory of him smoking a pipe, sitting in an overstuffed flowered chair at *Zia*'s house, looking out the window onto Catawba Street on the Northside.

Zia Rosa and *Zio* Joe had three sons—my mother's Vecchio cousins—Alex, Tony and Sammy. We called two of them uncle—Uncle Tony and Uncle Sammy. Since we already had an Uncle Alex—Mom's younger brother—we called Cousin Alex simply by his first name. Uncle Tony was the only one of the three who never married, and because of that, he spent time entertaining us kids with his stories, asking about school, our friends and what we wanted to do when we grew up.

When my sister, Nicki, and I were young, we spent some overnights at *Zia*'s house. We stayed there with *Zia*'s granddaughter, our second cousin, Rosemary. She was Cousin Alex's daughter and the only cousin in our age group.

Nicki, thirteen months older than me, was the firstborn of our generation. Rosemary came three months after, and I was born the following year. We have lots of childhood pictures of the three of us together—Nicki was taller with jet-black hair, while I was the shortest, positioned in the middle of the photo, with light brown curls, and Rosemary had long blonde ringlets, inherited from her mother's Irish ancestry.

During our childhood, and before the family got so large, we spent all of our holiday dinners with the Vecchios. Uncle Tony still stops by my parents' home every Thanksgiving, Christmas and Easter morning.

I've always said that it isn't Christmas until Uncle Tony shows up at the door. He has a quick cup of coffee, discusses whose *zuccadadi biscotti* came out better—his or my mom's—and then he dashes out, leaving us with some tale from our family history. I remember one about their summers, picking onions, *cipolle,* on *Zia* Concetta's farm. My father likes to joke with Uncle Tony about having slept in a room with him and his two brothers, Uncle Sammy and Alex, the night before he and my mother were married.

"They held me hostage," Dad always says. "They made me sleep on the inside of the bed against the wall so that I couldn't escape from marrying their cousin!"

Everyone laughs, including Mom. The truth is that all three of Mom's cousins have said over the years that Dad was more like their brother. Their mother, *Zia* Rosa, treated Dad like her own child, showering him with the same love and warmth she did her sons.

For as long as *Zia* lived, Dad remembered her with gifts on Christmas, Easter, Mother's Day and anytime he'd visit. With a wide, toothless smile, *Zia* Rosa would kiss Dad on both cheeks. He'd hug her neck, calling her *bella,* beautiful.

At *Zia's* 90th birthday celebration, Dad stood up and made a tribute.

"They just don't make them as strong as her anymore."

"Oh, *Nick-e,*" she responded, with her accent and reached for him, kissing one cheek over and over again.

Dad was referring to both *Zia's* personality and to her work ethic, which was important to any Italian immigrant who came to the United States in the early 1900s.

Zia was a four-foot-ten cleaning machine. After her husband, *Zio* Joe, died, she worked to support herself and buy things for her family. She loved her job and the people whose offices she cleaned.

When she was in her early eighties, there was a large picture of *Zia* on the front page of the Syracuse Post-Standard. She smiled proudly while reaching over to dust a corporate desk in one of the downtown buildings. In 1991, at the age of 97, *Zia* died, outliving my grandmother by five years.

"Uncle Tony," I say into the microphone of the camcorder, "There's your aunt's place."

Since it's boarded up, I know it would be difficult to track down any of *Zia's* relatives in the short time we'll be in Linguaglossa. But Salvatore is the Vecchios' cousin too, on their paternal side. At least they, like us, still have a relative connected to the old country.

****

Salvatore directs us down the road to Gaetano's house, and Stu parks the car between *Nonno* Stagnitta's old, gray stone homestead and the converted garage that was *Nonna's* house, growing up. Salvatore follows my father to the door of my grandfather's place. I hear him say something, in *dialetto*, about *Zio* Francesco, his uncle—my grandfather. Dad turns around and calls out to my mother.

"Mary," he says, and when she doesn't respond as quickly as he would like, he calls her name a little louder, "Mary!"

"What?" she says in agitation, trying to finish a conversation with Stu.

"Come over here!" he says with a lilt in his voice.

He turns toward the front door of the old stone house and peers in. Mom, Dad and Salvatore stand at the door. Dad speaks in English so that only she, and not her cousin, can understand.

"Come see your family," he says, glancing between the cracks in the wood that covers the entrance.

Even though my father can be funny, he can be fresh. His comment is in reference to what Gaetano told us last night about raising pet rabbits inside the old building.

"Dad's being a scorch," I say to Stu, as he walks up from the car. "We were so nice to him in Gualtieri."

Mom doesn't take the hook. And Salvatore—well, he has no idea what my father's saying. He doesn't seem to care either, standing there, puffing on his cigarette. After a few minutes, Salvatore announces it's time for him to leave and starts walking up the street back toward his home.

My mother calls out a reminder that she wants him to join us, along with Gaetano and Rosina, for the afternoon meal. Salvatore hedges a bit and says it isn't necessary. Mom, in her gentle, quiet, but firm tone insists that they have at least one meal together. He offers to cook, but she says that *she's* the female cousin.

Although the Italian culture is very patriarchal, there is definitely a matriarchal influence on my mother's side. Since my grandmother, *Nonna* Egidia, was reared by her sister, Barbera, Salvatore's mother, he doesn't argue.

As Salvatore walks backwards up the road, he agrees to be available *alle due*, at two. I pull out the camcorder so that I get a picture of him moving through the streets of Linguaglossa. When he sees the camera running, he calls out to Mom's oldest brother, *"Peppino, vieni quà."* He wants Uncle Joe to come here.

Uncle Joe is the only child of my grandparents who was born in Linguaglossa. He immigrated with my grandmother to America when he was five years old. My grandfather was already in Syracuse. Salvatore and Uncle Joe were born only a few weeks apart. The last time Uncle Joe saw his cousin was during World War II, when my uncle received special permission from his U.S. army commander to stop by the village to visit relatives.

Uncle Joe and Salvatore will both be eighty in January, only a few months away. They've aged well. The three times I've seen Salvatore, he's reiterated that he wants to see Uncle Joe again. I keep suggesting that he fly to the United States. He shakes his head back and forth and cackles. It doesn't work that way. Those who leave are also the ones expected to return, even for a visit.

Salvatore says, *"Salute"* to Uncle Alex, whom he met for the first time last year. But it's Uncle Joe, the oldest of Mom's siblings, the one that he knew as a child, the one he called out to, in *dialetto*, laughing and pointing with his finger to the ground, the land of their ancestry.

"Vieni qui, Peppino," he says, again, his voice deepening and shifting into a more serious tone, as he tells my uncle to come here.

Salvatore's brow furls and his eyes widen. Peering through, I see a deep longing for the past and the cousin he shared a childhood with, at least for the first five years of his life.

24) Mount Etna

Wednesday Afternoon, October 25

Mom greets Gaetano with a kiss on each cheek, and I point to Dad to follow. Stu takes a quick snapshot of my father kissing Mom's cousin, a little scheme that we planned. Dad smirks, glares at us, then steps through the entryway.

Gaetano and Rosina are dressed in their Sunday best, even though it isn't *domenica*. They're ready to take us to Mount Etna. First, we take photographs on their patio in the back of the house, overlooking a flourishing yard covered with plants, shrubs and trees.

In an outlying section, a vegetable garden grows, along with large cactus-like, prickly pear plants. As a kid, I wasn't so crazy about the taste of prickly pears. The seeds were too tiny and hard, and the pulp not sweet enough for my childhood sensibility. I grew into the flavor.

With the sight of the exotic pears, my mouth waters for the pungent zest. I remember the fruits and vegetables from my grandfathers' gardens—figs, grapes, zucchinis and other various produce from the Italian palate.

When *Nonno* Stagnitta was still alive, he had three gardens at his home on Townsend Street in Syracuse—two large vegetable gardens and one garden of roses, with at least thirty plants that bloomed rich, red buds every summer. The roses grew tall, up wooden trellises that paralleled the full depth of my grandparents' home. After a hard day's work maintaining his gardens, *Nonno* Stagnitta would meander through the rose bushes, gently checking each bloom.

****

Nonno not only had an extraordinary touch with vegetation, but he had a special talent working with people. *Paesani* from the Northside went to him for healing. Each would show up at the front door off the porch, usually with another family member, carrying loaves of bread or a sack of chickens, eggs, or bottles of homemade wine—all forms of gratitude payment, although I learned that the whites of the eggs were sometimes beaten and used for a natural cast.

My grandparents quickly moved the callers into the dining room and living room, closing the door that separated the front of the house from the family room and kitchen, where we would be. *Nonna, Nonno* and the visitors would stay in there anywhere from fifteen minutes to an hour or more. Of course as kids we were curious, but we also got accustomed to my grandfather's healing service.

If we were ever ill or fell and sprained an ankle or wrist, my mother brought us to see her father before even phoning the doctor. Nine times out of ten, *Nonno*'s cures worked. He sat quietly, holding the part of the body in peril or floating his hands gently on top of an organ. Sometimes he made a circular movement with his fingers, and then he flipped them, as if throwing something away.

Nonno's hands, hot as blazes, transferred the healing heat to the area of the body that needed help. Only my grandfather knew when to pull his hands away. Then he looked over at my mother and, in *dialetto*, said whether all was well—if the bruise needed rest or if additional medical care was warranted. Most of the time, we went back home without having to go see a physician.

My Uncle Alex's son, Frank, who was named after my grandfather and is a quiet man like *Nonno*, has the same abilities with animals. Although he uses scientific veterinarian medicine in the mountains of North Carolina, Frank laughs and humbly turns away when I tell him that he can heal animals just by looking at them.

My sister, Nicki, a nurse, also has healing abilities. Sometime in the early 1990s, when I was in the car with her, attempting to maneuver the vehicle into a parking spot, I snapped my neck and went into severe pain. No matter how I moved my head, the pain persisted. I moaned to Nicki.

"Sit still," she said quietly, and then she rubbed her hands together.

We both sat in silence while she held one hand over the right side of my neck for about two or three minutes. Then Nicki pulled her hand away and told me to turn my head to the right, then left. The pain was gone.

"What did you do?" I asked before jumping out of the car, spinning my body around in circles, turning my neck from side to side.

"Therapeutic Touch," Nicki said, reminding me of a course she took a few years earlier.

I'd forgotten about her course, and the childhood experiences with *Nonno*. Those memories of my grandfather's healing gift returned recently, after I spent a couple of years taking classes in Healing Touch.

Fascinated by the ability to sense and feel energy, I entered a year of apprenticeship and became certified as a Healing Touch Practitioner, incorporating healing into art and writing, and periodically, like *Nonno*, I actually perform Healing Touch on another person.

Once when working on a friend, I felt my grandfather's presence, standing at my side. I swore I heard his whisper, telling me to move my hands over my friend's right shoulder. I did. The energy emanating from the spot was hot. I held my hands still until the heat subsided, and then I looked over to be sure my grandfather wasn't really standing there. Only my friend and I were in the room.

After the session was complete, she sat up and reached for her right shoulder.

"I forgot to tell you before you started that I had a pain here," she said. "It's gone."

****

Full, lush vegetation behind Gaetano's house suggests that he's inherited my grandfather's love for the land, as well as his touch with various plants. The hot Sicilian sun is a real asset for plant life. Everything on this island has a long blooming cycle—much different from the climate of upstate New York. I wonder if the colder weather frustrated *Nonno* after he moved to the United States. If it did, he never said a word.

As we leave the sunny patio and walk back through the house, Gaetano shows us an old Victrola. He puts on Puccini. Dad lifts his hands and starts directing, as if conducting an orchestra. Gaetano sings out, *"balliamo"*—to dance, reaches for my mother's hand and, in tempo, turns her gently around.

Music has always been part of our family. Uncle Joe, Mom's older brother, is a musician and owns a music store. Each of my siblings, cousins and I have at one time or another learned a musical instrument from Uncle Joe. Stagnitta Music Company, located on the Northside in the middle of the Italian section of Syracuse, was only a few blocks from my grandparents' house.

Uncle Joe played music by ear before learning to read notes. He's
talented with numerous instruments, especially gifted with the old-
fashioned, stand-up bass. He is equally skillful with the piano,
accordion, mandolin, guitar, saxophone—and the list goes on. I've
watched him pick up an instrument for the first time and, in minutes,
play elaborate chords and tunes.

Uncle Joe has a more imaginative way of seeing life, intermingled
with old, Italian customs. He's also a collector of anything that comes
through his front door at home and at the music store. He has posters
hanging of musicians and musical performances as far back as the
1940s, maybe earlier.

A few years ago, he relocated his business two storefronts down.
After visiting him at the store, I relayed to my siblings, "Uncle Joe has
moved everything, including all the instruments—the cartons they
came in, guitar picks, strings, straps, sheets of music, newspapers, and
mail advertisements. You name it, it got moved and is sitting in the
same spot it was positioned in at the other location."

Despite his eccentricities, my uncle continues to play his music for
groups, weddings, hotels, festivals and fairs. I have fond memories of
childhood, when Uncle Joe played his accordion for family holidays,
birthdays, picnics and plain old Sunday gatherings. We all danced to
the *Tarantella*—an old, Italian folk dance, the Irish Jig and any other
songs he decided to throw in.

After Aunt Josie's death from Lupus in 1962, *Nonna* insisted that
Uncle Joe leave his accordion home. Aunt Josie, only thirty-three, left a
husband and two young children. The memories that the music
brought back was more than *Nonna* could bear. It was then that the
music stopped.

****

Outside Gaetano's front door, we wait for him to bring the car
around. I step next door to my grandfather's old stone dwelling. Mom
points out more holes on the side and in the front of the building.
Bomba, everyone keeps saying, referring to bombs dropped by
Americans on the village during World War II.

"This is a quarter of your mother's house," Dad says, smirking,
knowing that the other three-quarters belong to her siblings—Uncle
Joe, Uncle Alex and Aunt Josie's two children, Walter and Ann Marie.

I suspect Dad's trying to reel me in with some facetious idea floating in his head. But I refuse to be tempted. Instead, I inspect the aged wood of the front door. Extra pieces are nailed diagonally to cover up weathered holes.

Across the top is a small opening. I peer in. Streams of light shining through the back windows illuminate the rabbits scooting about. They jump and hide when the flash from my camera scares them. After we return from our outing to Mount Etna, I plan to ask Gaetano if I can get inside.

"Your mother's related to Bugs Bunny and his family," my father says, joking, still trying to rein me in.

"Dad!" I say, in a reprimanding tone and walk away.

Gaetano pulls up in his cobalt blue Fiat on the narrow path between his contemporary home and *Nonno*'s old, weathered one. Six of us divide ourselves into two vehicles. Mom climbs in Gaetano's back seat. Rosina rides in front. Stu drives the rental car, and I sit in the navigator seat. Dad is directly behind me.

I don't want to take a chance of motion sickness on the curvy mountain roads. As a young girl, I was the child who got carsick. It's one of the many reasons my family is surprised at my love for travel.

The last time I was in Linguaglossa, Salvatore and his wife drove me up the mountain toward Etna. I was embarrassed when I felt sick and had to ask Salvatore and Marianna to roll down the car windows. They stopped and insisted I get into the front seat, where I would feel less nauseous. This time, I came prepared and pull out a homeopathic remedy that I can pop into my mouth at the first sign of queasiness.

The drive up the road towards Etna is entertaining as we follow Gaetano's Fiat. Stu points out a go-kart, sitting on top of a car. Stu not only used to race go-karts, but for the first twenty years of our marriage, he owned a business that built racing karts.

"You mean to tell me we came all the way to Sicily and we see a go-kart?" I say, whimsically remembering my pit bunny days of hanging around, waiting for races to get over.

"Let me take a picture."

"Forget that," Stu says, "We have enough go-kart pictures to last a lifetime. Get a photograph of those lava terraces."

Hardened lava, positioned in layers, divides the landscape. I pull out the camcorder again to show my siblings the terrain. They'll be able to hear our remarks too.

I look over at Stu and joke.

"I've already given Dad a couple of lectures, and it's not even noon yet."

Stu smirks, despite admonishing me over the years that I had some gall, reprimanding my own father. Stu does not understand an Italian's mind. When I retreat, my father dreams up ways to pull me back into the jostling. Dad continues the commentary under his breath.

This time, I address my siblings directly.

"Dad is not being as cordial in Linguaglossa as Mom was in Gualtieri. Surprised?"

Stu laughs, which only encourages my father. Most of Dad's comments are harmless. When Stu turns the car around one curve after another, Dad starts singing, using the tune from the song, *I Left My Heart in San Francisco*.

"I left my stomaaaaaaaaaaach... at Mount Etna..."

My husband adds his own remark.

"The next shot you'll see is Gilda hurling over the camera."

Even I start laughing, although a little dizzy, my head is whirling from the altitude. Maybe I should have taken a Dramamine, but the drug would only make me sleepy, and I don't want to miss a thing. I pop the homeopathic pellets into my mouth. They keep the wooziness at bay.

Soon we're looking down onto Linguaglossa. Behind the red-tiled roofs and gray walled buildings of the town sits a backdrop of yet another towering mountain. The higher we climb, the brighter the leaves—rust, orange, red, yellow and amber.

We follow Gaetano's car until he takes a turn and stops. Everyone gets out of the cars. Over to the left sits a row of log cabins that turn out to be souvenir shops. To the right of them, Mom points out a *ristorante e l'hotel*. An old-fashioned tow rope suspends above the mountain. Gaetano and Rosina say that their youngest daughter, Stephania, comes here often to ski.

"Ask them if we can get closer to the mouth of the volcano," I say to Mom.

Once she does, we find out that all the buses that take people up to the very top are parked for the winter. Gaetano and Rosina, like Salvatore and Marianna the last time I was here, do not recommend that we drive any further.

I started thinking that maybe they've never taken the road to the opening. Maybe by living in the presence of a volcano, caution becomes second nature. Or maybe they know something we don't.

****

Nonna and one of her sisters, *Zia* Concetta, used to tell the story about how, as young girls, they carried umbrellas to keep ash out of their hair when Mount Etna erupted. They talked about the constant threat of an active volcano.

Boiling lava, which settled along the landscape, was part of their lives. It was the fabric of their town, the construction of terraces and the color of their houses. Over the centuries, the ash attached itself to everything.

Since he could not see smoke, Dad wonders if Etna has stopped erupting. From Gaetano's description, we decipher that the smoke still billows, but away from this north ridge area and over on the other side of the mountain. Dad's disappointed that we never make it to the top. He wants to look in, and so do I.

I rationalize it away with the notion that it might be a reason to return some day. As we meander around the ski area, Mom and I walk by ourselves for a few minutes, in and out of the souvenir shops.

"Did you see me pointing when I was in the car?" my Mother whispers.

"At what?" I reply, knowing that, as short as she is, I could hardly even see the top of her head in the back seat.

"Gaetano was showing me *Nonno*'s property," she says. "I wanted *you* to see it."

I missed that ESP message. But my Italian curiosity piques.

"Do you know exactly where the property is located and would you recognize it again?" I ask.

But Mom isn't sure about anything. Instead, she tells me how she tried to avoid the conversation by not responding. *Darn!* I think. *This could be a unique opportunity.* For what, I'm not sure. Then Mom admits that she's curious about the land that still belongs to her family.

"I'll try to point it out on the way back down," she says. "Watch my finger."

As we follow Gaetano's car down the mountain, all I can see is the tip-top of my mother's head, but I can't tell if she's pointing or talking with her hands. I never am able to decipher where the property is located.

By the time we travel back down the mountain and into town, it's close to two in the afternoon. We pick up Salvatore at *Un Bar* by the train terminal, less than two blocks from his house.

As he hops into Gaetano's car, my window is down, and I can hear him say that he's made arrangements at a *ristorante* owned by a friend. We follow Gaetano's car for about a mile back up the road we just came down, toward Mount Etna, before pulling into a parking area on the right.

When Mom steps out of Gaetano's car, she and I hold back and walk together.

"Mom," I say, "I never saw your hand point out your father's property."

"I decided not to bring the subject up to Gaetano again. I don't want to make any decisions on what to do. That's up to my brothers, especially Uncle Joe. After all, he is the oldest."

I don't say a word. Instead, Mom and I catch up with the others, who are crossing the road, heading to a villa-esque building with a large sign that reads, *"Ristorante Gatto Blu"*—The Blue Cat.

25. *Gatto Blu*

Wednesday Afternoon Continued, October 25

Cat sculptures, silhouetted and cut from flat metal—spray-painted iridescent cerulean blue—sit on every table in *il ristorante*. As we walk through the front door of a fairly large eating establishment for Italy, a couple comes running over.

"Buon giorno," they say, smiling and gesturing with their hands.

Even though Salvatore made the reservations, it's Gaetano who approaches the proprietor, gently grabbing his arm and turning him away. He says something in a low voice, for only the man to hear. Mom and Dad stand on either side of me, also aware of the interaction.

"Maybe Gaetano's telling the guy to bring *him* the check," Mom says, quietly in English. "I invited them, Nick. Make sure you pick up the bill when he brings it."

"I will, I will," Dad says with assurance, never shying away from picking up his share of dinner checks.

The couple that owns the restaurant turns out to be a brother and sister, somewhere in their sixties. They direct us to a spacious, long, rectangular table that holds seven comfortably. Salvatore sits at one end and Gaetano at the other.

Mom's inclination to invite her cousins out to dinner was sparked by an incident that happened last year when Uncle Alex and Aunt Barbara were visiting. It was the day they left their tour group in Taormina and traveled to Linguaglossa.

Gaetano and Rosina invited them for dinner, but Salvatore was not included. That bothered Uncle Alex. When he returned from their trip, he told me how he went all the way over there, in the hopes of spending time with both cousins. He barely spent any time with Salvatore and felt terrible that Salvatore wasn't invited to dinner, especially since Salvatore's wife, Marianna, had recently died.

Having lived with Salvatore and Marianna that summer in 1985, it was clear to me that Salvatore was a free spirit, a person with a life of his own. Being asked to Gaetano's house for dinner was probably not something Salvatore even expected. Since the two came from separate social classes, it did not necessarily endear one side of the family to the other.

I tried to explain all of this to Uncle Alex, but he felt that an exception could have made for that one time. Then I attempted to compare Salvatore to Uncle Tony.

"You know how Uncle Tony drops in for a visit and disappears just as quickly. He does it every Christmas when we're at Mom and Dad's house."

But Uncle Alex insisted that it wasn't like that.

So together Mom and I concocted what we thought was an ingenuous arrangement—to take *both* sets of cousins out to dinner. No one will have to cook and no one will be left out. Our hope is that, when we return home and Uncle Alex hears what we did, it will settle his discontent. Of course, neither Gaetano nor Salvatore have any idea what we're up to, and both Dad and Stu agree to go along.

Dad is very cordial and social at dinner, making small talk and participating in the conversation. Rising to the occasion, he treats my mother's cousins as amiably as she treated his in Gualtieri.

Everyone eats the customary afternoon meal of *primo piatto*, pasta. For the *Secondo*, some choose *vitello,* the veal. Others order *bistecca*— thin, minute steaks. There's wine, salad, bread, fruit, water—*l'acqua minerale senza gas* and *caffè*. Mom's cousins even order *dolci*.

When all is said and done, the host hands the bill to Dad, as expected. When we stand up from the table, Dad snickers under his breath, for only me to hear.

"And your mother thought her cousin was telling the guy to give *him* the tab—what he probably *really* said was, 'See that American sucker over there—hand *him* the bill.'"

I don't want to laugh, even though Dad's comment is funny. Instead, I come to Mom's defense again.

"Dad," I say, smiling, "we were the ones who did the inviting, remember? Don't say anything to Mom."

"I won't, I won't," he says, but I can tell by the glimmer in his eyes that he's filing away the incident to resurrect it at a later time.

Once outside the *ristorante*, Stu comes up from behind me and chuckles.

"Dad says he thinks it might be a cat house."

I whip my head around quickly toward Stu, who's the one more likely to have made a remark with a sexual overtone. I glare at him.

"Who really said it. Dad or *you?*"

"No, it was your father, honest," Stu says, defending himself.

Dad walks on ahead, toothpick hanging from his mouth, snickering at his own humor. I'm a bit surprised, since he's always been rather reserved around any of his children about any suggestive innuendos—but he did make that remark about the *sexophone* back in his region.

"He's a wild man, that Dad!" I say.

Mom gets back in the car with her cousins. Stu, Dad and I continue on the next leg of the journey. It seems that Salvatore owns some property that he wants to show my mother. We follow Gaetano for a short distance before he stops on the road and turns the car right onto a piece of land with a tall, wired fence.

Salvatore gets out and removes the padlock with a key. Behind the barrier, we enter a building and find the makings of a restaurant, larger than the one we just ate at. I'm not so sure Salvatore planned on showing this property to Gaetano and Rosina, but it appears they are about to learn something about Salvatore that's unbeknownst to them.

Inside are solid wooden tables that Salvatore built himself. In the corner, on one of the tables, is a checker set. Beautiful wood beams stand throughout the space, giving a contemporary rustic look, with an open feel. There's a long-wooden bar too, and another area, where *bocce* balls sit.

According to Salvatore, he and his cronies come here and play the old Italian game. I used to watch my grandfathers and their *paesani* play *bocce*, its ancestry coming from the ancient Roman Empire.

We follow Salvatore to the back of the building. Unlike the front, it's in disarray. A kitchen—more than halfway renovated, including appliances—is covered everywhere with drywall, dust and residue. There's a bedroom next to the kitchen and mattresses, doubled over and partially hidden by layers of more dust, drywall and other bits and pieces of trash.

There are a couple of bathrooms, *toilettes,* and there's a stairway leading to more rooms. The place, huge and spacious, sits on a prime piece of property, leading to Mount Etna, where lots of tourists pass by while visiting during the summer and skiing during the winter.

During our walk through the building, I hear Salvatore bring up Uncle Joe's name a few times. The place, at least in the back, definitely has touches of Uncle Joe's music store.

"It must run in their genes," Dad says.

Fascinating how two cousins have similar patterns even though they live more than an ocean apart! Granted, they were raised together the first five years of their lives, but they haven't lived near each other for almost seventy-five years—nor have they even seen each other since the end of World War II.

Nonna Egidia was raised by Salvatore's mother, *Zia* Barbera. My grandmother never lived with lots of extra stuff around, and her sister may not have either. I know for sure that my uncle wasn't raised with clutter. *Nonna*'s house was always clear of belongings—things were put away or thrown out.

Despite the collector gene of these two male cousins—at almost eighty years old, both are still quite productive—Salvatore with his own restaurant (although closed to the public) and Uncle Joe with his music store. They each have buddies they get together with daily, drink coffee and share tales. Salvatore plays a little *bocce*, Uncle Joe his music.

Then there's Gaetano, my grandfather's nephew. He walks around, shaking his head, scratching his brow and saying, in the *dialetto* of Linguaglossa, that he never knew Salvatore owned something as nice as this building.

Salvatore—well, he's indifferent to Gaetano's response and focuses more on pointing out things to his own cousin, my mother.

****

The two sides of my mother's family—the Vecchios and the Stagnittas—remind me of the Montagues and Capulets from Shakespeare's *Romeo and Juliet*. It must have been difficult back in the early 1900s, when my grandfather fell in love with a sharecropper's daughter, my *Nonna* Egidia.

Not too long ago, Uncle Alex told me that when *Nonno* Stagnitta went home to tell his father that he'd married my grandmother, his father slapped him across the face. It was the first time I ever heard that story.

Nonno Stagnitta had gone to America with his father when he was a young man. After they returned home to Sicily, *Nonno* had his own ideas about going back to the United States. He saw the potential for great opportunities and, despite his father's demand that he give up his dream, he never would.

Both his dream of living in the United States and choosing my grandmother for a wife became an obstacle between father and son. My grandfather's father was humiliated that his son chose a woman below his family's status. But no one in the family had ever talked about it.

Nonno Stagnitta, a strong, stoic and quiet man, was the only member of his immediate family to have emigrated. He never spoke of or even insinuated that my grandmother or her family came from a lower class.

The four of the five Vecchio siblings—including *Nonna*— who lived in Syracuse never mentioned the disparity. It wasn't until I traveled to Linguaglossa in 1983 that I started piecing my grandparents' story together.

Now almost a century later, two more people who loved each other and are long since dead, left behind relatives, still playing out their families' drama.

****

From what I can discern in conversation, Salvatore started renovating this building into a restaurant. After his wife, Marianna, died, the project came to a halt. Whatever the circumstances, Salvatore owns a major piece of land in town. Gaetano continues shaking his head as we move through the various rooms. His eyes and facial expressions widen with amazement.

He holds his hand up in the air, turning his wrists around in wide circles indicating all that's here—the space, the building and the land. He keeps repeating over and over to my mother how he didn't know that Salvatore had all of this—no more than a few miles away from where they both live.

I wonder whether the cobwebs of Gaetano's old perceptions, handed down from the Stagnitta's family roots, will begin to disintegrate.

Gaetano drops Salvatore off at the bar near the train station. When Stu pulls our car up beside him to say good-bye, Salvatore insists we not get out.

"*Ciao, Ciao,*" he says, waving good-bye, his fingers gesturing backward toward himself like Italians do when they wave.

We wave back, and Dad smiles with relief.

"*There's* one guy I got out of kissing."

I remind my father that he still has one more cousin to get through. Stu follows Gaetano on the road that leads to his house

"We just came from the cat house, and now we're heading back to the rabbit house," Dad jokes.

I tell Stu and Dad how I hope to get inside *Nonno* Stagnitta's old, stone, gray home. Once there, Gaetano is more than glad to open the wooden door and let us all step inside.

"Look," Stu says, and points out the construction.

A large round arch accentuates areas of the open space downstairs. It separates the main room from the back area, where we assume a kitchen was once located. There are barrel-arches, leading into various sections.

"This must have been an elegant home in its day," Stu says.

Stu, who taught Industrial Arts and Architectural Drawing when we first met and was the general contractor for our present home, has always been intrigued with blueprints and buildings, no matter how long ago they were built. To the left of the main room in the old Stagnitta homestead, my husband points out the stairway that leads to the second floor. It's impossible to climb, now that the house is used more like a barn.

The passageway is covered with hay and blocked with shovels, hoes and other farming tools. I envision my grandfather climbing those stairs, and wish I could go up and see the view my grandfather saw from his bedroom window. I think of him as a young man, standing on the small balcony above the main doorway, looking in the direction of where my grandmother lived, less than a half a block away.

We soon head down that same street, toward the steeple of St. Egidio's church hovering in the distance. An elderly woman, dressed in black, sitting on a chair facing the door, glances at us in her periphery as we walk down the road.

I once read that the reason Sicilian women sit facing doorways is so that they don't sexually tempt men by making eye contact with any that walk by. There are few women left, mostly older, who follow the custom of turning their chair away from the street. Those days are obviously dying, or in most cases, are already dead.

This street, where my grandparents once walked as young people, is the route that takes us to the church, a block away. At a small, triangular *piazza*, in the middle of a quiet intersection, stands an old, yellow-gray Romanesque building, a small walkway, a lamp post and a sign, with the words scripted—*chiesa di sant-egidio abate patrono della città*. The church of Saint Egidio Abate, patron saint of the city, is the same patron saint my grandmother and I are named after. I go up to the church doors. They're locked tight.

There's still no way to get inside. The first time I was in Linguaglossa with my sister, Teresa, and cousin, Marisa, they told us we could get in only on Wednesdays. The second time I stayed at Salvatore and Marianna's house, I made sure I was there on a Wednesday. I still couldn't get inside.

This time, Mom and I had hoped we could enter. Neither Gaetano nor Rosina knows how to get inside of the church. Mom will never push her cousins into finding out, and after three different trips and attempts, I am terribly disappointed. If the people who live here don't know how to get inside, how will I ever figure it out?

While my mother and father stand in front, talking with Gaetano and Rosina, Stu and I move around the exterior of the building, taking pictures from different angles.

Afterwards, we all meander down the side streets to the busier roads that lead to the main *piazza* and center of town. It's bustling with people and cars. We end in front of what is considered the major cathedral—*chiesa madre madonna delle grazie*—Church of the Mother Madonna of Grace.

As everyone continues smiling and chatting, it's obvious that Gaetano and Rosina have warmed up to my mother. I'm not surprised. Mom is a great listener and full of kindness. It's close to five in the afternoon when I hear her tell them we'll be leaving. They encourage us to come back to their house.

In fact, Gaetano starts wishing aloud that they had prepared a meal for us, and he even begins to question his wife about food. Rosina's eyes open wide, obviously surprised at his remark. In a calm tone, she tells him that she picked up sausages.

Mom insists that she did not come to create work for anybody, and that she's been delighted to meet them, to see her parents' hometown and to stroll the streets that her mother and father once walked.

Mom looks at me and says in English, "We've been here long enough and have taken up enough of my cousins' time."

While we wait in the main *piazza* in front of the Cathedral, Stu heads back up the street and into the old neighborhood to get the car. As I watch the comfortable gesturing that Gaetano and Rosina have with Mom, it's obvious they aren't ready for her to leave.

At the last minute, they throw in another place they want to show us—their older daughter's condo that she and her husband live in when they come from Catania to visit. By this time, Stu pulls the car up across the street and runs over to say his good-byes.

Mom suggests that we can see the condo and other sites we missed next time, although getting my mother back to Sicily seems unlikely. She thanks Gaetano and Rosina, and we all begin our rounds of kisses. When Dad isn't looking, I quickly take a camcorder shot of him kissing Gaetano good-bye. Stu and I snicker behind his back, knowing he won't see the clip until we get home to the states.

As we drive down the main street, the waning sunlight accentuates the ashen gray and black of the town. Just as I think of rusts and browns with Dad's hometown of Gualtieri, it's the lava grays from Mount Etna that I associate with Linguaglossa.

"I wish I thought of asking about going to the cemetery," Mom sighs,

"Do you want to come back tomorrow?" I ask.

"No," Dad says, vehemently.

"I didn't ask you, Dad," I say, staring at him as he sits in the back seat with my mother.

Stu pulls the car off the road and into a gas station to fill the tank. While he steps outside, I turn around in my seat and position my body to face my parents.

My mother hasn't answered my question. While giving her time to think about it, I look over toward my father.

"Dad, you were quite gracious at dinner."

A "humph" comes out of his mouth as he twists in his seat, acting as if he had a choice. Mom and I glance at each other sideways, aware that he's carrying on a bit for effect.

"He was good," Mom replies. "He can offer it up."

"Yeah, Dad," I say. "Offer it up for the souls in Purgatory."

He ignores our little dig and announces that he's ready to go back to the hotel. I tease him about wanting to watch *Walker, Texas Ranger* on television. Then I turn toward Mom.

"Did you see enough, Mom?" I ask, "Do you want to come back tomorrow for more?"

"No way," Dad says.

She giggles and says, "No, I've seen enough."

I'm not convinced, but I can tell her attention is returning to Dad.

"We need to get back to the hotel," she says, and I know it's because that's where Dad wants to be.

26) Leaving Taormina

Wednesday Night & Thursday, October 25 & 26

Exhaustion has set in. If Dad's watching *Walker, Texas Ranger* on TV, I don't hear a thing—neither the groan of the television nor Mom and Dad's voices. We all fall asleep.

It's almost 9 p.m. before we manage to get ourselves up and out for a late, light Italian-style dinner. We walk into town and down the stairs of the alleyway, past the tiered *ristorante* that Stu, Mom and I went to last night.

We take a left and decide to try another place, for variety. Variety in Italian food seems somewhat of an oxymoron. There are different sauce recipes for pasta. Even though salads, meats and vegetables are seasoned with similar spices—oregano, basil, parsley, olive oil and an assortment of wine vinegars—how they're prepared depends on the region of Italy.

Suggesting to a native born Italian that there are few differences is always an insult. People from the northernmost mountain towns to the southern tip of Sicily perceive their cooking and their way of life as unique.

At the *ristorante*, we sit at a sidewalk table by the doorway, where we can talk while watching people meander about the street. None of us are very hungry, so we order a few items to split.

But instead of bringing one small *antipasto*, the waiter appears with a vast array of *antipasti* on an extra-large platter. It holds cold cuts, cheeses, lettuce, tomatoes, olives and a selection of other trappings, including the customary fare of thick-crusted bread.

Behind our waiter, another server follows—not with the small salad we ordered, but with an enormous bowl of lettuce, tomatoes and a number of other raw green vegetables, enough to feed a family of ten. And the two sandwiches we plan to split between the four of us haven't even arrived!

I know we're being taken! When Dad questions the error, the waiter shrugs his shoulders without offering to make changes. He's playing what back home we'd call "possum" as he quickly disappears into the restaurant. I'm surprised Dad lets it go, but he's on vacation. Dad's often been quoted by one of my siblings or me as having said,

"If you can't afford to splurge a little on vacation and have to count every penny, you may as well stay home."

On the other hand, I'm irritated with this place's blatant disregard and want Dad to be assertive. Even though I go round and round about the food they choose to serve, despite what we ordered, Dad and Stu insist that it isn't worth fussing over.

"Fine," I huff. "*I'll* say something! I can make myself understood."

Stu looks directly in my face.

"Listen," he says, "I'm asking you as a favor not to say anything."

Uncomfortable and agitated, I shuffle side to side in my seat. Stu's so easy-going that he rarely asks me not to do something. I back off and think, *well, the waiter is young and may have been distracted.* As much as I try to convince myself, even I can't buy my rationale. I see how the owner maneuvers behind a table while watching the waiter deliver the food. He knows *exactly* what he's doing!

"Look," Dad says, to me, "If they need the money that badly, they can have it."

Mom doesn't say a word. The clenching of her teeth and hands may be a sign that she either feels the same way I do or she doesn't want to make a scene. Since Dad insists we let it go, she won't say anything. I sit there steaming.

Before leaving home, I told myself to focus on family history and not external affairs. It seems that my parents, especially Dad, are not the only force I'm confronting. There are other concerns related to my cultural heritage—money being one of them.

I think of what my brother, Gerard, said before I left.

"Remember—you are our *eyes.*"

I know he wants me to record my parents' responses while in Italy, and especially Sicily. Since money is such a high priority in the Italian culture, it's no wonder it becomes a force for me to reckon with. Facing my inherited perception of money is not something I want to tackle on this trip.

Why does it bother me so much to be taken advantage of? And why would the person who owns this restaurant set his patrons up to be ripped off?

At one point Dad says, "They've got to make the money when the tourists are here." And then, as if reading my mind, he says, "The guy is only ripping us off if we don't know he's doing it. I'm aware of what he's doing, and I don't care."

Money is the very ploy that I used to entice my father into taking this trip—by saying that Stu and I would pay—although by this point, my parents have spent as much on us as we have on them. But it was the attraction of the offer that made Dad say yes in the first place.

Money, wealth and currency has always been a pivotal center of the family. My grandparents moved to the United States to make a decent wage. They gave up everything else they loved by leaving their mother country to settle in a foreign place and create a better economic life for their children and future generations.

My reaction to the waiter trying to pad the bill is so automatic that it almost feels cellular. Could it be in my genes? Why else, at a sidewalk restaurant in Sicily, am I hell-bent against being taken advantage of financially, when forking over a few extra *lire* won't matter one iota to my pocketbook.

****

The last time Stu and I were in Italy alone, we eavesdropped on a tour guide with a broken but well-spoken English accent. Talking to a group of Americans at the Coliseum in Rome, she compared the differences between the Parthenon and other ancient Greek architecture to the Roman ruins we were standing in.

"For the Greeeeks," she said accentuating her *eeeks*, "Beauty was and is a central focus, each building perfectly constructed. Neither time nor costs mattered."

That made sense. I explained that same concept when I taught the Parthenon in Art History at the community college I taught at in North Carolina. But the next statement that came out of the tour guide's mouth was not part of my course curriculum. It made me cringe.

"Now the Italians," the woman stressed, "They were more interested in cutting costs, saving…"

And then her voice trailed off. She stopped talking, held her hand up in the air and rubbed her thumb against her first two fingers. The motion suggested money—*soldi*. She continued telling the tourists that Italians made decisions based on the dollar, the *lira*, the *drachma*.

Money, the value of it and the possessions it provides or represents, has been a high priority of almost every Italian I've ever known. It is part of my ancestry's sensibilities, so it must be mine too, whether I'm comfortable with it or not.

****

At the end of dinner, Dad pays the bill, which of course reflects the amount of food that was served. Nothing more is said. I don't know why it's bothering me more than anyone else. I keep telling myself that I hate being taken, and I do. I feel like a squirrel, chewing over and over on one nut, unaware of the exquisite tree it dropped from. At the same time, I can't seem to let go of my obsession.

When we get back to the room, I carry on some more with Stu about hating having anyone take advantage of me. He listens until his eyes droop. I write in my journal for a while, wondering on paper how to rid myself of the poverty mentality.

Thursday is a day off from traveling. We meander into Taormina late morning to look around a bit and cash some traveler's checks. Since the American newspaper never arrived yesterday at the hotel, Dad picks up one in town and finds out that the Yankees are ahead in the World Series. He's pleased.

It's only the second time during our entire trip that there's a light drizzle—the other being that first day in Rome. Stu runs back for umbrellas. Since the weather's getting a bit chilly, he's going to grab our sweaters too. We spend a good deal of time meandering in and out of shops and walk much further down into the town than we've been before.

To our surprise, we run right into a taxi stand. Everyone but me wants to return to the hotel and relax. I'm relieved that my mother won't have to trek back up the stairways. Her heavy breathing, from two nights ago, did subside and has not returned.

On my own, I move in and out of Taormina's small stores, boutiques and souvenir shops to do some Christmas shopping. I pick up calendars with various views of the island, Sicilian T-shirts for nieces, nephews and godchildren, and I purchase a slew of wooden and gold Florentine trays for my siblings, a few cousins, aunts, uncles and friends.

It's the first time on the trip that I'm by myself. At home, most of my day is spent alone in the studio. But I've grown used to having Stu and my parents near. It feels more like life growing up in Syracuse, where someone was always around to talk with. I easily fall into that way of living.

When I'm at my parents' house and kids are running around—dogs dashing in between, the phone and doorbell ringing—life seems more normal. When I return from being with family, I'm lonely. I'll call my siblings or parents, weaning myself slowly from the family energy.

Having stayed up into the early hours of the morning to talk and play catch up with everyone, I get less sleep in Syracuse. So bedtime back at my own home in North Carolina is usually early for a few nights. The other part of the story is that I wear myself out with extra external stimuli.

Walking through the streets of Taormina is like being in a world that falls in between Syracuse and my own life. I don't feel totally alone here on the streets. People passing by have features like me—short of stature, dark eyes and hair, Roman looking noses. And everyone has something to say along the way. Clerks in the shops comment about things I buy or someone else buys.

A stranger on the street remarks about a dog off its leash, a car cutting someone off, or the taste of a drink they sip. Italians address strangers, just because they're there, and I'm included. At home, I may be more suspicious about anyone who wants to know too much about me. In this environment, it feels normal. If someone realizes that I'm an American, they ask where I'm from, how long I'm staying in Sicily and when I'm flying home. We'll be in Sicily for only one more complete day before catching the train back to Rome early Friday morning.

****

When we awake in Taormina on our final day here, we see snow settled on the summit of Mount Etna. The warm autumn of a few days ago has cooled overnight. We gather all of our additional purchases and stuff them into the folded cloth suitcases that we brought along for souvenirs and gifts. Before we drive down from the mountain town, there are two more places to see.

Stu drives out of the eastern-most town gate on *Via Cappuccini* and *Via Fontana Vecchia*, through a very small *piazza* and onto *Via* David

Herbert Lawrence. We're heading for the villa that D.H. Lawrence, the writer, once lived in back in the 1920s.

The roads leading there, like most others in Taormina, are narrow. We periodically pull over to the side, letting other cars coming from the opposite direction pass by. If it weren't for the plaque that reads, "D.H. Lawrence, English author, lived here 1920-1923," I would never figure out that the pink and cream-colored building, which now appears to be part of a condominium, is that villa.

Now a private residence, we only stop long enough to take a quick glance then turn around and head back up the same roads we came down. In looking at the map, it appears that our final destination is a distance from the center of town.

But to our surprise, we end up back at the entrance to the pedestrian only street. Less than two blocks away is the archeological Greek theater, *Teatro Greco*. Stu finds a tight and perhaps not-quite-legal parking spot. But there are cars parked every which way, and no one, including the *polizia* standing there, seems to care.

In our early planning stages, when no one was sure what to expect from relatives, we left the door open for the possibility of driving further south to *Siracusa*, where larger and grander ruins can be seen. Dad talked about the ruins there when he came back from his trip, thirty years ago. Now that our time in Sicily is coming to a close, *Teatro Greco* will be our only opportunity to see one of the many archeological sites on the island.

The Greek Theatre was carved out of the hillside, sometime back in the 3rd century B.C. According to the historical information available, it was rebuilt at the end of the first century A.D., under the Roman Empire.

We walk up a slight incline before reaching the ticket counter. When I casually mention that my father came from Sicily, the woman only charges Stu and me for tickets. Mom and Dad get in for free.

We enter under a colossal arch and through the front passageway to the site where the animals and gladiators once fought. In the distant hillside, we can see sections of spectator seats. At first Dad acts enthused, and then, with a quick twist of mood, he changes his tone and comments, sarcastically.

"How exciting."

"You don't like this theatre?" I say, surprised.

He mumbles something under his breath about the theatre in *Siracus*a. Mom stands behind Dad, listening to his every word, even ones I can't make out.

"Well, this is better than driving down to *Siracusa*, right?" I question.

"Yeah," he says, "We didn't have time to go all the way down there."

I can't figure out his change of heart and watch his hand move up to his chin. He walks around, pacing a bit like he does at home when he has something on his mind. Stu's disappeared around the outside perimeter of the ruins.

There's no way Mom and Dad can scramble up and over the stones and columns that have fallen over the centuries. The trail is broken and unstable. In a short time, Stu reappears, talking about the remains that he saw.

"I paid to see ruins?" Dad questions.

"You didn't pay for anything," I reply, "Stu and I paid. You got in for *free*."

"Oh, because I'm old," he says, as he shifts from complaining about the ruins to a more melancholy tenor.

I pick up on his sadness.

"It isn't because you're old, Dad. It's because you came from here."

"Yeah," Mom says, in a lilting voice.

"Really?" Dad says.

"Didn't you hear me tell the woman out front that you were from here, and when she heard that, she said you didn't have to pay?"

"I thought it was because of my white hair."

"That too!" Mom says, trying to lighten the mood.

That's the part of Mom that I must have unconsciously seen in Stu when I married him—the two of them were always trying to shift conversations into a lighter mode. I appreciate that part of their disposition.

I wonder about Dad, though. Is he reminiscing about his times in Sicily at a younger age, when he could still climb ruins and hike roads that were easier for him to reach? It doesn't seem to bother Mom. Then again, she's never been in *Taormina* or *Siracusa*, *Linguaglossa* or *Gualtieri* as a younger person. It's Dad musing over his past.

We stand at the floor of the *Teatro* to scan the view. Pieces of pink marble columns lie on the ground. Nearby, large stones are carved in either Latin or Greek letters. I'm not sure which—ΦINSTOYΣ AB.

I take a couple of quick photos, hoping that when I return home to ask my sister JoAnne's husband, who teaches Latin and other languages, the translation. Mom's on the same wavelength.

"You can ask Tim what that means," she says, when she sees me taking the photo.

"Well, we're about to leave the Linguaglossa-Taormina area," I say.

Dad who's sitting on one of the large stones says, "*Linguaglossa, Lingua piccola.*"

Piccola means small in Italian. I look at him and I know that in that nanosecond, he's shifted from melancholia back to being a scorch. His comment is for Mom's sake. She knows it and pretends to ignore his remark. Still, she meanders over close to him.

The two of them have a running debate about whose family came from the larger town in Sicily. When I returned from my first trip to Sicily, Mom broke into a wide smile after I announced how much larger Linguaglossa is than Gualtieri Sicaminò.

Now that the two of them have seen the actual sizes of their towns, Mom pretends to ignore Dad while still snickering at his commentary. I ask my mother to tell me what she thinks about Linguaglossa and how she feels about leaving her region. I turn on the camcorder, wanting to capture whatever she has to say. Mom starts to squirm. She hates being the center of attention.

"Well, here's the region," she says. "I saw where my parents were born."

As we all listen intently, she turns her head away, smiling shyly. I try to get her to say more.

"It was interesting," she says.

"I came, I saw, I conquered," Stu comments, reflecting the mood of the Roman ruins.

"Yeah," Mom says, "That was it—although I don't know if we conquered."

"We came, we saw, we *paid!*" Dad jumps in.

Stu laughs. I do too. There's no way Dad will never let the bill that he picked up for dinner in *Linguaglossa* be a thing of the past. That would be too easy. But I insist that Mom have the last word.

"It's your region, Mom. Dad will have another opportunity."

He stays put, sitting on the same stone. She stands next to him. Dad's smiling again.

"My region?" Mom says, shrugging her shoulders, scrunching her nose and mouth. "I didn't buy it."

I laugh. *Ah, that money thing!* It just sneaks in when least expected.

"But did you enjoy seeing your parents' hometown?" I nudge.

Mom stands quietly, her face a little more sober now.

"Yeah, very good. It was very good."

Dad quickly comes to her rescue. He uses an intimate language that belongs only to them.

"*Sai contenta?*" my father asks my mother, in *dialetto*, wanting to know if she's content.

"*Si,*" Mom responds, more strongly to him.

"*Va bene,*" Dad says firmly. *It's good*—suggesting an end to my inquisition.

Then Mom comfortably raises her hand, as if saying good-bye to the air. Just like many of the relatives we've met, she holds her hand with her fingers pointing back toward herself.

She waves goodbye to her family's town and smiles.

"*Ciao,*" she says.

27) Taormina to Messina

Friday, October 27

By mid-afternoon, we're in Messina, battling the traffic and checking back into the *Hotel Paradis*, where we stayed when first arriving in Sicily. There are fewer people around, especially for a Friday. The front desk staff seems less welcoming while they busy themselves with chores.

To reach the elevator, we maneuver around a cleaning crew, washing and polishing the marble floors. It feels like the autumn tourist season has come to a close. Minutes after we check into our room, Dad comes knocking at our door.

"There's no hot water," he says.

As it turns out, there's no hot water in their room only. We have plenty. The hotel staff tells us that the boilers for the other side of the building were turned down earlier in the day. It's going to take hours before they'll work again.

They move Mom and Dad down the hall, kitty-corner from us. Their accommodations have only an angle view of the water. Ours has a straight-on look at the bay. We offer to trade, but my parents are satisfied with hot running water, a clean room and a bed to sleep in. Their attention is shifting toward home.

The four of us go together to drop off the BMW at the *Europcar* office, which is within walking distance of the main cathedral. Messina is a good sized place to transition from town to city life before we leave the next morning for the more frenzied metropolis of Rome.

Because Messina is still fairly busy, I find myself particularly attentive to my parents' physical well-being as we walk toward the *Duomo*—Messina's main cathedral. At one point, they lag behind. I stop, look back and check to be sure that they are cautious of cars zooming around a corner where we need to cross.

After I feel confident that my parents cross the street safely, I see my father's head disappear. The next thing I know, he's on one knee. I hurry back. Dad is tying my mother's shoe.

"I could have done that," I say, to him. "Why didn't you ask me?"

As soon as the words come out of my mouth, I wish I'd tended to my own business. I can see by the look on my parents' faces that they are in a personal space of their own.

I'm surprised that my father doesn't seem to mind leaning down and tying Mom's shoe. His tenderness catches me off-guard—when he softly tells her to be careful and hang onto his shoulder.

I want to cry. Since the night in Taormina—when Mom was breathing so heavily and I feared she'd have a heart attack—I've obsessed off and on about her health. I hate even acknowledging that she isn't the same spry mother etched in my head.

It's odd that it's her health I find myself concerned about, since it's Dad who's had the various operations—two heart, one torn-leg ligament and a number of other surgeries and procedures. Dad's been dying since I was eight years old. He was one of the first people in central New York to have open-heart surgery. Despite or because of his health problems, he's been very conscientious about eating and exercising.

Mom, who's never had a hospital stay outside of nine deliveries, is the one who's not as conscientious about taking care of herself. A typical Italian mother, she puts the rest of her family's needs before her own. Whenever I get angry over what Mom is doing, I make myself shift and think of her finer qualities—kindness, caring and her unconditional love for others.

My sisters and I have tried for years to talk to her about exercising, eating healthier and putting herself first. Sometimes Teresa, because she's the one living near my parents, has taken the bull by the horn.

Together she and Mom get on a health regiment—no cookies, no chips and no bread. Teresa's rationale is two-fold—one to help my mother and the other to keep her own health in check. I'm sure my mother loves it, because it gives her something to do with my sister.

Whenever I call home, Mom tells me about how she and Teresa food shop together, share recipes, talk and organize around their new health routine. It supports my already existing belief of how much Mom's interest revolves around spending time with family, in any way she can. A benefit for us, but what about her?

****

My mother was ninety-five pounds when she married my father back in 1947. Dad still teases that her parents never fed her as well as he has—which, of course, we've all known is just not Italian.

I have an abiding image of my mother, when she *wasn't* pregnant, soon after her 30th birthday. She's moving quickly and gracefully down *Nonna* Egidia's front porch in Syracuse. Her long jet-black hair rests gently over her shoulders onto a soft-pink, chiffon shirtwaist. The dress, belted in the middle, highlighted her narrow waist.

Mom's Greta Garbo legs, accentuated by the seamed stockings that ran, perfectly-straight, up the back of her leg, and stylish, thick, high-heeled shoes, reminiscent of the times, made her appear taller than her five-foot frame.

I was only eight years old at the time—it was five years before Aunt Josie died. Mom and Aunt Josie were close as sisters and were like best girlfriends. My older sister, Nicki, and I listened to their conversations as we sat around kitchen tables over cups of coffee.

There must have be even more intimate discussions, when we got up and went out to play—the kind of talk that only exists between women who feel secure with each other.

Mom had a real soul connection with Aunt Josie. They were from a generation that rarely analyzed every thought and feeling, like Mom says us girls do. Over the years, I've shared my most intimate joys and fears with one or more of my five sisters, as well as Aunt Josie's daughter. Mom and Aunt Josie were the role models for that intimacy.

I first noticed my mother shifting away from taking better care of herself after Aunt Josie's death. When I was thirteen years old and only weeks away from starting my freshman year in high school, my aunt died. I remember how my mother came home from the hospital and turned her head away as she ran into the side door of the house— while my father encouraged us kids to stay outside for a while. Mom must have needed time to gain her composure.

My mother had two more children. JoAnne, named after Mom's sister, was born eighteen months after Aunt Josie's death. Four years after that, Bridget, the youngest, was born. Caring for eight children and a traditional Italian husband couldn't have been an easy task, although taking care of children suited Mom. No matter what our calling, if our most intimate confidant is gone, and there is no place to express our deep feelings and frustrations, we either give up or find another source.

Over the years, my sisters and I have tried all kinds of ways to get Mom to take care of herself. My brothers have participated in their ways too. We've sent gift certificates for manicures, pedicures, massages and facials. But Mom's grief for Aunt Josie, like her own mother's losses, must be deep.

Mom, of course, used every certificate we've ever sent. Not only because she wants to acknowledge our gifts, but she would never want to see our money go to waste. Her focus now, more than ever, is Dad—the good things that he does, but most especially, the things that drive her crazy.

I've often blamed my father for not providing the emotional support that my mother has needed. After fifty-plus years of marriage—watching my father bend down in the streets of Sicily, in his own region of Messina—makes me see how Dad cares for my mother in the warm tone he uses when telling her to hang on while he ties her shoe.

Watching Mom accept this gesture adds a softness I never knew existed between my parents. The two of them share something that, even I, as their offspring, could neither reach nor explain.

For decades I've focused on my father's shortfalls. Finally, in Sicily, I'm beginning to balance his shortfalls with his strengths. Perhaps by accepting *all* of who my father is, I can forgive him for not being what I thought he should have been, and in this process, accept the human frailties of my mother and myself.

Scaffolding encases the exterior wall of the 12th century *Duomo* now being renovated. We walk around the outside of the Cathedral on a fairly wide street for Italy and come to the main *piazza* in front of the church. I feel sure that the bell in the detached *campanile*, or bell tower, rings on the hour.

Because there are not a lot of people gathering, my timing must be off. We all look up and study the elaborate *campanile*. Below the highest steeple, and flanked by two smaller peaks, is one of the largest astronomical clocks in the world.

On one side, two dials show phases of the planets and the seasons. Above it, a globe indicates phases of the moon. About one-third of the way down the bell tower begins a series of seven sections of niches.

In the top two niches are bronzed bells. The first are tucked behind a gilded lion that represents Messina's ancient symbol. The lion is known for letting out its terrific roar. In the second niche, two female sculptures stand on ledges, positioned inward. The niches below house a gilded skeleton and figures—the replica of a church and a chariot with horses. Messina's Duomo is known for its full mechanical performance of these figures, going into the tower through one niche and returning out from another.

****

In 1985, with Aunt Mary and Uncle Peter, I actually saw the figures moving in and out of the niches. Uncle Peter's nephew picked us up in Gualtieri to visit Messina. The bustling of the streets that day contrasted the quiet countryside, *campagna*.

Like all other Italian drivers, Uncle Peter's nephew drove madly around corners, over curbs, dashing frantically through the streets. He pulled the car up into the *piazza* and told me to jump out just in time to hear the noon bells ringing and see the figures moving around, like an old Swiss clock.

The lion roared. It was the peak of the summer season— quite different from now—as today's quiet *piazza* has only a few tourists winding about outside of the *Duomo*. We ask a local walking by if the figures will move and if the bells ring at five, but he explains that only happens at noon each day. We missed our chance.

We scoot inside to see the *Duomo's* interior. It's fairly modest and simple. A few sculptures rest against the walls. After walking up to the main aisle, we discover that a priest is getting ready to offer a Mass at the left altar. I watch my father shuffle around with anticipation.

He approaches Stu and me and says, "I'd like to stay for Mass and hope you don't mind."

That's a turn of events, Dad asking me if we'd mind. When my father wants to attend Mass, nothing ever stands in his way. Before both of us have a chance to say it's perfectly fine, Mom hurries over and comes to Dad's defense.

"Your father hasn't had much opportunity to go to Mass. It won't take that long."

She must be expecting me to react disapprovingly, like I've done in the past, but I don't feel that way. I do tell Dad that I hope he's okay with us looking around the church at the sculptures instead. He seems relieved.

It finally dawns on me that, at seventy-six years old, my father shouldn't have to put up with my resistance. I'm his offspring—not his parent, his adult daughter—not his child. Like my practice back home of getting into the studio early and drawing angels—Dad's ritual of attending Mass is equally important to him. Are the struggles we've had beginning to disappear? Is the on-going conflict between us vanishing?

Mom, Stu and I head to the other side of the apse, tracking a few artifacts along the way. Tucked into a corner, we discover an exhibition space that houses art and other archeological remnants of the previous churches that stood in place of this cathedral. A tour guide, included in the admission fee, explains the history of objects from various Medieval Norman churches that have come and gone on this site. Sicily's history is one of invasions and inhabitants of various cultures.

In 1908, an earthquake devastated the church that stood in this spot. Rebuilt after World War I, that structure fell victim to the American bombings of World War II, and another cathedral was reduced to ruins.

It's humiliating to be an American listening to the destruction caused by our bombs. This part of my history—from my American roots—that I've not known about. Then again, there is still more history, including my own family's past that I long to discover.

After leaving the *Duomo,* we return to our hotel and have a quiet meal downstairs—in the same place where we ate when we first arrived in Sicily. Bedtime is early tonight.

The next morning, Stu and I awake long before the travel alarm goes off. Stu can wake, doze and fall sleep again. I cuddle next to him for a short time before stepping out onto the balcony.

Below us stands a large beige, rust and yellow building. It must be occupied by a number of families. There are two layers of patios—one is on the roof, the other, a level below, extends out on the side of the main structure. Greenery and awnings cover the lush terraces.

Beyond the building lies The Straits of Messina, the water calm and still. Within a few hours, we'll be sitting in the belly of the ferry on the train that will take us back to the mainland, then north to Rome.

There are no sounds of motors whirling in the streets below. A golden-morning light, della Francesca-like, makes the experience surreal. Peace and gratitude wash over me.

How fortunate to have this time with my parents, to have been with them in the towns of our ancestors. Growing up, I never dreamt of coming here to Sicily. As far as I knew, it was out of reach. I don't know why, but back in the early 1980s, I had this passionate urge to prepare for a trip to Italy.

I was merely stopping by my families' hometowns to see what they looked like. My interest in traveling to Italy was mostly for the art. Maybe the inner voice that prodded me here all those years ago did it under the disguise of seeing Italian art but was, instead, slowly leading me down the path of discovering my own past.

****

We settle into our first-class compartment, knowing we have a full day of travel before we arrive in Rome early this evening. Dad announces that he would love to return to Gualtieri the following August and attend the St. Nicholas feast. Mom sits quietly on the right of Dad, trying to stay inconspicuous.

"Do you want to come back, Mom?" I ask.

"I'm fine," she says, "I may not come back."

Her voice is low. She is still smiling, but I can tell at this point that Mom is satisfied with her experiences and is ready to head home.

I understand. As much as I love being here, I'm *also* ready to go home. I'm getting tired of thinking in another language, even though Dad has taken the task of speaking.

Being back on the train and knowing that we'll be traveling up the coast and into Naples makes me think of my father's story of going there as a young boy. I still can't believe my grandmother let him travel alone at such a young age.

"Dad, tell us about your trip to Naples again."

"I was thirteen, and I took a train from *Pace del Mela e arrivai a Napoli*."

"In English, Dad," I say.

He's done that a number of times now, speaking to us in Italian— or to some of the relatives in English. We all laugh, including Dad himself. He continues telling us about the man who was supposed to have met him in the train station in Naples, but the guy never showed.

"People were walking and trying to distract me, so they could take my valise," he says.

"Valise?" I question, he's never before referred to a suitcase as a valise.

"Yeah," Dad says.

"Is that like a valance," Mom says, laughing.

Stu laughs too, but Dad ignores their comments and keeps telling his story.

"Next, I went to the police station. When I got there, I stood next to the building. In case someone tried to do something, I'd run in. But the police officers, they closed the shades and turned off the lights. This was four o'clock in the morning. So I got a taxi—a horse taxi," Dad says. "A horse and carriage. The driver took me to the place, and…"

Then he stalls. I imagine that he must be thinking about where it was he was going.

"To the Black Madonna," Stu chimes in, humorously.

Mom, Dad and I laugh. Dad looks at Stu, who snickers. I can tell that Dad is amused with Stu's slight disruption.

"No," Dad says, and keeps on as if he hasn't been interrupted. "…the place where this guy lived. He'd forgotten about me and overslept. But he walked me into his house. When daylight came, he took me where I had to go to get the papers done that I would need to travel to America. Then he put me back on the train and I was able to return home."

"And did you go via Messina on the train?" I ask.

"*Si*," Dad replies, and stops briefly before both he and Stu translate the word in unison.

"Yes," we all laugh.

"Thank you, Dad, for that story," I say, looking over at Mom, and then at Stu. "Any commentary from the peanut gallery?"

"I'd rather have the peanuts," Mom says, with that open-wide grin of hers—shrugging her shoulders, laughing slightly while she wiggles her hand, like Groucho Marx used to do with his cigar.

Stu replies a simple, "No," unable to top my mother's performance.

"I returned back home to Gualtieri safe and sound," Dad says.

While listening to Dad's story, the ferry has already started moving.

"*Messina bellina*," Dad says. "We better head up."

Since I promised Dad an opportunity to give final remarks in his region, Dad, Stu and I made plans to go up to the boat's deck and wave goodbye to Messina. Mom has decided to stay and watch the luggage.

When we were children at the beach, Mom would tell us all to go ahead into the water with my father while she stayed at the blankets.

"Someone has to watch our things," she would say.

And now, smirking, she says, "You're all going up and leaving me in the hole."

Her comment stops me cold.

"That's what *Nonna* used to say, remember?"

"I traveled the *whole-a* way in the *hole-a*," were the words my grandmother, *Nonna* Egidia, used when describing her trip in the under part of the ship from Sicily to the United States in the early 1900s.

We head upstairs and leave Mom for a short time by herself in the *hole-a*.

28) *Ciao, Messina*

Saturday, October 28

"*Ciao, Messina!*" Dad says as he looks toward the mainland.

The ferry has already pulled away from the dock before we arrive on deck. The day is as blue and clear as when we first entered Sicily—a bit chillier though, with the month of October now coming to a close.

Dad continues his farewell.

"If I don't see you here anymore, I'll see you in the next life."

"Yeah, but you're coming back next year," I say, trying to keep Dad focused on life versus death.

"*Mia figlia dice torneremo* next year!" Dad says, exclaiming that *his daughter states he'll be back next year!*

"For the feast," I add.

"*Per la festa di Gualtieri Sicaminò,*" Dad proclaims, holding his head high, his hometown's name rolling perfectly, in fluid *dialetto*, off of his tongue.

"And one of your other children will come back with you," I reply.

"And one of my other children will return with me, if they can *afford* it," he says, laughing at his own remark before repeating himself in Italian.

Then, in distinct English, and still chuckling, he added, "I hope they save their money for both of us."

"Is that the only way you travel?" I ask.

"I only travel free."

"Dad," I say, "I think you spent a few bucks of your own."

"Maybe a few," he responds, brushing it off and changing the subject.

"Hey," Dad says. "We didn't see the whacha-ma call it."

Stu has laughed at me when I use the same expression while grasping for the name of a person, place or thing. If Mom were with us, she would quickly fill in the blank.

"What did we not see, Dad?"

"The statue."

We walk around to the backside of the boat. The day has an even more glorious azure cast from the stern, where the Straits of Messina widen behind us. The ferry leaves a broad, white wake. There are few clouds in the sky. The air is sharp and crisp. Since we arrived on the deck late, I'm afraid we've traveled too far. But there she is—the statue of Mary, protecting Messina's harbor.

"This is nice," I hear my father say, while looking out into the sea and up at *La Madonna de Messina*.

"According to legend," Dad says, "there's no bottom under all this water—only fire. I asked the taxi driver this morning if the legend still exists. And he told me that it does and that they've never been able to find bottom."

I stare down into the water to see if there really is fire below. At first, there are only reflections of light, and then the shadow of my body twists and shifts across the waves.

I try to see deeper beneath the surface, past that shadow of myself and through legendary flames. There aren't any. The harder I stare, the more the ferry bumps and turns. Only translucent water mirrors my form. There's so much more to discover. Between the mainland ahead and the island behind, in these rough waters of the Straits, there must be a bottom, somewhere down there.

Dad turns and looks at the view of Messina. As the ferry pulls farther and farther away, his profile floats against the backdrop of the island. Boats, yachts and the docks, where the train was loaded onto the ferry, become smaller. We can still see glimpses of the train station, its tracks and a few additional cars.

Behind all that are terraced houses and buildings, the *Duomo* hangs high above the town, and I see the section of the *autostrada* that we first drove on when heading west, toward Giammoro, and then Gualtieri Sicaminò.

Dad becomes exceptionally quiet. Creases on his brow come and go. His features flip between tranquility and contemplation as he looks back at Messina.

"You'll return," I say.

"Yes, I'll return," he replies, flipping out of his meditative stance. "If someone can afford it."

Stu and I smile. My father is unrelenting.

"I want to specify," he says, as he consciously changes the mood and breaks out laughing. "I don't want to give anybody any ideas…"

Then both Dad and Stu laugh hard at Dad's insistence that he'll return only if someone else pays his way. Ah, even *soldi* is used as a distraction. Knowing my father, it will be him paying someone else's way before it's all over.

"Dad you're a trip," I say, and then I prod him along to the starboard side.

"Face me," I tell him, hoping to capture him in the camcorder, with Sicily as a backdrop. "This is a beautiful shot."

Dad turns and looks toward the island.

"No," I call out. "I want *you* in the picture."

"You're looking at Sicily, but I don't get to see it?"

"Turn around Dad and face the camera," Stu says warmly, "and tell us a story."

Being the ham that Dad can be, he turns,

"What kind of stories do you want?"

"Well it has to be Messina-related," I answer, "because this is your goodbye story. Your goodbye to Messina, goodbye to Gualtieri. *Tutti!*"

"Well…" Dad says, before falling speechless.

I prompt him.

"Did you have a good time in Gualtieri?"

"We had a good time in Gualtieri," he responds. "We had an *okay* time in Linguaglossa."

My father is biding time, trying to control his emotions, and he is using Linguaglossa as a deterrent.

"Dad, we're not talking about Linguaglossa,"

"Okay," he says, raising his hand slightly—having pulled himself together enough to continue.

"We'll talk about Gualtieri."

He starts, in *dialetto* first, saying that they had accepted us with open arms. I stopped him and made him translate into English.

I know my father is trying to compare his cousins' greetings to my mother's family's reception. I also know that the comparison is like apples to prickly pears. Dad's cousins knew him, grew up with him, and were a part of his life.

Mom's relatives, who I thought were quite responsive, met her for the first time—a long-lost cousin they never saw before. I'm not sure I'd be as willing to give up any of my days if someone called me from a nearby hotel before showing up on my doorstep.

Since I'm not a very willing participant in Dad's game, I ask him questions to keep his farewell speech focused on his town and his region.

"They wanted to do things for us," Dad says.

"Yes, they did," I say.

Then Dad starts listing his cousins' names.

"Especially Maria, *moglie di*, wife of Pasqualino. And Pasqua."

Remembering the various *antipasti* at the *ristorante* the Sunday night before we left, I add, "Carmella and Nicola, and that wonderful dinner they treated us to?"

Dad jumps right in and repeats their names.

"Carmella and Nicola. Nicola *piace la machina*."

"Dad—English."

"He likes to drive a car, and I thought I'd heave my guts out. But I fooled him."

"What did you do?" I ask.

"I kept them in," he smirks.

Through Dad's quick review of his town, he flips between English and Italian. When I point it out to him, he laughs.

"I'm so messed up," he says, holding up his hand, "When I get back home, I'll be talking to my customers in Italian."

I focus the camcorder on a small rowboat in the distance and address my siblings.

"See that little tiny boat in front of us?" I ask. "That's Dad, returning to Sicily."

The three of us chuckle, although I am fully aware that my father is now slowly shifting between thoughts of Sicily and his everyday life at Eastwood Barbershop.

All of us have begun thinking about heading home. Instead of looking back at the island, we're looking ahead at the mainland, to where the ferry will be unloading our train traveling north.

"There's Reggio di Calabria," I say, looking toward the town on the other side of the Straits of Messina.

It's time to wind up my interview, so we can get back downstairs and onto the train's car, where Mom's patiently waiting.

"Dad—you have the last word," I say as I point the camcorder at him.

"Well," he says, "we had a good time. It's been enjoyable. And Gilda behaved immensely."

"We got along, *didn't* we, Dad?"

"Eventually, I suppose, the *real* Gilda will come out, and she'll pull her hair out," he says. "Well, as long as she doesn't pull *mine*."

We have gotten along. I'm quite amazed at myself for not having flown off the handle more often, having done that with Dad so many times in the past. But I was determined this time to find a new way of relating to my father, of accepting him, of not taking whatever he might say personally.

I don't always understand my dad. On this journey I realize he's his own person, and so am I. I'm not just a product of my father or my mother.

I am a mixture of the two—the good, the bad, the beautiful, the less and most attractive elements of both parents, both families. I'm not just a product of Gualtieri and Linguaglossa, but a result of the American culture that I was raised in—the northeastern part of the United States, the Baby Boom generation, the Catholic school phenomena of the 50s and 60s.

My history is layered with elements of ancestry, religion, family, education, profession, gender and the present world environment. It's too complicated to pinpoint myself into one hole. Ah, the hole. That's where Mom is waiting downstairs for us—in the *hole-a*.

Dad looks over at me, raises his hand and waves the same wave his father—*Nonno* Antonio, used to wave, the same wave being used throughout Sicily, the same wave Mom used before she left her region—the whole hand operating as one unit, instead of individual fingers, the palm and fingers moving up and down together.

"*Ciao*, Messina," Dad says. "*Ciao*."

29) Return to Rome

Saturday p.m. October 28

"Did you forget me in the hole?" my mother says, smiling.

"We'd never forget you," Stu answers.

We settle into our seats, Dad next to my mother, Stu and I across from them. When purchasing the tickets in Messina that day we first arrived, I was sure to request both window and middle seats, so that we could see the scenery while traveling up the west coast.

The two places next to the hallway door were empty on the way out of Messina, but once we reach Reggio di Calabria, two gentlemen join our six-person compartment. They appear to be professional men, in their late-fifties, wearing suit jackets over sweaters and carrying briefcases. One has his jacket draped over his shoulders, like most men do in Italy.

At times, our travel companions get up and step outside the compartment into the hall, only a few feet away. They often turn their whole bodies toward the wide open windows facing east, speaking intently in pure Italian.

I am less interested in their conversation and more intrigued by their hand and body movements, by the look of a suit jacket, draped over shoulders. I imagine, by the subtle conversation and temperate gesturing, that the men must be conversing over a private business deal or engaged in a philosophical discussion.

Relaxed, the four of us speak only periodically, resting our eyes or reading. Mom's rereading the *Farmer's Almanac*. She mentions off and on what kind of winter to expect in Syracuse, North Carolina or another state where one of my siblings now lives.

The scenery is lush, with groves of vegetables and fruits—grapes, figs, oranges, apples and pears. It's truly harvest season. Sometimes, the train slows down and I can see rows of tomatoes, hanging from racks and terraces, still decorated with plants and foliage. Beaches are now empty. On the right side of the train, we see sporadic rounded and peaked forms of the Apennine mountain range.

When we arrive in Naples, one of the gentlemen in our compartment gets off. After a while, the man still sitting with us starts a conversation with my father, in Italian. Before long, he switches to English so that everyone can participate. He speaks English well, only stalling when grasping for a more difficult word. He is a *professore* of History at a university in Rome.

Dad tells him how I was a *professoressa* in a college at one time. I explain how I had taught art at the college level. I don't bother to mention I was an adjunct professor and that some of it was at a community college.

It was just as well, because the man made sure to mention the difference between teaching at a college versus a university. I am fully conscious of his innuendos. Having been a professional in the educational system for almost thirty years, I'm familiar with its hierarchy. I'm not surprised that the divide is alive and well, soaring even in the old country.

I'm gracious, however. My Italian-American parents raised me to be polite, and after all, they are sitting right here. My father, the total extrovert, loves telling the man about the professors, politicians and members of the clergy who've come into his barbershop over the years. I've always assumed it's not just the great haircuts, but also Dad's ability and eagerness to communicate about any subject.

We all enjoy talking to the professor, including me. I especially enjoy the chance to throw in a few side digs, since I know the vulnerable places for an Italian male. After clearing up the hierarchy of institutions, *il professore* wants to set the record straight on the differences between the northern regions of his country and the southern, like Sicily.

I've been round and round in this dialogue, often with friends who moved to the United States from Italy.

"I think the differences are more obvious to the people here," I respond. "For those of us coming from the United States, there are a lot more similarities between the regions than Italians can see."

The articulate professor does not seem to know how to respond. The lines in his brow crease. He fumbles a bit before answering.

"Maybe that's true, not seeing it from the outside looking in."

He then steers the conversation into another direction.

"Our country's young couples are having less and less children. So now the concern for productivity and care of the elderly is becoming a political issue."

Having moved past a few bristly subjects, the conversation becomes easier. Dad's in his glory, comparing the United States with

Italy in the company of a professor from his native land who's knowledgeable about contemporary and historical Italy.

The professor also verifies the legend about the bottomless sea below the Straits of Messina, passed down from native to native through word of mouth.

"Below the whirlpools, in the narrow stretch of water between Sicily and the mainland," the professor says, "is a bottomless sea, where fire brews."

As daylight starts to dim, everyone sits back and rests quietly. My mind wanders between the last hints of land that I can see and the lines from T.S. Eliot's poem, *The Four Quartets*.

> *"And the way up is the way down, the way forward is the way back..."*[1]

Trains, heading in the direction from where we'd been, pick up speed as they pass our window.

> *"When the train starts, and the passengers are settled*
> *To fruit, periodicals and business letters*
> *(And those who saw them off have left the platform)*
> *Their faces relax from grief into relief..."*[2]

The sounds of rattling from the tracks become more prominent as we approach Rome. During this last bit of time on the train, my mind floats, remembering pieces of sights, sounds, smells and moments with relatives in Sicily, and memories of grandparents, great aunts and uncles.

> *"To the sleepy rhythm of a hundred hours.*
> *Fare forward, travellers! not escaping from the past*
> *Into different lives, or into any future;*
> *You are not the same people who left that station..."*[3]

We enter Rome just past dusk and wish our companion a farewell. Within minutes, a cab driver is heading to the Hotel Columbus in

---

[1] Eliot, T.S., "The Dry Salvages," *Four Quartets*, New York, Harcourt, 1943
[2] Eliot, T.S., "The Dry Salvages," *Four Quartets*, New York, Harcourt, 1943
[3] Eliot, T.S., "The Dry Salvages," *Four Quartets*, New York, Harcourt, 1943

Vatican City. The staff welcomes us back, and we feel like we're at a home away from home.

One of the attendants hurries to get the suitcase that they stored for us. Unfortunately, the cab driver who brought us to the station when we left for Italy never did find my father's money clip. I file in the back of my mind a new money clip as a possible birthday gift for Dad.

Our present hotel suite is a bit larger than the one we had when we first arrived in Rome. But it still has two bedrooms and one bath to share. This time, Stu and I have a double-bed, instead of twins.

Since we didn't eat much on the train, we're anxious for a full dinner and head downstairs to the restaurant, located only a few yards away from the archway that leads into the hotel. We ate there during one of our meals at the front-end of our trip. They treated us well, and Dad always returns to eating establishments where the staff gives him attention.

Once again, I feel they are taking advantage of us. The waiter brings bread and adds a few other accouterments here and there. Dad thinks they're just being nice, until the bill appears and every one of their extras is added.

"How can you let them take advantage of you like that," I say, to my father.

"I told you before—they only take advantage if I let them. I know what they're doing, but it doesn't matter to me."

Before the bill is paid, I leave furious, feeling like the check has been padded here too, like the one in Taormina. I walk back to the hotel alone. Mom, Dad and Stu soon follow.

Stu comes into our room and closes the door. The expression on his face is firm, and it's the first time he's gotten mad at me on the trip. I back off and let him talk.

"That wasn't fair, Gilda," he says.

I know I'm in trouble when he calls me Gilda—since he always calls me Gilly, and usually with a lilt in his voice. This time it's a hard guttural G.

"But," I say, "I hate to be…"

Stu doesn't want to hear it and stops me mid-sentence.

"Your father doesn't deserve that," he says. "He knows what those guys are doing and sees right through them. But he doesn't *care!*"

"What about you?" I ask.

"I don't care either. What difference does a few extra dollars matter?"

Then I feel embarrassed with my own husband.

"Your father deserves an apology," he says, and then he never speaks another word.

He goes into the bathroom, comes out and gets right in bed. I'm not used to Stu being so adamant, so don't know what to say. When I try to talk, he says he's tired and is going to sleep.

I fiddle through some of my things, get dressed for bed, and then I go over to my parents' room. Mom is reading a pamphlet about Rome and Dad's sitting at the end of his bed, watching *Walker, Texas Ranger*.

"Dad," I say, during a commercial. "I have something to say."

"Yup," he says, taking off his glasses and looking at me, as if nothing has transpired.

"I'm sorry for having been so peeved at those waiters and taking it out on you."

He stares into my face, his bathrobe hanging around his shoulders and down toward the floor. It's tied loosely in the middle, and Dad's pajamas hang as freely as his robe. My father's facial expression reminds me of my grandfather's—his father, *Nonno* Antonio. Instead of a reprimand in his eyes, I sense compassion.

"It's okay, Gilda," Dad says, calmly. "There's nothing to apologize for."

"I don't know what my problem is, Dad. I hate to be taken."

I can tell by the tone of his voice and the way he's looking at me that he knows something about these feelings that I must not yet understand. Sometimes, I attribute it to a poverty that I've never even experienced. If my nose or my brown hair and eyes can be inherited, can't some of these old mental attitudes be genetically inherited too?

Maybe that's what Dad understands. Maybe, in some way, he's overcome some of this. Or maybe the trait is from Mom's side. I don't really know and don't want to lay blame. I just want to rid myself of the flaw.

As I sit down on the floor between my parents' twin beds, my father reassures me.

"I haven't thought another thing of it—nor did I take it personally."

My mother sits there, listening to my father. Then she comforts me too. I can feel their empathy—it's deep. Perhaps they've been haunted by the same feelings over the years.

"Let it go, Gilda," my mother says, in a warm tone. "We've had a great day."

30) Day Before Leaving

Sunday, October 29

Daylight Savings Time, and we are blessed to be getting the extra hour where we need it most—in Rome. There is so much to do in our final day here in Italy. We rise early and are sitting at breakfast by 7:00 a.m. The *prima colazione* at the Hotel Columbus continues to be elaborate—large long spreads of food, from eggs to platters of cold cuts and cheeses, fruits and juices, breads and pastries.

About ten minutes before eight, we enter St. Peter's Basilica for a Sunday Mass. The only early Mass available will be spoken in Italian at one of the altars toward the upper left-hand corner of the cathedral. A Mass spoken in English will not be available until later in the morning, but we want to see the Sistine Chapel at the Vatican Museum, and it will only be open this morning.

After Mass, we wait in a long, winding line for an hour and a half before finally getting through the museum's front door. I forgot that the museum is free on Sundays—the only day we were able to schedule our visit.

The tourists and people in the tour groups who wait in line with us are fairly courteous to each other. Sometimes, a pushy tour guide bumps the line if the *polizia* aren't looking and, in Italian style, shoves in their group of people. It doesn't settle well with many folks, who make faces or mutter under their breath to anyone close by.

Only a rare voice, usually in Italian, calls out. The tour guide goes into some justification, waving her or his arm and a flag, defending the position. It's usually about money and time.

I'm intrigued how some folks stay so calm, while others huff and puff. Most fascinating to me are the languages being spoken. I think of the Bible story of the Tower of Babel—everyone talks but no one understands each other.

My lower back aches from standing on my feet for so long. I recall having read in one of my mind/body books that problems with the lower back are about fear over financial security. I bet there's some connection to last night's tirade and the bill from the *ristorante*.

I ask my mother how her back is doing. She's had her own bouts with back problems. She says she's fine. Mom's not a complainer about any of her physical ailments. She reminds me of Stu. Both of them are able to suppress pain until they come to critical points that could threaten their long-term health. Dad and I, on the other hand, have both been accused of borderline hypochondria, of running to a healthcare professional at the first sign of an illness.

Dad never complains about his back though. It's not a part of his body that has given him trouble. My father's issues have been with heart and feet. That same mind/body books says that the heart represents the center of love and security, and feet—an understanding of life, in others and ourselves. I stand in line, shifting from foot to foot, resting periodically against the brick wall that circles around the corner, down the street and to the Vatican Museum.

Once inside the main door, we walk through the museum as swiftly as we can with the amount of people heading in the same direction. Our main goal—the Sistine Chapel, something Mom asked to see. Since she had few initial requests while planning, and I'm not sure we'll get her back to Italy, I'm determined to make it to this museum despite the long line.

Although the rest of us have seen the frescoes, we're all interested in seeing Michelangelo's paintings, again, including Dad who hasn't seen them since they were restored and cleaned after he was here in Rome

We follow signs through the museum and the circuitous route that points to *la Cappella di Sistina*. We stop at only a few key frescos and artifacts, lingering longer in the *Stanza della Signatura*—Raphael's room.

The Renaissance artist's infamous School of Athens from the 16th century covers one whole wall. He and his apprentices also painted the other frescos that cloak every surface in the room. I've seen this room five times, but I never tire of viewing the perfectly-formed figures that Raphael created of Socrates, Aristotle, Pythagoras and other great philosophers and scientists of ancient times.

By the time we reach the Sistine Chapel, there are crowds of people, standing shoulder-to-shoulder. Italian guards keep whispering, *Silenzio*. In spite of Michelangelo's frescos being a major tourist attraction, the Vatican security is determined to keep this space sacred. When the crowd's voices begin to rise again, the words *Silenzio, Silenzio!* ring through the jammed-packed chapel.

We stand and strain our necks to look up at the rounded form of God's hand, reaching out for Adam. A few people stand up from the wooden pews lining the walls, and we sit down, cricking our necks, again, this time from a sitting position. There's the panel of Adam and Eve, hovering around the tree, wrapped by the serpent, luring them into eating the apple.

In the same panel is the Genesis account of Adam and Eve turning away, hiding their faces after being expelled from the Garden of Eden. Other Biblical accounts are illustrated in additional panels—Noah and the Ark, the Passage through the Red Sea and Moses receiving the Ten Commandments.

I point out Michelangelo's self-portrait in The Last Judgment fresco to my parents and Stu. The artist created it twenty-five years after painting the ceiling. Michelangelo portrayed himself as a grotesque piece of skin, hanging from the hand of St. Bartholomew, who had been skinned alive. These later figures of more mature bodies contrast with the youthful, airier forms floating in the ceiling overhead.

I think our bodies have also aged over the morning's activities. We are worn out by the time we make our way out the chapel, through the museum and back through St. Peter's *piazza*.

Along the way there are hustlers with trinkets, books and religious ornaments. Dad buys a souvenir, with acetate pages that flip over on top of each other, showing how some of the ancient monuments were constructed. The vendor takes a liking to Dad and tells his own stories about having lived in the United States.

All the tourist stores are open, and we work our way past the number of pilgrims on the streets, head down the *Via della Conciliazione* and finally reach the hotel. Too tired to eat a huge meal, we take a fifteen-minute respite in our suite before heading down for a light lunch.

In the quiet surroundings, only steps away from the busy streets on the other side of the once-upon-a-time monastery walls, we enjoy the natural setting of trees and vegetation in the garden *ristorante*. It's our last afternoon meal in Italy.

After considering a tour of the city by bus, we agree that we're all too exhausted. So we go back to our rooms, and we each take a long, deep siesta. I sleep so heavily that I awake with that sense of not knowing where or even who I am.

By the time we awake, dusk has set. We freshen up and get ready to take our own evening monument tour. We walk up toward St. Peter's *piazza* to the cabstand and grab a *tassi* that takes us directly to the Coliseum. Of course it's closed, but I know my parents can't struggle up the steps anyway.

We peer through one of the lit-up, large rounded arches and can see enough of the stands where ancient spectators sat and watched the different games played during the Greek and Roman era.

It's a perfect night to walk—sweater weather. We do the evening *la passeggiata* past the illuminated Roman Forum, stopping in spots to look down into the ruins where we can see ancient stones and columns, still standing after all these centuries. It feels just right, peaceful and relaxing, with a touch of history.

That's probably why I don't propose we try to find the site, on the other side of the Coliseum, where a legendary Pope Joan supposedly gave birth in the streets during a procession from St. Peter's Basilica to St. John Lateran Cathedral. Although the Pope Joan spot is definitely something on my list to search out, I foresee three possible problems.

It's dark and I don't know exactly where the site's located. I have a street name, and I've read that there's a landmark on a side street along the way. The spot is not on any conventional tour map, and I probably will need light to find the location. Secondly, our remaining time in Italy is coming down to a matter of hours, and this is not one of the places I think my parents are interested in seeing.

Third, and the biggest of all concerns, is that I have not mentioned to either of my folks about this historical legend and my interest in finding any remaining artifacts. To bring it up now could break the peaceful mood we've established and start a feud with my father. In the light, my mother might be willing to go along. There's no point in pushing Dad about something that will only ignite a flame between us.

As I walk the streets of Rome with the people I love, I think of the psychic, who told me about being that forlorn aristocratic woman in another lifetime, who wandered the ancient streets alone. Whether this is true or not, at least I'm not by myself now. I feel at home in our casual walk around the Coliseum, past the Roman Forum, down to the Victor Emmanuel monument and the Royal Palace.

It's a magical journey with illuminated lights leading the way. There are places I still want to see, but I know in my soul that I'll be back again someday, like I have been time and time and time again.

For now, it's important that my parents get to see whatever sites tempt their interest. Dad asks to view and take photos of the balcony of the Royal Palace, where Mussolini stood during the World War II years, echoing the era of his youth and one of the nemeses that brought him, as an American soldier, to war.

We all know that soon we'll end our evening at the Spanish Steps, a promise I made to Mom when we first arrived in the country. The night air is comfortable and lots of people are out walking and moving about. Cars and Vespas—small Italian scooters, zoom up and down the streets.

Eventually, we hop a cab to the Spanish Steps, where Rome's nightlife booms. People are sitting, standing and climbing up and down the stairway. When a tourist guide comes by with a group, I eavesdrop, listening as he points out the corner building to the right of the famous set of steps and the apartments, where the writers Keats, Shelly and Byron once lived.

The guide also talks about the public fountain at the bottom of the steps. Pietro Bernini, father of the famous architect, Gian Lorenzo Bernini, designed the fountain in the shape of a boat. As we stand in the small *piazza*, looking up at the Spanish Steps, I mention to Mom about her program, *Everybody Loves Raymond*.

She smiles and doesn't say much—just that she recognizes the setting. My heart still feels heavy from my biting comment that first night we arrived in Rome.

Fashionable boutiques and shops flank the area. Somehow, I lure Stu into an upscale men's store so that I can buy him something before leaving Italy. We walk out with a silk brown shirt, woven with a touch of tweed, wrapped in an elegant, tan-colored box.

Next door, we grab a couple of sandwiches from *un Bar* to split in our hotel room before grabbing a cab and heading back.

****

At 7:30 a.m., the cab that will take us to the airport for our 10:45 flight is waiting outside the hotel walls. I drop off an envelope at the front desk for Stephania, the woman who had found rooms for us.

Dad, the only one with any *lire* left, handed me 50,000 *lire*—about twenty-five dollars—to give her. He also put in some memorabilia coins like the ones he gave his cousins. By 8:30, we're at the airport loading our luggage onto roll-around carts.

The lines for international flights are not terribly long yet. Stu and I go first through a security question-and-answer session before lining up for the counter. I turn around when I hear my father answer the attendant about whether or not he has sharp items in his luggage.

"My razor," he says, and then his voice turns slightly higher, as he motions toward his face. "I have to shave."

Stu and I chuckle. The woman's eyes widen with amazement at some of Dad's answers.

Mom stays quiet and lets Dad do the talking, although I do see her head nod back and forth once to the woman. Since Italians have the utmost respect for their elders, the woman in charge shows that reverence toward my parents.

When we finally reach the desk, we discover that, just like in Philadelphia, our seats are separate again. This time, I'm not willing to take the chance that we will find passengers on the plane who might change seats.

I also decide that Dad is not responsible for discussing this in Italian, since I'm the one who made the reservations. I am going to handle this situation. We've been in Italy long enough to remind me what stops need to be pulled out.

"Look," I say to the Italian USAir attendant, "we booked these tickets months ago. They separated me from my parents on the way over. I am *not* accepting that mistake again!"

The attendant is very apologetic, but insists there is nothing she can do. The line behind me starts to get longer.

"I'm traveling with my elderly parents," I say, "and I'm not sitting somewhere else in the plane without them."

I look over at my folks and give them one of those facial expressions that only they would understand—eyes opened wide, lips turned up only on the right side. It means, *leave this up to me and don't be insulted that I just called you elderly.*

"I'm sorry Madame," she replies, as if in rote, "but the plane is full and there is nothing that we can do about it."

I keep insisting that she find us four seats together, but she will not budge. Finally I erupt.

"Let me speak to your supervisor."

She looks around and huffs. I hate putting her in this position, but I would hate worse being put in the position of being shuffled around again. She picks up the phone and calls a man she addresses as Mario, and then she looks down toward the other end of the counter.

She's obviously communicating in Italian with a gentleman about six positions away. Despite the attendant's anxiety to move the line along, I stand there, without budging, and wait for Mario to show up.

31) Flying Home

Monday, October 30

"Wow!" Dad says proudly, after walking through the security gates, "I've known you for over fifty years, and I feel like I'm just getting to really know you for the first time. Where did you get that gumption?"

It pleases me to have my father notice that, over the years, I've learned to take care of myself in the world. Mario, the airline's supervisor, understood our situation. We had to wait to see if anyone would be checking in with children. They had first dibs on bulkhead seats.

While Mario surfed through the computer, we exchanged friendly chatter, despite my resolve to correct the present seating arrangements. I wasn't going to sit back and take it this time. Mario recognized the importance of Stu and me sitting with my parents.

A line Dad often used must have been programmed in my mind.

"First time, shame on them—second time, shame on *you!*"

Whatever was running in my hard drive, it was my intention to finish this whole trip to the end at my parents' side. I sensed that Stu might have been a bit embarrassed with my insistence. He's gone through this with me before, and sometimes it makes him uncomfortable.

But there are other times he uses it to his advantage. When we go out to dinner and end up waiting well past the allotted time we've been told, it's usually Stu who'll say, "Well, it's time to send in the big guns." Then he looks at me and says, "*You* go say something."

After having looked out into the crowd of people standing behind us, Mario decided not to wait any longer.

"Let me go ahead and give you these four bulkhead seats. Everyone taking this flight needs to be here by now."

Mario put us in the first row, four seats across the middle cabin, directly behind First Class.

As we continue toward the gate, Dad seems almost gleeful.

"Well, you told off that taxi driver on that first day here in Rome, and now this. You really are my daughter, aren't you?"

We pass down the ramp to the plane and have one more checkpoint. Standing there is the same lady who checked us through security in the terminal. It was the person Dad told about the razor in his suitcase. When the agent sees us coming, she turns around and says something to the young man next to her, and then they grin at us.

"It's us again," Dad says.

"I remember you," she replies, still smiling before turning to the guy next to her. "They're fine."

We're not only fine, but we are delighted with our seats. The bulkhead gives us room to stretch our legs and move more comfortably during our nine-hour trip back to the states.

Mom and I sit next to each other in the middle again. Stu sits on my left and Dad is on Mom's right. After having eaten so well in Italy, it's hard to process airline food. I need to start withdrawing from eating so much anyway. Once lunch is served and the food trays are cleared, the commotion in the cabin settles down.

Dad falls right into an afternoon snooze. Mom, Stu and I watch the movie, *The Gladiators*, which begins with the last day of Marcus Aurelius' reign. How appropriate after our visit to the Coliseum and The Roman Forum last night.

Once the movie is over, I look through the book that Dad bought on the street. Acetate overlays of the Forum and the Coliseum show how they both looked when they were fully intact.

There's time to sit back and reminisce. I think of how Mom seems grateful for the chance she had to see her parents' village. Her trip was a courageous step.

It reminds me of her mother, *Nonna* Egidia—she flew for the first time, at ninety years old, to one of her grandchildren's wedding. Two years later, when another grandchild got married, *Nonna* responded.

"I *don't-a* know about you, but I *go-a* fly. Driving *take-a* too long. I *mee-ta* you there."

Perhaps my mother has more of her own mother in her than she's let on over the years. At the age of seventy-three, this is Mom's first cross-Atlantic fight. Still, there were times when she's been quiet and more reticent outside of her comfort level. Dad, on the other hand, has been happier, like he always is when he goes on vacation.

As the years have moved on, my parents have grown more Old-World Italian—Mom catering to Dad's every need, and Dad expecting it. During this trip, they've stretched beyond their own limits. Dad gave up his daily dose of Mass and Communion to keep the schedule moving smoothly, while Mom challenged her own *status quo* by having taken this trip at all.

Mom says more to me after she's sure Dad is asleep, as she ponders aloud questions that she didn't think of when we were visiting her parents' town.

"I wish I asked where my grandparents were buried," she says.

"I never thought of that either, Mom," I tell her, "and I wish I figured out a way of getting us into St. Egidio's Church."

It bugs me that after three trips to Linguaglossa, I still didn't get inside the church named after my own patron saint.

Mom continues to mention things she wishes she'd done when we were there—like actually having driven onto her father's property, finding a way to the mouth of the volcano and, most significantly, tracking down a picture of her grandmother on her mother's side.

"Well, Mom—maybe we'll have to go back," I say, and she doesn't say, "No."

The closer we get to the United States, the more activity begins to pick up around the cabin. Mom is unusually assertive when the government forms are passed out. She grabs the one for her and Dad.

It's been a discussion for days about how Mom wants to tuck the thirty-four 18-Karat gold necklaces into her bra—whether Dad wants her to or not. He's been insisting that they declare every last cent. I don't think it is necessary, since together, our amounts are so close that it wouldn't be worth taking the time in customs to declare an extra dollar or two.

Of course, my father's concern is the Seventh Commandment—*Thou shalt not steal*. Once I insisted it was a waste of our time, it made an impression on my mother. She's going to handle the custom form her own way. Dad threatens Mom about agents strip searching her.

"I'll just take off my blouse," she says, laughing. "They'll tell me to stop right there!"

Mom does have that wonderful sense of humor, even though some of her other remarks still surprise me. I wish I could read her deep-seated feelings better. It brings me back to the day I labored over the word, "enigma." Perhaps I can somehow lure my mother into going back to Linguaglossa to find more pieces of that puzzle, to get a clearer understanding of her.

We land in Philadelphia only a few minutes late. Customs is a breeze for Stu and me. Mom and Dad are directed to the far right, behind a wall. There's no way I can get in there and protect them now. Why in the world were *they* chosen?

While I stand at the baggage carousel for arriving domestic flights, I worry about my parents. Now Stu's becoming anxious, choosing not to put our luggage on the conveyor belt, opting to carry it instead in the hopes that we'll catch an earlier flight home.

My husband is back in work mode—the part of him that is not so different from my father. During the last few days of our trip, Dad has been talking about getting back to the barbershop. The two of them understand each other's business minds. The premise that we marry a person who is a combination of our parents holds true in my marriage.

After fifteen minutes, my mother and father walk out—Mom, dressed casually with stretch pants and a light gray sweater that hangs to her knees, is smiling. Dad, in his jeans and old, teal, Charlotte Hornets' jacket, has a scowl on his face.

"What happened in customs?" I ask, "I couldn't get back in, and I've been concerned about the two of you."

"Oh," Mom says lightly. "We got behind a couple who had to open all of their luggage."

"What about you?" I ask nervously.

"When we got to the front of the line, they just waved us through," Mom says, matter-of-factly.

"Why is Dad grimacing?"

"Oh him—you know your father. He needs to use the bathroom."

Some things never change, *Thank God!* My parents place their luggage onto the carousel and Dad uses the men's room. Then we all walk toward the gate, where the earlier flight for Charlotte will depart.

Mom and Dad still have a three-hour layover before flying to Syracuse, and our actual scheduled flight is supposed to leave an hour after my parents' flight. I feel bad leaving them early. If we wait, we won't arrive home until almost midnight, and Stu wants to get going so that he can get some sleep before work tomorrow.

"Don't be silly," my mother says, as we all hustle down the corridor. "Your father and I can wait here together. We'll be fine."

"How do you feel, Dad, about our leaving you?" I ask.

"Your husband's got to get ready for work tomorrow. He needs his rest."

That's my father—the old traditionalist. When we reach the gate, Mom and Dad sit relaxed in a corner, away from the chaos of people waiting to get on flights.

Stu goes to the desk and puts us on the standby list. My usually subdued husband is now moving about, unable to stand or sit still, anxious to get on the plane. Once the engines start revving, our chances don't look very good. In a quick nanosecond, however, they call our names. Stu rushes over.

That's when Dad stands up and starts to pace as restlessly as Stu has been pacing. My father comes up close to hear what the status is for us getting on the flight. He's obviously uncomfortable.

"What's the matter, Dad?" I said. "Are you all right?"

"I don't know about these past two weeks," he says. "I'm not used to us getting along so well."

Just then, the attendant says that they don't have the two seats. I stop and relax, aware of my father's concern about our relationship taking a major shift.

"Well," I say, "Would it make you feel better if I start a tiff with you when we come at Christmas?"

He chuckles, although I can see he's still uncertain. My mother sits, smiling, and Stu is dancing between the desk and me. The attendant rushes over.

"Hurry, hurry," she says, "They're closing the doors. You can get on, after all."

It happens so suddenly. I kiss my parents goodbye and Stu hugs them. There is no time to analyze or say anything else about what my father has just said and about how momentous the last two weeks have been for me too.

But this intense feeling of sadness about separating wells up. I don't know what to do with it. *God! I'm not leaving home for the first time, I'm just saying goodbye to my parents after our sojourn together.*

Halloween is the next day, the beginning of the holidays. Christmas is only a short time off. I'll be seeing them again soon, although at this moment, it feels like it's an eternity.

Dad's encouraging me to go ahead, not wanting me to miss the flight—saying they'll call when they get home. Mom, who's been sitting comfortably, cheers me on, like she's always done, knowing that I'll break down if she shows any emotion.

Stu and the attendant hurry me onto the plane. I turn around and grab one last glimpse of my parents, waving me on, before the door that leads down the runway closes.

Epilogue

"...in my end is my beginning..."
Four Quartets
T.S. Eliot

I made a pilgrimage home, not only to the towns that my grandparents and father came from, but to Rome, to the Vatican and the church where I was raised. Although my frustration about the hierarchy of the church has only increased, I fell in love with Italy all over again. After returning home, it was all I wanted to think about— the time spent with my parents, the country, the culture, the people and the villages of my ancestors.

I wanted to return right away, learn the language and attempt to communicate with the one cousin close to my age—Carmella from Gualtieri Sicaminò—now living in Sorcorso. The anxiety and worry that I experienced before having left for our trip became a distant memory. Whatever divine force exists must have known I was about to experience something big.

And big it was. It turned out to be a healing for my father and me— an acceptance of him, no strings attached. It was something I've been trying to achieve for a very long time. A continuous narrative unfolded from Rome to Gualtieri, Linguaglossa back to Rome and home.

When Stu and I went to Syracuse for Christmas, I didn't pick any fights with Dad, nor did he with me. Our relationship has changed. It's not that he doesn't ever fly off the handle, like he's done in the past, and it's not like I never react like I have before. Both of us are better than we once were, at least around each other.

Dad sees the difference. On occasion, after he's carried on about something, he'll look over at me and smile. It's as if he knows I know him now. And in that recognition, there is an unconditional acceptance of each other.

During a phone conversation soon after our trip, my father told my brother, Anthony, what he said to me in the airport the day we left Rome.

"I've known your sister for over fifty years, but I never really knew her at all."

Despite the fact that I've heard it from my father's own lips, I was delighted to hear it again from my brother. I realize that the way my father tells one of us what he thinks about the other is not necessarily healthy, though it's part of our new acceptance of each other.

And I know that if Dad told my brother—the oldest male from my generation—that he saw me in a new light, then our time together in Italy made a difference. I suppose one would say it shouldn't matter what your father thinks or doesn't think. It has been a lot easier knowing that we will have passed through this life together, having healed any wounds that have held me back.

Dad has stayed in fairly good spirits since the trip. The following year, he went through some turmoil when he sold the building where his barbershop of fifty-five years had been housed. His concern was for Mom and my sister Teresa. He didn't want to leave them with excessive legal and paper work if he were to die. He struggled through a lot of uncertainty about retiring. Luckily, he hasn't had to move out of the building, so Dad is still cutting hair.

He phoned his cousins in Sicily a number of times after our trip and called me afterwards to tell me about their conversation. Mom was happy to get on the phone and talk when Dad finished. And the truth is: I love any excuse to talk to either one of them.

Dad did not return to the feast the following August. The morning after 9/11, the phone rang at my home in North Carolina at around 5:30 a.m. It was just before noon in Sicily. It was my cousin Carmella, calling from Sorcorso.

Speaking in Italian was not always that easy for me, so trying to articulate in a foreign language after waking up from a deep sleep was a challenge. I could hear Carmella's anxiety and concern as she asked if everyone in the family was safe from the bombings in New York and Washington.

I tried to respond, but I sounded hyper—even to myself—from the unexpected overseas call so early in the day. I struggled to figure out what verbs to use, whether a noun was masculine or feminine, how to control my excitement about hearing from Carmella, while still trying to give her the information she wanted.

I took a deep breath, calmed down, and said, "*Tutti bene*," which means "everyone is fine."

"*Tutti bene?*" she repeated in a questioning inflection.

"*Si, Si,*" I said, "*Tutti, tutti* bene."

Later, I phoned Dad and asked him to return the call and let Carmella know that we were all safe—that my siblings living in and around New York were out of harm's way, and that no one in the family had been injured or physically affected.

Soon after 9/11, I started thinking that, with the threat of terrorism and war, there was a chance we wouldn't get to Sicily any time soon. Maybe I *did* have a premonition when I thought I might be an older woman before I saw Carmella again. I'd hoped it was only a fear.

After having been back from our trip for well over a year, I was surprised when Mom brought up some of the same questions about Linguaglossa that she pondered on the flight home. As we were sitting around her kitchen table, I wondered if she was hinting about returning to Sicily.

"Do you want to go, Mom?" I asked.

She wasn't so direct as to say "yes," but she didn't say "no" either.

"We can try to get into St. Egidio Church," I continued, "and look up some distant relatives who might have a picture of your grandmother. We could even go to the cemetery where she and other relatives are buried."

Dad, who was sitting on his chair in the family room adjacent to the kitchen—supposedly watching television—interjected his opinion.

"No way!" he said, "If we go back, I am *not* going to Linguaglossa."

"It's okay, Dad," I said, "You can stay in Gualtieri with any one of your cousins, while I'll drive Mom over to Linguaglossa."

"But if we go back, we're going for the festival," he said.

Mom looked at me with fire in her eyes, her lips squeezed tight, an expression of vehemence across her mouth. When she got quiet, I knew she was angry.

"Dad," I said, "We can do *both*, and you don't have to come with us. It will work out okay. Your cousins will be happy to put you up."

I was surprised that Mom suggested we return. Her health had not been as strong as it was during the October we traveled. I also thought that maybe if Mom had something to look forward to, she would take good care of herself.

My husband's optimism must be wearing off on me. Returning to Linguaglossa would definitely give me an opportunity to dig deeper, to find out more. Even though I spent a lot of time with my mother's family growing up, I realized there were still aspects of Mom to uncover. I don't know if I'll find them in Linguaglossa.

The way Mom was raised—her beliefs and attitudes—came over with her parents, brother, aunts and uncles. And there could be another clue or two under that booming volcano. Or maybe it wouldn't be about going to Linguaglossa as much as going there with just Mom. If Dad stayed back in his hometown, maybe I could prod more things out of her, find out the mystery—the enigma my mother holds close to her heart.

The trip has yet to be planned. Dad, now in his early eighties, and Mom soon approaching the same decade, do not drive long distances by themselves anymore. Someone, usually Teresa, takes them to the shore, to Boston or to New York. And they have been willing to fly down to North Carolina to stay with Stu and me. They even flew to Los Angeles to attend the Bar Mitzvah for the son of my brother, Anthony. (Anthony, who lives in California, married a Jewish woman.)

It's unlikely Mom and Dad will make another trans-Atlantic plane trip. If they do, I'm going with them for the feast, and then onto Linguaglossa. There is still more hidden family history in those brown, rust-colored mountains of Gualtieri Sicaminò and the gray lava stones around Etna. Plus, that Roman aristocratic woman living inside of me has a craving to walk the streets of Rome again. She hasn't walked them for much too long.

I hear a voice calling me back to the Roman Forum, the Pantheon, the Coliseum and the site nearby, where remnants still linger of a possible female pope.

My Father's Daughter
From Rome to Sicily

Discussion Questions

In Gilda Morina Syverson's memoir, the reader is transported on a fascinating journey from Rome, down to the island of Sicily. The author pulls us through struggles and joys of the past and present, along with sharing places, scenes, people and memories of ancestral heritage. Along the way, we are captivated with ancient sites of Rome that contrast the landscape of the picturesque countryside.

As time moves forward, the journey resurrects cultural folklore and accentuates the family's dynamic. Like many families across the globe, Gilda's ancestors have a history that exerts both obvious and hidden influences. The questions below are intended to encourage dialogue about the memoir for book clubs, readers groups and for dialogue among friends and family.

1) As the reader sits alongside our author on the cross-Atlantic flight to Rome, what emotions are evident? What does this adventure of a lifetime potentially entail?

2) Some of Gilda's strengths as well as her challenges came from a more traditional Italian-Catholic upbringing. Were you raised in a culture that did not always fit the new beliefs that you discovered on your life's path?

3) When Gilda sits in St. Peter's *piazza*, she has glimpses of appreciation for her religious upbringing, despite her feminist leanings. Are there aspects of your spiritual upbringing, or lack of one, that give you strength despite the differences you may now have as an adult?

4) For years, our author had asked her father to travel to his hometown roots, in Sicily. Has there been any country or part of the world associated with your own heritage that you've had a desire to visit? Is there anything about your past that you would like to discover?

5) A psychic once told Gilda that, in a past life, she lived as an ancient, aristocratic woman in Rome. Is there a city, country or certain area of the world that you have a yearning to visit, even if you have no idea what is calling you there?

6) On the train from Rome to Sicily, Gilda, her parents, and her husband find themselves in a compartment with a German couple. Watching them, Gilda feels that there are cultural differences. Have there been times in your life where you have encountered someone speaking another language or participating in a tradition foreign to you? How did it make you feel? How did you respond?

7) On the ferry from the mainland of Italy over to Messina, Sicily, Gilda is aware of a quiet that overcomes both her parents—especially her father, when he sees his homeland again after 30 years. Is this silence in any way an indication of what may lie ahead as they step onto the island of Sicily? What kind of mood do you find yourself in when you're about to step into a new place, or step back to an old one?

8) When all four travelers arrive in the small town of Gualtieri Sicaminò, the cousins—who haven't seen Gilda's father in decades—receive them with open arms. How do we, as a culture, receive unexpected guests that knock at our doors? Have you ever shown up at someone's door and realized, *Uh-oh, I should have called first?*

9) When Gilda's father says good-bye to his cousins, Pasqua and then Pasqualino—probably for the last time—the feelings

expressed by those present run a gamut of emotions. What is it like for you to say goodbye to a close friend or relative, a child who is leaving home for the first time, or a parent or partner who is dying?

10) When our travelers leave Linguaglossa, Gilda's mother mentions that there were still things that she wished she could have seen or found. Are there questions that Gilda's mother had that you still want to know about? If you are a mother or grandmother, what wisdom do you want to impart?

11) Both Gilda's parents had a chance to say farewell to their regions—her mother, when standing in the ancient ruins of Taormina, and her father, when on the ferryboat from Messina back to the mainland. This pivotal scene provides the backdrop for us to ponder our family roots and travel adventures. Share any thoughts that surface from reading about this experience.

12) Back in Rome, Gilda's father wanted to see the balcony where Mussolini, while still in power during World War II, addressed Italy. Are there any historical figures—positive or negative—you would like to meet or see in action?

13) How do you think Gilda and her father's relationship changed over the course of the trip, from the United States through Rome, Italy, Sicily and back home?

Gilda Morina Syverson, artist, poet, writer and teacher, was born and raised in a large, Italian-American, Catholic family in Syracuse, New York. Her heritage is the impetus for the memoir *My Father's Daughter From Rome to Sicily*. Gilda's story was a Novello Literary Award Finalist previously entitled *Finding Bottom, An Italian-American Woman's Journey to the Old Country*. An excerpt was published in *Topograph, New Writing from the Carolinas and the Landscape Beyond*.

Photo by Kerry Dale Long

Gilda's award winning poems and prose have appeared in literary journals, magazines and anthologies in the United States and Canada. Her commentaries have been aired on Charlotte, N.C.'s public radio station.

Gilda moved to Charlotte, after having received an MFA in Fine Arts from Southern Illinois University. She has taught in the creative arts for over 35 years and teaches memoir classes and workshops for Queens University of Charlotte, The Warehouse Performing Arts Center in Cornelius, and in various other locations. Her fine art has been exhibited regionally, nationally and internationally. Her angel drawings and prints are in a number of collections throughout the United States, Canada and Italy.

Gilda lives outside of Charlotte, with her husband, Stu. Connect with Gilda at www.gildasyverson.com and on Facebook.

CPSIA information can be obtained
at www.ICGtesting.com
Printed in the USA
BVHW04s0608070618
518367BV00002B/249/P